ABOUT THE AUTHOR

Born in Zambia to Iri[illegible] taste of success was wi[illegible] Championships at the age of eighteen. His crew were then selected to row for Ireland.

Bryan joined the Army as a soldier before being commissioned from the Royal Military Academy Sandhurst as an Officer in 2nd Gurkha Rifles. He served all over the world including service on operations.

After leaving the Army, Bryan worked on a diamond mine in Angola, West Africa. When the mine was attacked by UNITA rebel army, Bryan and his team were taken into captivity. Four days later they were released and flown south to Namibia. Bryan immediately volunteered to return to civil war torn Angola and took his team back with him.

After a successful career in wealth management, Bryan was invited to join the marketing training team of a FTSE 100 company and was quickly promoted into the leadership of that team.

Bryan established his own leadership development business thirteen years ago. He has built a prestigious client bank from scratch. His clients include Kelloggs, Standard Life, Microsoft, Coutts and Company, and Prudential.

Bryan is a business mentor for the Princes Trust and an Ambassador for the Management and Leadership Network.

LEADERSHIP
WITHOUT RULES

20 HABITS OF EFFECTIVE LEADERSHIP APPLIED IN CAPTIVITY

BRYAN DUNLOP

PG Press – PGP

Published by PG Press (PGP)
Mountain Farmhouse, Marden Road,
Marden, Kent TN12 9PZ
Telephone: +44 (0) 1622 831310
info@pgpress.co.uk
www.pgpress.co.uk

Printed by
Berforts Group – Stevenage and Hastings
ISBN – 978-0-9575476-5-0

Dedicated to Poppy, Harry and Tom

ACKNOWLEDGEMENTS

I'd like to thank a number of people.

My Mum and Dad. I am sure I caused you anxiety on more than one occasion but I didn't mean to.

Robert Northridge for being an inspiring school master and rowing coach. What I learnt while rowing at Portora Royal School made a very positive impact on me.

Richard Dawnay for inspiration when I was a young soldier, attempting to become an Officer.

Rob Archer in Queensland, Australia, who gave me an incredible opportunity and taught me a lot about leading people in a tough environment.

Sandy McNeil for his support during my time as an Officer in 2nd Gurkha Rifles. He showed us all how strong leadership can transform a body of men.

Sarat Chandra (Simon) Rai, who typified the Gurkha spirit.

Roger Brown and Brian Harrington Spier, mentors and friends in Angola, West Africa. I learnt a lot and took great encouragement from their support.

My close friend and mentor, Alan Jones, who had a big influence on my commercial career and subsequent success.

Teena Lyons whose support in the writing of this book has been immense.

Finally, to Poppy, Harry and Tom, to whom this book is dedicated. I enjoy everything that I do but I enjoy being a husband to Poppy and a Dad to our boys the most.

CONTENTS

INTRODUCTION

I have led and I have been a leader, as a soldier, an officer in the Gurkhas, an employee, a manager, a leadership development consultant and a business owner. In each of these roles I have confronted challenges, which have ranged from being attacked and held captive on a diamond mine in Angola, West Africa, to working in a big and stable financial services company that lost a High Court appeal leading to a complete change in direction, just when everything seemed stable.

Challenges are part of life. Our ability to meet them is based on a combination of how confident we are and how confident we are in the people who lead us. We all know it is possible for great leaders to inspire their people through times of great uncertainty and danger, whether we have experienced it for ourselves or seen it from history.

The apparently mystical ability of a leader to inspire others when most others would be terrified into submission (or inaction) has led to the opinion that leaders are born and not made. The assumption is people are born with specific personal characteristics that set them apart from others. This isn't true. Everyone has the potential to lead. This may sound like a bold statement, but it is the basis for which I chose to write this book. I firmly believe we all have the capacity to 'step up to the plate' and be effective leaders.

It is human nature to wonder how you will react in an extreme or challenging situation. Would you be able to think and act beyond the usual boundaries and make a real difference? How likely is it that you would be able to work your way through the fear and limiting beliefs which haunt everyone, so you could see what needs to be done and then do it? Are you leadership material?

I was fortunate enough to get all the answers to these questions – and probably a few others too – when I spent four days in captivity in Angola.

On Friday 30th October 1992 at about two o'clock in the afternoon, the diamond mine I was working on at Luzamba in Angola was attacked by nine hundred soldiers from the UNITA rebel army. I had no idea that we were about to be attacked and neither did my boss. We were taken by surprise by a force with overwhelming numerical advantage. I will explain more about how the story unfolds throughout this book, but suffice to say we had very few options other than to negotiate with the rebel commanders.

I was there because I had been asked to take a team of retired Gurkhas to Angola, to provide security to the diamonds being produced on a mine near the borders with Zaire and Zambia. When fifteen of us took the job, we had no idea we'd be caught up in the furore over the democratic elections there, which were scheduled for late October 1992.

At the time I spoke to a member of the French army, who was serving with the United Nations force overseeing the election, who predicted a win for the newly reformed communist party. It was apparent this would create implications for the opposition UNITA Party, led by Jonas Savimbi, particularly if the results were very close. Worryingly, although the United Nations were to oversee the actual voting, they were not around for the declaration of results, having withdrawn to the comparative safety of their compound in Luanda.

During the two days of voting, we sealed off the compound and watched the ballots disappear by helicopter towards the airstrip at Cafunfu, We had various views on the potential risks that we were facing. It wasn't just that we were in a diamond mine that made us attractive to terrorists. The fact we had lots of vehicles, food, oil, lubricants and weapons was equally appealing.

Early on the morning of Friday 30th October, it was rumoured that UNITA had rejected the outcome of the election and had a large force of seven thousand men in the town of Cafunfu, which was only thirty miles from Luzamba. We had nine hundred expatriates on the mine at this time, including thirty women.

By Friday lunchtime, plans were being made for

the evacuation of the women initially, and then the entire nine hundred expatriates to Luanda. This would have entailed approximately six return flights, with turnaround times and crew fatigue; it was going to take about two and a half days to complete the evacuation exercise. By this stage my team had grown to twenty-nine Gurkhas and myself. We developed a contingency plan, which involved commandeering a series of vehicles and driving into Zaire. The border with Zaire was about three or four hundred miles to the north and our expectation was that we would be able to take this convoy through to Zaire, possibly fighting as we went. What we would have found in Zaire, had we been forced to take this action, none of us knew. Our perception was that it would be better to do something rather than nothing.

One of my men had rather enthusiastically started burning classified documents in what he thought was a yellow metallic dustbin. It actually turned out to be a yellow plastic dustbin, which promptly caught fire emitting the most extraordinary black clouds of smoke. As our compound was slightly removed from the main one, everybody saw the smoke and thought we had already come under attack.

We had been told to start to make preparations to leave the mine. I was unsure of the exact detail of this departure plan, other than expecting us to be the last to leave. I went in search of the new head of security, a retired Brazilian Special Forces officer, called Victor. As I knocked on the door of his Portacabin portacabin office, we came under very heavy automatic fire. This was supplemented by a couple of loud explosions, which were very near and were caused by either mortars, or grenade launchers. We were unsure who was attacking, in what force and with what objective. With the bullets flying around it was very confusing. I tried to find out the direction of the attack, the 'enemy's' progress and our odds of repelling the assault. If it was the UNITA troopers from Cafunfu, we were unlikely to offer any armed resistance. If, however, it was a renegade group of bandits then that was a different story.

Once we ascertained it was UNITA we agreed that offering armed resistance was not the best course of action. For that reason, we started to pull out of our compound and headed towards a prearranged rendezvous about five hundred metres out into the bush. I was the last to leave and came under direct enemy fire on two occasions, during which I was obliged to take cover. When I reached the rendezvous point and had accounted for everybody we sat tight and waited for the shooting to die down. It was at this stage that we were presented with a dilemma. We were going to have to get out of Angola that was certain. It seemed that if UNITA were now in control of the mine that exfiltrating to Zaire was our best option. There was one major problem, my men were not appropriately dressed or armed to escape on foot to Zaire. Being focused on our preparations for leaving the mine had meant that we had dropped our guard. In addition, one of my men had been hurt climbing over a barbed wire fence, sustaining a very long, deep and ragged laceration to his lower leg. It was a nasty wound and we did not have enough sutures in our first aid kits to deal with his wounds. There was a risk of infection if he had to stay in the bush for any length of time.

Victor and I, and one other British security expatriate, decided that we must go back into Luzamba and speak to the commander of the forces that had just attacked us. With a degree of trepidation, we walked into Luzamba not knowing how we would be received. We left orders with the Gurkhas in the bush that if none of us came back within three hours, then they were to do their best to escape out of Angola. It wasn't much of a plan but if the three of us were going to be murdered by UNITA, then there was no point in my Gurkhas potentially suffering the same fate.

We were greeted by the UNITA troopers with suspicion and after a short discussion we were directed to their commander. Victor, our Brazilian head of security, was able to have a fluent conversation in Portuguese with the UNITA commander, most of which I was able to understand. As anticipated, it appeared that their main objective was not only the diamonds, but also all of the assets on the mine site. They were actually very keen to get all of the expatriates off the mine as quickly as possible.

At this stage there was a force of about two or three hundred UNITA troops both in our compound and in the main accommodation area. The commander assured us that no harm would come to our people. He seemed reasonable enough, so we agreed that bringing the guys back in to await evacuation was the best of the two fairly limited options available to us.

At around seven o'clock on Friday evening, as three of us headed back to the bush to bring in our team, we watched the first Hercules plane taking off with about one hundred and thirty members of the mining community on board. I remember thinking 'normal' life in Luzamba had come to an end. What bothered me more was that we were no longer in immediate control of our own destiny.

Having recovered the team safely and brought them back into our own compound, we were given five minutes to pack the most basic bag of clothing. We were then marched up to the main compound and put into a separate holding area. The UNITA troopers knew the reputation of the Gurkhas, and for very good reasons were isolating us from the main group. It added to my concern that our group might merit additional unwanted attention.

There was, however, a more immediate issue. For the first, and I hope the last time in my life, I witnessed the complete breakdown of social order. Suddenly people who had lived harmoniously together for nine months were fighting over water, the meagre amounts of food that had been left, shelter and shade. It was an unusual and unsettling experience.

I persuaded the soldiers who were guarding us to allow me to go to the Mine Manager's House to look for medical supplies. They allowed me to do this as long as I was accompanied by two troopers. We had had a couple of parties in the Mine Managers House in the past; it held happy memories for us all. When I went there that Saturday morning, it had been completely trashed. People had urinated and defecated on the floor. Everything had been looted by the local population. It was a mess. Less than twenty-four hours earlier I had had a beer on the veranda, and now it was an empty shell. I left and didn't go back.

During our four days in captivity, from Friday through to Monday, there were two very alarming incidents. On one occasion three drunken troopers came to our pen and asked for the leaders of our group. They told us that we had an hour before they were going to come back and shoot us. Then they walked off.

Obviously we spent a worrying sixty minutes trying to evaluate the likelihood of this actually happening. Part of me thought it was very unlikely, but another part of me wondered what I'd do if they were serious. There weren't many options. We were being guarded day and night. That group of soldiers didn't return, but the threat never really went away.

The second incident began on Sunday evening, when we discovered that the air charter company were no longer prepared to fly to Luzamba. This came as a bit of a blow as it meant more time in an increasingly hostile environment. One of my concerns was that those of us from the security team would be left with no "civilian" employees to protect. If this was the case, it increased the threat level against us. We had been stopping all kinds of theft and civil unrest, so we were never going to be the most popular people on the mine. We did, however, learn that our employer was now negotiating with the Brazilian Air Force to send a Hercules C-130 to rescue us.

On Monday morning, the UNITA Commander told us that he and his force were leaving to conduct an attack on Malange, the nearest large town, about two hundred miles away. He and his men would be pulling out and leaving us to await our own extraction. While our initial reaction to this news was very positive, when we sat down and reflected on it, we realised that it had been UNITA who had been discouraging the local people from coming into the mine to loot. With UNITA preparing to leave, we now had responsibility for our own security. Victor Motta and I agreed a plan. My team would be responsible for keeping the runway open and for ensuring that no villagers got onto the runway or into our compound until we had left.

I placed a roadblock between us and the villagers with a Portuguese speaking security guard. I ordered the guard to explain that we would be leaving within forty-eight hours. The villagers could then have everything. If anyone attempted to pass the road block or went onto the runway the implications would be very severe. We were very clear about this and we had to be. We were outnumbered by about a hundred to one and every house in Angola has at least one AK47. Our situation was very precarious and now called for desperate measures.

We ran security patrols for about twelve hours. No one from the village caused too much bother. On one or two occasions we put down some harassing fire at groups of armed men who were seen about one hundred yards from our road block. At the back of our minds we were aware our runway had no lights and we didn't know if the Brazilian Air Force pilots had night-vision equipment. Keeping the villagers out for a night was something we wished to avoid. At about five o'clock on Monday evening, around an hour from last light, the Brazilian Air Force C-130 appeared overhead and banked to land on our strip. There were about sixty of us left.

The plane that collected us hardly stopped and lifted off before we had even had a chance to sit down, let alone strap in. We knew we were still vulnerable until we had reached a certain altitude and it took a few minutes until we started to feel safe. We had been in immense danger and under considerable pressure for three days but everyone had got out safely.

Within four hours we arrived at Windhoek Airport in Namibia. I've still got my old passport from the time with its Namibian entry stamp bearing the somewhat extraordinary reason for 'purpose of visit' – evacuation!

Back in Angola, the situation in Luanda was appalling and thousands had been killed. Pro Government people were roaming the streets, killing indiscriminately. Anyone who was suspected of being a UNITA supporter was summarily executed. Tanks were on the streets.

My story didn't end there though. We had only been in Namibia for a day when Victor Motta asked for volunteers to go back to Luanda. He needed people to provide security for those members of staff who were still occupying the compound there. My initial reaction was that he was mad and I wouldn't go back, let alone take my men with me. It was the fairly obvious response, given that it was such a short time since we had escaped with our lives. However, I sought advice from our directors in London about whether we should return. They told me that as the man on the ground I must make the decision.

I spoke to my Dad, a man any son would turn to for guidance. As a father myself now, I know exactly what my instinctive advice would have been. To his credit, and I am sure at some cost to himself, never mind my Mum, he told me that only I alone could make the correct decision. I was now faced with one of the biggest choices of my life.

I chose to go back to Luanda to honour our contractual obligations. The next step was to encourage my team to come back with me. Their decision would be a direct reflection of the faith they had in me as a leader. I sat down with the guys and told them about Victor's request. I was completely open in saying that I didn't know the precise situation in Angola but that I had made the decision to go back. I then took questions from them, most of which I wasn't able to answer and left them to make up their own minds.

I remember sitting in a pretty plush bar having a glass of excellent German lager in my soiled and dirty shorts and T shirt, when one of the senior Gurkhas came in and said they had all decided to go back to Angola. It was quite an emotional moment. These men were older than me, with a lot more operational experience. I took it as a compliment.

The next morning we gathered in the hotel foyer,

ready for a coach to take us to the airfield. By now the reality of our return to Luanda and all of the threats we were likely to meet when we got there had really sunk in. My mood wasn't helped when one of my British colleagues, who had chosen to return to England, caught hold of me by the arm.

He started shouting at me in front of my men, saying: 'You'll all be killed. Don't go back.'

It was difficult. I respected and admired this man; he had been decorated for gallantry on operations in Aden in the 1960s. It also challenged my resolve in front of my men. As it was I was scared. I didn't know what Luanda would be like. It was dangerous at the best of times. Thousands of people were running through the capital with hardly any control. In spite of this unhelpful interlude, I stuck with my decision, told him my mind was made up, wished him well and got onto the bus. It was clear that his outburst had had a negative effect on my men though.

It was a surreal experience to return to Luanda. Even though I did not know what we would find when we touched down on the airstrip and whether we would come under fire as we attempted to leave the aircraft, the situation was by now largely under control. I left Luanda in late December 1992 having fulfilled my obligation to my team and to my employer. I returned in February 1993 on direct contract to my Brazilian employer, but that is another story.

Obviously, following my experience in Angola, I spent a long time reflecting on what I did in that period and whether I could have gone about things differently. I really wanted to be sure I'd done all that I could in the disarray, order and disruption that marked those few days. This period of self-examination also involved looking long and hard at my performance as a leader.

While the chain of events at Luzamba could never have been accurately predicted, the fact that the mine had employed me and my elite group of Gurkhas meant everyone was expecting trouble. We certainly weren't there for cosmetic purposes. Therefore, I had plenty of time to plan and even predict certain courses of events. However, from the moment I arrived I became aware that a certain leeway was required. I had to allow for disruptions to my plan and the odd unwelcome surprise, which, of course, we got at every turn.

In short, although I had plenty of training to fall back on, thanks to my schooling at the Royal Military Academy Sandhurst and my subsequent military career, there were no hard and fast rules about how I should act or what I should do. In fact, the only rule was there were no rules. And, as I discovered, that suited me just fine.

Since Angola, I worked in many roles before setting up my training consultancy. In one of those roles I led a team of people in a financial services company when we were taken over by a competitor. I knew my team were unsettled, I was unsettled too. Once again, I was in a position where everything we had taken for granted was taken away in an instant, although this time there were no weapons involved. I realised that my experience in Angola and my service as an officer in the Gurkhas taught me how to respond and how to behave. I was able to apply certain skills again, so that my people would feel that although life had changed, everything was going to work out well.

It was these experiences that prompted the realisation that leadership is learnable. Each of my experiences, although some were more extreme than others, imparted an important lesson which I was able to apply again and again in different situations. I'm not, and never have been, the textbook 'perfect leader'. A fact, I'm proud of. However, I do know that a combination of the lessons I learned and my own fast-thinking, innovative and occasionally left-field style of leadership has not only sustained me through countless difficult situations, but has probably saved lives too.

In 2001, I set up my own leadership training consultancy and since then have I have had the good fortune to work with hundreds of people who are either in leadership roles, or aspire to be. I didn't set out to teach a one-size-fits-all style of leadership, because I don't think there is one. I believe that instead there is a rich central vein of knowledge, which a resourceful and innovative leader can adapt and make their own. Taking my own experiences and those of other leaders I have worked with, I've observed that there are a number of habits among those who are willing to challenge convention and lead innovatively. It is those habits, which I have used to help hundreds of new leaders find their own approach to leadership that I have now laid out here in this book.

My view is that in the modern, fast-moving, business environment a new breed of leaders is required. This era of constant change, technological revolution and discovery needs people at the top who are able to think fast, adapt as necessary and find new ways to motivate their teams to greet these new challenges with enthusiasm not fear.

Leadership without rules is not an ABC guide on how to lead. The twenty habits detailed here are merely a toolkit and some may well be more relevant to your style or circumstance than others. There is advice on everything from running and inspiring a team, to securing full engagement of those around you, to learning how to change tack quickly when things don't first go to plan. I've also included thoughts on how to behave like a leader and speak and listen effectively, because in my experience too few leaders ever really manage to do this well.

The final part of each chapter is devoted to sharing

some ideas and exercises that I have used with our clients. They have been chosen because they are simple, practical, effective and proven to add value. If you want to help your people to develop a more inspiring attitude these exercises should help. Each exercise has an objective and a method. If you would like to talk through any of them further, email us at bryan@bryandunlop.com and we'll arrange to speak to you.

Many of the ideas in this book will prove to be a highly effective part of your armoury, although quite possibly at different times in your career. The book doesn't have to be read sequentially. It is perfectly fine to dip in and out of it to find the information you need. How you use these habits is up to you.

This book is an invaluable toolkit any modern leader can't afford to be without. If you want to make a big difference to your organisation, here is how.

CHAPTER 1

GIVE IT SOME ATTITUDE

I remember sitting in a conference room when I was a salesman and about to become a training officer. I had just been promoted and was soon to start learning how to teach sales skills to people who were joining our business.

For a moment I let my mind wonder back to my own training as a salesman four years earlier, when I was at the beginning of my journey to become part of a well-respected team.

I recalled how the single most significant factor that had contributed to the significant upward shift in my sales results was when I realised it was my attitude and not just my skills that would dictate my outcome. This realisation came about not only through my own training as a salesperson, but also through a conversation I had with an ex-army colleague who had come to visit me early in my sales career.

We were chatting about the differences between

army life and life as a civilian and, in particular, my life as a salesman. It was still early days, but I was already confident that I was doing quite well. However, at some point in the conversation, I let slip that I used to leave the office quite promptly on Friday afternoon and not think about work all weekend.

'You weren't like that in the Army,' my friend remarked. 'You were engaged in military stuff all the time, even at the weekend.'

Following this piece of unsolicited feedback from someone who knew me quite well, it suddenly became clear to me that since I had become a salesman I had rarely been as engaged to my profession as I had been when I was a soldier and an army officer. In fact, for the majority of time, I was considerably less focused on the job in hand.

It may help you understand how problematic this should have been, if I tell you my pay as a salesman was directly related to how hard I worked and how well I did. So, if I wasn't fully on board, I was directly impacting my back pocket. Yet, I wasn't nearly as engaged as I could have been. On a scale of one to ten, where one is completely disengaged and ten is fully engaged, I was probably working at about a seven.

Don't get me wrong. I did all that I was required to do. I always saw the number of clients that my employer told me to see; but as I told my army colleague, I had no qualms about leaving early and rarely thought about work outside the office. On Monday mornings, I'd be at my desk for about eight o'clock, which was still relatively early in comparison to my colleagues, but it was only when I was in the office that I truly switched on to the task in hand.

My results were still pretty good, but they could probably have been better.

I contrast this with my time as an army officer where I definitely worked from at least a nine, if not a ten out of ten.

> It suddenly became clear to me that since I had become a salesman I had rarely been as engaged to my profession as I had been when I was a soldier.

A prime example of this would be from 1988 when I was the duty officer in Hong Kong for two weeks and practically on my own in the Officers Mess. My contemporaries were either in England attending courses, or on overseas postings with their own teams.

I could have sat around and done nothing, it was after all hot and sunny and there was a swimming pool in the barracks, but I chose to try and learn how to do two things:

1. use a high frequency radio
2. develop my tracking skills

These were skills that would have been defined as 'nice

to have' for an officer, but as the commander of the reconnaissance platoon, I deemed them particularly relevant to me in my capacity as a soldier as well as a leader. A team in a typical reconnaissance platoon is four-men strong. Traditionally, each man has a specific expertise, such as, communications, demolitions, tracking or first aid. My view was that by doubling up on my own essential skills, alongside the command and control skills I already had, this would help me to be a greater asset to the team.

Gurkha soldiers don't celebrate Christmas, but it is still a holiday for the British Officers and Non-Commissioned Officers. This meant that while I might have been the only officer in the barracks, it was easy to gain access to the best instructors and all of the equipment that we would need for me to develop these skills.

I was therefore lucky enough to receive one-to-one training from some real experts, and as a direct result of this I managed to develop high levels of capability with each skill. This one-to-one training enabled me to go more deeply into both subjects, which satisfied my desire for greater knowledge and ultimately meant that I would be an asset to my team.

Embarking on something like this may seem like a relatively sensible thing to do if you are in a profession where additional skills might save your life, or the lives of the people around you, and I accept that. However, it doesn't wholly explain my dedication. It is not the main reason behind the engagement score of nine or ten.

When I was a salesman selling wealth management, do you think there was any chance at all that I would take the Inland Revenue's guidance notes on inheritance tax with me when I was going on holiday? There was absolutely no chance of that; none whatsoever. This is despite the fact that my knowledge of taxation could have had a *direct* and *significantly positive* impact on my pay.

It wasn't therefore that my newfound sales career didn't invite, or even demand, dedication and effort. There had to be more to it than that.

We had top performers in our office and they were easy to identify. For a start, their results were better than everyone else's. You didn't often see them in the office where we were based, because they were usually out seeing their clients. When they were in the office, they were doing things of value: phoning clients, completing paperwork, planning with the boss or their assistants. They tended not to go out for lunch with the rest of the guys, or stand around chatting.

On one particular occasion, I remember leaving the office on Friday afternoon at about three o'clock (so that was late for me) and one of my colleagues was at his desk with a big pile of client records. He was one of our top performers.

'What are you doing?' I asked him.

'Phoning clients, I've only got nine meetings scheduled in for next week,' he replied, as he shuffled through his papers.

'You've *only* got nine? I've got six,' was my response. Prior to that conversation, I was thinking that six was pretty good, even though our target was ten.

'I'll get one more then head home,' he said brightly, as he reached for the phone.

He had all of the reasons to go home early. He was married with two lovely children and they lived in a beautiful house in the country. The sun was shining and the weekend beckoned, but he was going to stay until he had done what he'd set out to do. He wanted and needed to ensure his success continued. Nothing was going to distract him from that.

Yet, if anyone should have been staying in the office, it was me, not my colleague.

I left, he stayed. His results were better than mine.

Simple? Of course it is.

He had something that I clearly didn't have, well not in that profession anyway.

It was now very clear to me that attitude was extremely important.

It was around this time I started analysing the document that reported the sales across our business. It was produced monthly and I started reading it with great interest. The same top-performing names were on the front sheet, which listed the top twenty sales people, month in and month out. How were they able to produce such good results so consistently?

The inescapable answer was that they were consistently working from a nine or a ten.

Having looked at the individual top performers, I decided to take my research further and began looking at the branch results to test my theory. Again, month on month, the same branches featured at the top of the list. It didn't take long to see that the top performing branches were made up of the top-performing sales people.

It occurred to me that effective leadership could well be at the heart of these great performances. The top branches were full of people who appeared to work from a ten and the other factor they had in common was that the successful ones all had strong and inspirational Branch Managers.

It led me to think about how I could train people to understand that their attitude was the key to their success. I drew inspiration from a selection course I had designed when recruiting Gurkha soldiers from within my own battalion for a military skills competition I was going to take part in – in Australia in 1988, the Australian Bicentenary.

I had created the selection programme to help me identify people who were determined, driven, focused and resilient, with characters full of perseverance and self-belief. Although once we had selected them we would then train them for three months, the selection process was of vital importance because it had to identify a certain type of person; one who always worked from a ten.

I adapted my bicentenary selection technique into an exercise where I would ask any audience to identify the traits or characteristics of top performers. The definition of 'top performer' was someone who has the ability to consistently get excellent results, specifically when the environment is challenging. It is clear that there are people who are capable of delivering strong results when the environment is easy, but not everyone is capable of delivering when times are tough.

So what is it about some people that enables them to deliver these high levels of performance? What do they have that the average performer doesn't have?

The answer is very similar to the traits we saw in the Gurkhas who did well on my selection process. Top performers tend to be:

- tenacious
- persistent
- focused
- positive
- determined
- driven
- optimistic

- open-minded
- confident
- adaptable

I've done this course frequently in my leadership seminars and some people often suggest that it is necessary to be organised to be a top performer. Of course, being organised can help, but it is worth noting that there are people who are both top performers and disorganised.

Occasionally people suggest that being knowledgeable is important. Like being organised, being knowledgeable will make a contribution. Having knowledge can help, but it is when you start to *apply* that knowledge that your results can begin to change. There are many people who have all the knowledge they need but, for some reason, they do not apply that knowledge. This theme will be developed in a later chapter.

The point is that being knowledgeable and well organised are important, but not vital. The characteristics that separate top performers from average performers tend to be a rich combination of the ones described above.

Now ask yourself this question, when you look at this list of traits, how many of these traits are skills and how many of them are attitudes?

The answer is that they are all attitudes.

It is a person's *attitude* that primarily dictates whether they are able to deliver high levels of performance when the environment is challenging, and this is the point this exercise illustrates very neatly.

This isn't to say that skills aren't relevant because, of course, they are. Top performers combine a powerful attitude and high levels of skill. Yet, it is predominantly the top performer's attitude that helps them create highly developed skills.

People with certain characteristics are inclined to go out and get the knowledge they need long before they are required to. As a leader, you've got to demonstrate the traits listed above (and others), consistently, plus you need to inspire them in those who follow.

Before we get on to how you might go about doing just that, it might help to delve a little into why those around us have such different attitudes.

In its most simple form, people's attitudes are described as being either glass half-full, or glass half-empty. It's an old adage, but how is it that different people can see the same thing in two completely different ways? This disparity is attributed to what some people call conditioning. In this context, the expression conditioning means the way people are, or were, encouraged to think and to perceive things.

All human beings have been, and continue to be, conditioned. They are conditioned by people they've met and experiences they've had. One view is that this starts from birth and continues from there. It never stops, regardless of how old one gets.

A lot of this conditioning goes on during a time in early life when we have very little conscious understanding. Our first memories are not of the moment of our arrival into this world. Our first memories tend to be linked to an age of about three, four or five. Memories are usually linked to specific activities, glimpses of what went on, as opposed to a switch being flicked that starts conscious understanding of what is going on around us.

Through all of this, the conditioning process is taking place. People are conditioned to think in a certain way, to perceive people and things in a certain way and to behave in a certain way. The sources of this conditioning are obviously different for everyone, but there may be some constants.

> All human beings have been, and continue to be, conditioned.

Parents will clearly have a big bearing on conditioning. There will be other sources as well. Grandparents, teachers, friends, sports coaches and lots of other people and experiences all play a role and contribute to the individual developing an attitude of some kind.

The question we need to pose is this. How much choice do we have over the people and experiences that shape us?

The answer is it varies; in our formative years, probably none. Our attitude is shaped by people and things, over which we have very little, or absolutely no, control. This can change as we grow older. We can start to consciously choose who we spend time with and the types of experiences we are exposed to. In essence, we can control the sources of our conditioning, which means that we can control the development of our attitude.

While the idea of any type of change is often unsettling for people, we are incredibly adaptable. As you will see in a later chapter, change is easy when you want to change.

The obvious conclusion is that the way is wide open for a leader to exert some influence over the attitude of his team. And this is exactly the case. It really is possible to enable members of a team who might have a glass half-empty perspective, or attitude, to develop a glass half-full view of the world.

To illustrate how this might happen, let me share an experience I had when I was a fourteen-year-old boy.

I was lucky enough to go to a very good school in Enniskillen in Northern Ireland. While I was there I met a number of really great teachers and sports coaches. One man stood out for me. His name is Robert Northridge.

Robert was an old boy of the school himself. He had been to university, and then travelled around the world working as a teacher before returning to the school he was clearly very attached to. I experienced Robert both as a maths master and as a rowing coach and I learnt a lot from him in both areas.

Robert had many great attributes and skills. His results on the river and in the classroom bear testimony to that. One thing stood out for me though. At the beginning of our two year maths 'O' level course, Robert took the time to give my class his insight into how he thought we could gain success. He explained carefully what he was going to do and what he expected from us. Robert confidently set out how an 'O' level maths paper was constructed and therefore how we would study only topics that he felt sure would appear.

He said there were four questions that always appeared in some form every year and we would concentrate on those. He also explained how the ten questions that we would face were structured. Apparently the first six marks (out of the ten) were quite easy to gain, the next two were more difficult and the last two more difficult still. He told us that our objective was to gather marks as quickly and as easily as possible and the goal was to gather forty-six marks, not to get lots of questions completely correct.

In the space of about ten minutes, Robert had outlined a strategy that clearly made sense and which gave us all a sense of confidence that we hadn't had when we went into his classroom for the first time. It is worth emphasising here that Robert was addressing a class full of boys who had been consistently told that maths wasn't a strong point. He was no doubt very aware of this, but he never once let it show.

When we got started on the first topic Robert took great care to set us off on a simple aspect of that subject. His teaching approach was clear. He would explain the mathematical theory involved, and then set us a question to work on. When we had finished our work, we took our answers up to his desk and he marked it there and then. If we had got aspects of the question right he'd explain how many marks we'd have got in the 'O' level exam in a very positive way. If we got something wrong, he'd explain what we needed to do to get things right. There was never any criticism and he was always very upbeat. Looking back, I am sure he chose those initial questions very carefully because we all did very well, very quickly.

Knowing what I know now, I can see his strategy was to build our confidence. When we all started to think that there was a chance we could pass the exam (and don't forget the exam was still two years away at this stage), our level of engagement soared.

Two years later everyone in the class acquired an 'O' level in maths and that was a direct result of what Robert had done for and with us. While we all worked very hard, the person that led us through was Robert Northridge. He had a plan, he was calm and he instilled great confidence in us. He made sure we worked and he pushed us hard, but that was what we wanted. Most importantly, he took time to build our confidence and that's what really mattered.

I have often thought about Robert's process of engagement when I'm working with both individuals and teams. That is why my initial focus has always been the building of that early confidence and engagement to the task.

All leaders should have a relentless focus on building and maintaining their people's confidence. As we've seen with Robert Northridge, the development of skills will make a contribution to people's confidence. Even if, like Robert, you inherit a group where some or all of those within it don't have the confidence or attitude that you'd like them to have, it is possible to change things markedly.

Effective leadership is the catalyst. Depending on the individuals in question, it may take time, but all leaders must hold the belief that inspiring and developing their people is possible.

SUMMARY

1. It is our attitude that has the greatest impact on our results.
2. Remember Robert Northridge. His key objective was to build confidence in the team. Even though the

exam was two years away, he was able to demonstrate that passing was not only possible but very possible.

3. Build confidence by getting your people to focus on what they do well and share this with the rest of the team. They may need your help and support, but that will be time well spent.

PERSONAL DEVELOPMENT EXERCISES

EXERCISE ONE

The difference that makes the difference

Business benefit

You will develop your people's understanding of the relationship between perception and reality. With your support, your people will overcome issues that they perceive to be challenging

Resources

Time with the team and the F hand-out (see below)

Method

As the leader you should complete this exercise yourself before using it with your team.

Give yourself fifteen seconds to count the number of Fs in the text below. You are not allowed to mark the paper with any form of pencil or pen.

»

peak performance is the result of laser like focus,
adopting a fizzy of certainty and operating from
maps that guide us towards the
achievement of our desired outcomes

How many Fs did you see?
Copy the text above onto small pieces of paper, one for each member of the team. Place the pieces into envelopes and seal them.

At a team meeting, tell your team you are going to give out envelopes with a piece of paper inside and all of the pieces of paper are different. Explain they will have fifteen seconds to open the envelope, read the text and count the Fs. Emphasise they are not allowed to write on the pieces of paper. Finally, ask them if they have any questions and, if they don't, start the exercise.

When the fifteen seconds is up, ask the team members to place the paper back into the envelope and put it down. Now request feedback on the number of Fs each person has seen. There should be a variety of responses.

If you look closely at the text in question you will see that there are seven. If there are a variety of scores across the team, the point to be made is that we all see things differently, even something as simple as an F on a page. If we don't see seven the first time, we develop a perception that there are, for example, four, but the reality is that there are seven. We just can't see them.

Allow the team to open their envelopes again and take them through the locations of the seven Fs.

»

Stress that if you hadn't shown them the seven their perception would have been that there were four, or whichever number they came up with. Without your input they would have maintained this (incorrect) perception forever.

Set the exercise into a business context by asking the team to think about business challenges where perceptions they hold might be incorrect. An example of a perception is that many people assume the business environment is challenging. Another way of looking at it is that a challenging business environment sorts the wheat from the chaff.

PERSONAL DEVELOPMENT EXERCISES

EXERCISE TWO

The difference that makes the difference

Business benefit

Your team will understand the power of focus

Resources

Ten minutes with the entire team in one location

Format

Focus is an incredibly powerful thing. The reason the glass half-full/half-empty example is so effective is because it tells us what our focus is allowing us to see.

»

Try this yourself and then try it with your team. Find a piece of paper and something to write with. Look around the room and count the number of circular things you can see. For every circular thing you see, make a mark on your paper. If you are in a room that has lots of circular lights, then make one mark for each of the circular lights that you are able to see and so on.

Take a couple of minutes to do this. How many do you have? While you were counting the circular things, how many rectangular things did you see?

The answer to this question is usually not very many. Why is that? Because you were focused on the circular things that you were consciously looking for.

As Plato said: 'You see what you look for' and scientifically he has been proven to be correct.

The next time a member of the team focuses on something that is negative, remind them of this exercise and ask them to identify something positive.

CHAPTER 2

BEHAVE LIKE A LEADER – ALWAYS

You have done all the right things. You know the job inside out and backwards. You know everything there is to know about your company's products and services. You know each of your team's CVs so well, you'd be happy to take a twenty-question quiz on each member.

But, you don't have the full attention of your team.

Somehow, and you can't seem to put your finger on the exact reason, you just don't seem to be inspiring those around you. Why? Well, there is more to leadership than ticking all the right boxes procedurally. There is also an intransient, yet vital, quality of how you behave in front of the men and women. It is the leadership polish that will take you to the next layer of success.

I got my first real taste of this six days after I first arrived in Angola. I accompanied the head of security

– let's call him Tom – on a lengthy drive to a remote industrial plant in Mucussuca. Our vehicle was a clunky Portuguese-built UMM vehicle with the acceleration and power of a arthritic tortoise and it didn't help that it was weighed down with rations, weapons, ammunition and cooking oil.

As we approached the only bridging point on the Cuango River, three or four armed men appeared from underneath the bridge. From this moment on and throughout the subsequent incident when we came under fire, it was obvious Tom was in a complete 'flap'. We escaped OK that time, but by then I was already having serious misgivings about the man who was leading the security team.

The journey back from Mucussuca was even more troubling. On this occasion, the UMM actually broke down, because Tom, clearly panicking, was driving it so hard. We had to abandon the vehicle and set out on foot to Luzamba, which provided yet another opportunity for Tom to unwittingly demonstrate how unprepared he was to withstand any sort of stress whatsoever. He very visibly fell apart at the notion of being stranded in hostile territory.

Finally, when we were picked up by a friendly vehicle attached to the mine project, Tom was so effusive and grovelling in his thanks it was humiliating to everyone concerned. It was blatantly obvious (if it wasn't before) how frightened he had been and that he was in no way up to the job.

Although none of us truly knows how we will react to stressful situations, we can all learn a big lesson from this. My early experience with Tom completely destroyed my trust and respect for him and made our subsequent working relationship very difficult. To be honest, it never really recovered.

As a leader, you must be constantly aware of the impression you are creating.

As a leader, you must be constantly aware of the impression you are creating. What are you doing that affects others' perception of your ability to see a project through to its conclusion? Are you giving enough thought to your attitude, skills or characteristics as a leader, so you can inspire confidence in those around you?

To be an effective, all-round leader, the skills you need to think about are:

- Act with integrity – always
- Commit to what you say and follow through
- Listen to those around you
- Be ready and willing to be accountable for everything that happens

One of the most eye-opening exercises I run in my leadership seminars is to ask delegates what they look for in a leader. The word that comes up time and time again is 'inspirational'.

The word inspirational can mean many things, but most people attach that expression to leaders they have enjoyed working with and for. Delving deeper into the term inspirational is even more illuminating. Invariably, the words or expressions associated with inspirational leaders are, they:

- walk the talk
- lead by example
- are passionate
- are consistent
- are honest

To better understand how a leader might be expected to behave, let's take each of these expressions and explore them in a little more depth.

WALK THE TALK

If you are going to lead effectively, you have to have an ability to personally demonstrate the core skills that you expect from your people. This is obviously quite demanding and nowhere more so than in the military, but whoever said leadership was easy? In the infantry, for example, there are two basic objectives:

1. Be fit because you'll probably have to march to the battle carrying a very heavy load.
2. Be a good shot with all of the weapons available to a platoon.

An officer has to develop many other skills as well. They also have to be able to navigate by day and night, use a variety of radio systems, including using secret codes, and deliver orders clearly and concisely. That's just to name a few additional skills.

When I was an infantry officer, I invested a lot of time in building my fitness so I could lead from the front. I volunteered to be officer in charge of the cross country team and one of my roles was to train with the squad each morning. They ran further and faster than anyone else in the battalion. It was hard work for me, but it helped my fitness.

I couldn't ask others in the team to develop their fitness, if I wasn't fit myself. I took this stance, despite being fully aware there were other officers whose standard of fitness was well below par. They were happy to be mediocre, but I didn't think this was acceptable.

It was the same with shooting. I took every opportunity to practice my shooting skills, with all weapons. While being a good shot compliments the essential skills an officer should have, I wanted to be able to compete with the best shots in my platoon. Once again, I was very aware there were other officers who avoided shooting, because they were bad at it and didn't want to embarrass themselves. That wasn't where I wanted to be though. That wasn't walking the talk.

I've carried this attitude into everything I have done

subsequently too. When I coach sales people in client meetings, I always offer to actively participate if the person I am coaching wants me to do so. I have had the benefit of sales training skills and know I can add value to the client and the coachee.

This open and direct, walk the talk, type approach has enabled me to demonstrate that I am prepared to place my credibility on the line. This is not an arrogant stance. I am not perfect and when I coach I am not looking for perfection. I am looking for the coachee to progress though and walking the talk has definitely helped me to deliver that.

LEAD BY EXAMPLE

I learned this lesson while I was in the junior division at the Royal Military Academy, Sandhurst in April 1985. Her Majesty the Queen was the Guest of Honour at the Sovereign's Parade that marks the day when the Officer Cadets in the senior division are commissioned. In other words, it is the day they stop being trainees and start being Officers.

One aspect of Her Majesty's speech to the entire Academy was particularly memorable. The Queen said that she was sure we would all find ourselves in situations that we had never encountered before and could possibly be tired and even quite scared, In addition the Queen said that if this happened and we led by example, then we would have done all that was required of us.

Leading by example is very much the British Army way of doing things, whether you are a senior officer, or the most recently promoted lance corporal, yet, for some reason, this isn't always the case in business. To demonstrate how important it can be, let me give you an example from my time in Angola.

During our time there, one of the most dangerous tasks we had to undertake was the fortnightly distribution of a food parcel to every member of the workforce on the mine. This was known as cabaz, which is a Portuguese expression. Cabaz came in the shape of a cardboard box that weighed about forty pounds, but was awkward to carry. Cabaz contained tinned meats, flour, oil and sugar amongst other highly desirable foodstuffs. In addition to the cabaz, each member of staff was entitled to twenty-four cans of soft drinks.

Cabaz was very highly cherished as it could be consumed, sold or traded and this in a place where there were no shops. The disorganised nature of the distribution of cabaz to around 500 members of staff meant that opportunities for theft or the allegation of theft were many and the potential to cause uproar high.

There was a senior manager in the diamond mine, called Harry, and he was a very experienced man who had worked and fought in many countries and wars. Harry decided we were not going to allow 500 people into the compound at the same time as this represented too much of a risk to public (and our) safety. Groups of thirty people would be allowed in and when they had all left with their cabaz, another thirty would be allowed in.

Harry predicted that this strategy would cause problems, certainly for the first couple of times we implemented it. My team and I were tasked with policing groups of thirty and providing security at the containers where the cabaz was stored.

As Harry predicted, on the Saturday afternoon when cabaz was due to be distributed, there was a very angry group of about five hundred people standing outside the administrative compound. I was responsible for keeping them out and glad there was a fence between me and the irate mob. We did our best to placate some of the anger, but when we let the first thirty people in, the others became even more restless.

Harry appeared at the gate.

'How's it going Paddy?' he asked me.

'They're angry and annoyed Harry,' I said. 'They haven't been told why we are doing what we are doing and I'm not sure they'd listen anyhow.'

'Fine, open the gate,' said Harry briskly.

The gate was opened and, to my astonishment, Harry calmly walked out into the middle of the baying mob, raised his hands above his head and started shushing them. I almost couldn't believe what I was seeing.

Very calmly, Harry explained why we were only allowing groups of thirty people in. He emphasised that someone's cabaz had been stolen the last time it was distributed, adding that he didn't want any of them to go without their cabaz so that was why we were doing what we were doing. He finished this intervention by asking everyone to sit down and offering them drinking water while they waited.

When Harry came back through the gate, he told me he would get water organised and duly did so. The next time we opened the gate, the next 30 came through without any trouble at all. By then, Harry had disappeared, but he had done what he needed to do.

I was inspired by this demonstration. Harry had shown real courage and great instinct with that crowd of people. He had used great leadership to resolve a potentially very difficult situation and shown the employees and his team that he was prepared to confront challenges head on.

Too often in business, when people move into a management or leadership role, they adopt the mindset that they are now removed from the day-to-day challenges faced by the front line. Managers often hide by explaining that their work load requires them to stay in the (often nearest) office and that they don't have time to support their people in their roles. This is particularly the case with mediocre sales managers, especially when times are tough. These are generally businesses where clients are unhappy and the client-facing teams are getting a lot of grief.

It is the leader's role to confront the challenges faced by any business by leading by example. This takes courage, as Harry demonstrated, but the long-term impact on a team can be incredible.

BE PASSIONATE

'Nothing great was ever achieved without enthusiasm': so said the American essayist and poet Waldo Emerson. Enthusiasm and passion are fundamental qualities in a leader. Being passionate about the industry they work in, the business they work for and the people they work with is essential. Yet, too few leaders spend any time thinking about the type of impact they want to have.

Whether leaders know this or not, they have an impact every time they interact with their people. A passionate leader can electrify a team and push it to new heights.

When I was about two years into my job as a salesman a manger called Alan Jones took over our branch team. I already knew him from my time as a trainee, because he had spent some time training me and he had already impressed me and others on many levels. It's possible that I was biased in his favour, because he had previously served in a very good unit in the army, but nevertheless, when I was told he was going to be our new boss, I was very pleased indeed.

Part of Alan's role was to accompany us on client meetings. He had an obligation to supervise us and also help us develop our skills through coaching. None of the team had ever really enjoyed joint visits with the previous two managers. They either took over the meeting completely, which wasn't great, or they sat in the corner and said nothing, which wasn't brilliant either. At the end of the meetings, we would be given feedback, which was basically criticism of our performance. While most people in the sales team had broad shoulders, no one enjoys being put down and I certainly didn't.

From the beginning of my first day of joint visits with Alan things were different. To begin with, we had a really good chat during the car journey. We talked about his time in training and about what I knew about the team. Alan asked me what I wanted from my sales role.

'I'd like to go into training at some stage,' I replied.

'I think you'd be good in a training role,' was his instant response.

Then, after a few moments reflection, he added: 'If you're going to be a credible trainer, you're probably going to have to get yourself into the top 25 per cent of the salesforce at some stage.'

In the previous chapter we looked at the power

of questions to create focus and, in this example, he was taking this technique one stage further. He was using language to create a focus for me. His use of the word 'credible,' for example, was well chosen and very effective. Of course I wanted to be a credible trainer, who wouldn't?

By very reasonably suggesting that I'd have to get myself into the top 25 per cent of the field force, he was also setting a certain goal for me, without having to go into the actual, all important, figures.

'What levels of business would I need to do to get into the top 25 per cent?' I asked.

'About five-hundred thousand should do it,' he said (This referred to our units of business measurement). 'How much did you do last year?'

'Four-hundred-and-ten thousand' I replied.

'So, we just need to find the same amount and another ninety thousand to get to five-hundred thousand' was his confident response. 'Give some thought to what I can do to help you get to five-hundred thousand and I'll do my best to help out. Now tell me about the client we're about to meet.'

This exchange really got me thinking. While it isn't necessarily unusual for a new leader to ask his people what they want, my first two managers had never asked me. In fact, they'd barely spoken to me on our first day out on joint visits. Yet, from the start, Alan had done enough to demonstrate to me that he was going to try and help me achieve a professional goal. The achievement of this goal would directly impact my private life and the people I cared about outside work too.

The bottom line was that Alan was saying that he would help and I believed him. It quickly became apparent that he was having similar conversations with all of the people in the team too. Alan had a passion for people. Specifically, he had a passion for understanding what they wanted from the business, so that he could work with them in the achievement of their professional goals.

There was an upside for him too. The goals of the team were aligned to his business goals. Clearly, it suited him that I now needed to deliver five-hundred thousand where four-hundred thousand might have once been just fine for me.

Passion for people and the job is a pre-requisite of true leadership. I meet too many people, many of them leaders, who have fallen out of love with the sector they work in and the company they work for. They often try to mask this lack of love from their people, yet this never works. When you are truly passionate about something, it is obvious from what you say and do and the energy and intensity that you bring to everything.

BE CONSISTENT

People often say that they want to work with someone who is going to behave in a consistent way. In actual fact, what they really mean is they definitely don't want to work with someone who behaves in an *inconsistent* way. Inconsistent behaviour creates uneasiness among a team. From day to day, even hour to hour, the team feel uncertain about which version of the strategy the leader will present. This obviously unsettles people, discouraging empowered behaviours and encouraging hesitancy.

Clearly one of the objectives of effective leadership is to release and harness the potential within the team, the individuals within that team and the individuals as part of a collective. If a leader's inconsistent behaviour inhibits their people, they will be setting themselves up for average results at best and, at worst, potentially high levels of attrition amongst their most capable people.

> Passion for people and the job is a pre-requisite of true leadership.

I once worked with a director of a large financial services company. It was quickly apparent he was the most inconsistent man I have ever encountered. I knew a good number of his team very well and they commented on this every time we met.

'We don't know which version of Bill is going to turn up, so we have developed an ability to try and establish this and then let the rest of the team know if they should approach him, or if they should avoid him,' they would say.

Of course, Bill's behaviour changed fairly frequently, so it was a constant challenge to keep abreast of his moods. The impact of this inconsistency was that everyone who reported to him was constantly 'on the back foot'. Every time anyone undertook a task, their default mindset was: 'How will he view our actions if he is in one of his moods?'

The root cause of the inconsistency was Bill was a bully and that is very damaging to those on the other end of this behaviour, whatever their age. Do you remember that school playground expression 'sticks and stones may break my bones but names will never hurt me'? It's not true is it? It is very difficult to deal with emotional abuse, which is why bullying, in any environment, is reprehensible, but especially in a person who has been given a position of authority and responsibility.

The way Bill 'motivated' people was by making them feel bad about themselves. Fortunately, he didn't remain in that senior role for very long.

Inconsistency destroys confidence, which is so important to great business performance. If you want your people to operate with confidence, they must know that they are going to be treated in a fair and consistent way at all times.

BE HONEST

In the context of leadership, honesty is telling your people the truth, even when that message can be difficult. If people are going to trust a leader, they are going to want to know that everything the leader tells them is the truth.

One sure fire way to lose loyalty very quickly is to lie (even if you think it is the best thing to do), or to avoid telling the truth. People want to know the truth, especially when times are tough. While the truth might unsettle them, knowing that they are not being told the truth, or not being given the full picture, is guaranteed to unsettle them. People who are unsettled can't operate with certainty. They will operate with hesitation and hesitation benefits no one.

Constant and open communication from the person on top is critical. Even if a team is spread across a wide geographical area, there will be times when the correct thing to do is for the leader to go and see their team and talk to them face to face. I have been shocked to find this is apparently too inconvenient for some leaders. Instead, they prefer to rely on conference calls, email, or even videos distributed among their people.

I know personally what this feels like from the other

side from a time earlier, during my commercial career, when a company I worked for got into trouble. The downward spiral went on for about eighteen months, but the workforce only learned details via the media. We were in the somewhat unsatisfactory situation of receiving information about our future job security from the radio news.

Our employer was nervous about media leaks; he wasn't prepared to tell the workforce anything before he told the press. In other words, even though it was clear to everyone the company was heading for disaster, the management didn't trust its own workforce. That would challenge anyone's loyalty.

Eventually, we were all gathered together into a meeting room and shown a video from the managing director. It was carefully made and full of spin. We didn't really know the MD, who had assiduously avoided the workforce for many months, but it was clear that we were seeing a PR-driven version of him. Of course, a video doesn't allow for questions and answers, so we were no nearer to getting to know him either.

To add insult to injury, we were given a printed sheet of frequently asked questions (FAQs), which was of limited value, and told the meeting was over. As an act of leadership, this ranks pretty close to the worst example I can remember.

However desperate the situation, real leaders would

get themselves in front of their people, deliver the corporate message and then answer questions with honesty. Our future was unknown, but we didn't hold that against our MD. It was his unwillingness to talk to us that was less easy to stomach.

All we wanted was for our MD to come and talk to us and to be honest with us.

Of course, leaders are privy to information that must remain confidential and I am not suggesting that a leader divulge this in any inappropriate way. However, it is a true leader who puts themselves out in order to engage on a face-to-face basis. That makes all the difference.

SUMMARY

1. The way you behave in front of the team is the leadership polish that will take you to the next layer of success.
2. Inspirational leaders walk the talk, lead by example, are passionate, consistent and honest
3. …And are never reluctant to engage face to face with their team.

PERSONAL DEVELOPMENT EXERCISES

EXERCISE ONE

Behave like a leader

Business benefit

You will be able to improve your leadership capability

Resources:

Non required

Format:

Take a piece of paper and write down at least five things that you think a great leader needs to be. For each word write down what you mean by that word or expression. For example, if one of those words is something like 'inspirational' then write down exactly what that means to you. When you think of someone who is inspirational, what is it that they do that makes them inspirational? Exactly what do they do that makes them inspirational?

When you know what it is that makes them so inspirational, start to think about how frequently you demonstrate that type of behaviour.

Using a scale of one to ten, where one is low and ten is high, rate yourself based on how often you display those traits or behaviours. For example, if you think that being a good public speaker contributes to being inspirational, rate yourself on your ability to inspire people by speaking to an audience.

»

If you rate yourself lower than your desired rating, you now know that you should be working on this skill. The next step is to ascertain exactly which skills you need to develop, i.e. what do you need to do to speak in an inspiring way and then start to take action.

This exercise raises your awareness about what makes a great leader and the extent to which you frequently exhibit those types of behaviour. If there are gaps, you should work on getting better.

PERSONAL DEVELOPMENT EXERCISES

EXERCISE TWO

Behave like a leader

Business benefit

Enable your people to develop their leadership capability

Resources

Up to sixty minutes needed with each member of your team

Format

Explain to each member of the team that leadership isn't a position or a title; it is a state of mind. For a team to deliver results, it is necessary for every member of the team to think and behave as if they were a leader. Take the time to talk to each of your people to establish what leadership

»

traits they admire.

When they have identified one leadership trait, encourage them to develop that trait. Ask them to identify what type of circumstances will provide them with an opportunity to apply this trait. When they have identified the occasions when they can apply this trait, ask them to consciously identify what type of behaviour they will actually need to exhibit. Ask them to be specific.

When this behaviour is known, ensure you are aware of both the circumstances and their behaviour so that you can look out for it and support individuals in the application of this behaviour.

CHAPTER 3

TEAMS DON'T WORK – UNLESS YOU DO

Since I've started working with leaders outside a military environment, I've been constantly amazed at the widely held views about what changes occur when people take up a position of responsibility or leadership. Misconceptions abound about how behaviour and communications should change to reflect this elevation. Then, rather like a warped game of corporate Chinese Whispers, this misinterpretation of how a new leader should act and react frequently leads to some extraordinary and wholly unnecessary behaviour.

My most memorable example of this is when I worked with a new manager who proudly installed a rather ostentatious standard lamp right at the front of his desk. I couldn't help but say I thought it looked very out of place and told him I was curious as to why he thought it added something to the ambience of his office. Do you know what he said?

'I think it adds a degree of gravitas to an otherwise slightly dull room,' he replied in utter seriousness.

I didn't agree and neither did my colleagues. However, our greatest concern was that our new boss had taken the time to buy a tacky standard lamp and bring it to Windsor from Brighton. What sort of a statement was he trying to make?

Another negative side to this trend of imagining how a true leader might work is that people very often volunteer to move into a management role because of the perception of the benefits that will come from the elevation. I don't mean the extra income, although that is always a big draw. What I mean is they view it in terms of the respect, status and kudos that come with the job. In their eyes, promotion comes with a degree of control and comfort. It is as though they naturally assume it is their turn to give the orders and they can now elect others to do the unpleasant things. In short, they believe their life is about to become, or should become, easier.

Great teams are built around great leaders. For a team to work well, the leader must work well.

I couldn't agree less.

There is nothing about leadership that is, or should be 'easy'. Leadership is not an excuse to sit back and bask in the glow of an inexpensive standard lamp. Nor is it about all the goodies you can lay your hands on. Leadership is an opportunity to serve others. It is only once a leader embraces the fact that a core function of leadership is to get the best out of all of the people they influence that they will ever get the most from those around them.

In my experience, having had the opportunity to observe hundreds, if not thousands, of leaders, both in the military and in a commercial life, great teams are built around great leaders. For a team to work well, the leader must work well. A team is only ever as good as their leader. If the person out in front is not prepared to take personal and professional risks to set the team's direction, then the odds the team will succeed are massively reduced.

I had an interesting experience with a senior team in a financial services business a couple of years ago. The business was in a challenging place and those on the front line were getting a very tough time from all sides. They were constantly under fire from clients and from people within the company.

The leader of that business decided to get the leadership team together for a two-day event to create a bit of morale and team spirit. I was asked to deliver the first day's event. I flew over from my home in Ireland to meet the boss beforehand so we could chat through the content for the day.

Our meeting coincided with one he was holding

with his eight direct reports, because this was the only time he could spare. I already knew some of these managers and welcomed the opportunity to listen to their views on the challenges being faced by the business.

I joined their meeting just after lunch and presented my views on how my day should run. The format was agreed with some minor adjustments.

They asked me to stay while they discussed the agenda for the second day of the two-day event. It emerged that the agenda for day two had been agreed via an earlier conference call. The manager responsible for the agenda was tasked with sharing the ideas that had come from that earlier call. Those ideas had been devised by a working party of four managers, all of whom were present at the current meeting.

It didn't start well. The manager in charge of the agenda hadn't actually thought to bring any copies of the agenda. This meant we were all in the rather frustrating position of listening while he read out what was going to happen. As the agenda manager stumbled his way through the agenda, I spotted the boss shaking his head. He looked deeply concerned. Seconds later, he interrupted.

'Are you really saying that the session on leadership is going to start with a video and then be followed up with a group workshop for seventy people?' he demanded irritably.

The agenda manager, in desperation turned to his

colleagues for some support. Unfortunately for him, there was none forthcoming.

'Well, on the conference call, we did discuss..." he began to stammer before being interrupted again almost immediately.

'I thought we said on the conference call that the session would open with me talking about business performance,' said the boss.

'I thought we debated that and decided to replace that with something a bit different?' responded the agenda manager with a tinge of anxiety in his voice.

'I don't remember that,' pronounced the boss. Turning to another manager, he said: 'Bill do you remember that?'

This was starting to look a bit like a confrontation now.

'I can't remember to be honest,' said Bill, shifting uncomfortably in his chair.

The conversation continued in this vein with the boss pulling the agenda apart and telling everyone there what he thought they should do. Of course, it wasn't really what he thought they should do; it was what they were going to have to do. At the end of this monologue, the boss left the meeting to go to another one.

I remained in my seat and the somewhat dejected agenda manager asked me if I had any ideas. I put forward some ideas that might work and we discussed each one. As every idea was formulated, they kept coming back to the same question: will the boss like it? If the general view was that he wouldn't like it, the idea was scrapped.

I have real issues when a senior team containing some very accomplished people behaves like this. Here we were, discussing an event with the objective of raising morale in a challenged business environment, yet everything that was being done was having the opposite effect. The boss's approach clearly wasn't doing much for the morale of his senior team.

A sure fire way to damage morale further was to deliver a conference that hadn't been thought through and was poorly organised. This is what they were in danger of delivering and to their most influential seventy people. So, what could the boss have done differently in this case?

I have a couple of views.

The first is that this disorganised approach to the conference was a reflection of the priority, or rather lack of priority that was being given to this event. For a start, the timing was all wrong. Everyone knows that when leaders interact with their people, they always have an impact; therefore it is important to make sure that the impact is a good one. With that in mind, I was curious why the format for the event was being discussed on a conference call just four weeks before the day itself. For something with this level of importance, I'd have recommended that the boss chair the working group and the working group meet face to face a minimum of three months before the event was due to be delivered. Three months allows for ideas to germinated, tested, adjusted or discarded. If the boss is going to have such an influence, including the final say, he should stay close to the organisation to minimise the risk of demotivating his people through last minute, wholesale changes.

Another difficulty with this approach is that it is not a good idea for the person in charge to give the team a perception that they have absolute control over something this important, if they are then going to use their authority to ride roughshod over all their ideas.

The team should have agreed the meeting objectives and also any specific planning boundaries within which they had to operate, with clarity. The team I observed in the planning session described here didn't even know which one of three possible venues they actually had for the conference. All venues were completely different in layout and this would undoubtedly have had a bearing on how the event would be managed. Yet, in the chaos of the discussion, this didn't seem to have occurred to anyone.

The boss, or someone to whom responsibility had been delegated, should have worked closely with each of the people who were involved in planning the event. The day before the conference should have been set aside for a full run through, as opposed to being used for last-minute final preparation.

This was an example of poor prioritisation leading to poor planning. Or, to put it more memorably, this was, without a doubt, a case where the seven Ps should be applied: Prior Planning and Preparation Prevents Piss Poor Performance.

On a very serious note though, the seven Ps apply to everyone, *especially* the boss. The leader's involvement should begin from the moment a team is formed and they should maintain a healthy presence from then on. Parachuting in to criticise at key occasions is not going to do it.

What is a 'healthy' leadership presence? After all, it is a fine line between trying to help guide individual members of a team in the right direction and driving them mad with your constant micromanaging. It is certainly something I have had to juggle when I was a member of the training team in a large UK insurer. Part of the role was to observe colleagues in sales meetings with real clients.

Our colleagues had no say in this process because it was a regulatory requirement. Most of the time it was OK, because the manager did the sit-ins; but every so often someone like me had to be brought in. These people had no prior relationship with me and regarded my presence with suspicion because, in their eyes, I was a suit from head office. They overlooked the fact I had been a relatively successful salesperson, who had previously benefited from the training that we all knew was effective when applied in a client meeting.

When I turned up for a day's client meetings with a colleague I had never met before, a pattern of behaviour started to develop. The person I was about to spend the day with would often tell me that they were busy preparing for the day and would point me in the direction of the office kitchen where I could make myself some tea or coffee. Whether they were busy or not, it was clear that they were trying to impose a degree of control over a situation where they felt they had very limited control. I fully understood their position. I had been in their shoes after all. However, I knew that if the person I was coaching was going to get any value from our time together we had to get over this phase of deep suspicion and form a healthy working relationship as quickly as possible. We didn't have the luxury of time.

I developed the habit of tackling the unspoken issue of my uninvited presence head on, usually as soon as we were in the car. My approach was simple and direct and usually sounded a bit like this.

'I've done your job and had days out with people like me from the training department,' I'd say. 'Some people like these days and some don't. I think I know that you'd prefer to be going out with the manager you know, but I'm here to help. I'd like to try and add some value to you today if that is possible, so to begin with

I'd like to discuss very openly what you want from me during our time together today.'

The alternative, as I saw it, was that we didn't have this open conversation and we poked a stick at trying to add value to the salesperson. Every time I had this conversation I'd get a different response.

The most direct response to my question of what the salesperson wanted me to do during the client meeting was; 'Sit in the corner and shut up!'

My response to this direct statement was relatively direct as well: 'I will sit in the corner and shut up as you have requested. I usually only offer to participate if the client gets confrontational; and if you want to pass the issue over to me, that offer remains. Either way, I will give you some feedback when the meeting is over. In what format do you like your feedback?'

The person I was with on this occasion actually responded very well to this statement and we went on to have three very good meetings together.

One lady I worked with was more aggressive, but in a passive way. She was polite, but never pleasant and avoided eye contact with me at all times. When we got into her car I asked her not to start the engine immediately. This caught her attention and she asked me why not. I told her that I didn't know whether I needed to take my car with us. We were leaving Bristol for three meetings all over Gloucestershire.

'It is clear that the idea of our spending a day together with three of your clients is not very appealing to you and I think I can understand that,' I explained, honestly. 'I do want to try to add value and I have, after all, been a salesman. The reason I asked about taking my car was very simple. If, after the first client meeting, you feel you haven't had some value and haven't enjoyed the process, I will not come to the other two meetings. I can then use my own car to go back to my office. I've cleared this with your boss who says it is fine. What do you think?'

This lady, who was now on the back foot, replied: 'I don't think you'll need to take your car, I am sure it will be fine.'

'That's great,' I said, smiling warmly. 'Where are we off to first?'

We then had a good conversation about the client we were going to see. My objective was to quickly create an environment where we could get over the usual issues and excuses that had dogged this type of coaching experience on previous occasions. I knew from experience that sales people responded well to my being direct, and generally welcomed my offer to get involved in client meetings and volunteering to leave if we weren't making progress. I like honesty and openness and I respect others who are honest and open. I'm not unusual in that. Similarly, I don't like people who habitually focus on what's wrong with a situation;

however, leaders do have to understand what is wrong before they start to try and create a solution.

In an environment like this, it's fine to let people have a short moan if it means that everyone can then refocus on the objective. If the issue isn't addressed early on, it can fester. This leads to a lack of honesty, which impacts on the results that can be achieved.

As it was, the saleswoman and I did have a good day together. In fact, she asked me to participate in the second and third meeting as well. As we drove back to her office, I thanked her for her openness during the day and asked her if she had had some value from our time together. It was only then that it emerged that she'd had a very bad experience from a previous trainer from head office. She'd been left with a very strong impression that my predecessor had only been interested in demonstrating how good a salesperson he was.

THE BOTTOM LINE?

Even though they were a small group of two people, the previous person hadn't been focused on, or prepared, to work for her or their benefit. He was only interested in his own benefit. While he held a position of some authority, he wasn't behaving as a leader. His objective was to try to add value to that salesperson by developing her skills, or by delivering some form of encouragement in what is quite a lonely job. Instead, what he did was overlook the team and focus on himself. That isn't leadership. It is selfish competitiveness.

The success I had with that salesperson was down to the fact I had no secret agenda, or interest in being right, or proving myself to be superior in any way. My only objective was to add value and work with the team to achieve this.

I have come across far too many leaders whose core objective appears to be to demonstrate how important they are. They do this by hogging the limelight and unfairly diverting their team's efforts in a direction that will place them in a good light.

I had one boss who was fundamentally lazy. He preferred hobnobbing in head office to anything else. It was very apparent that any work that was being done by me or any other members of the team was being show-boated as his work. You could say that this is what delegation is all about. It is to an extent, but not if there isn't any recognition for the people who have done the work. That isn't leadership.

Effective leaders are those who are very good at identifying where good ideas and good results come from. They are careful to say thank you to the people who have really made it happen too. This is an important skill because people in managerial roles often exist to support the people on the ground. In the military, the person on the ground is the soldier who is eyeball to eyeball with the enemy. In a bank, the person on the ground is the cashier, or the person at customer services who is eyeball to eyeball with the customer. In a public sector business, it the person on the ground is the one who is eyeball to eyeball with the public. If you are a leader in any of these circumstances, you should be doing everything you can to enable those people on the ground to be as effective as possible. You should be supporting their efforts at all times and taking as much time as you can to get in front of them and thank them for their efforts. The value of a sincere thank you from a leader who genuinely cares is huge. A lot of leaders are too busy schmoozing, or hiding in head office, to make this happen in a meaningful way. It is to their and everyone else's detriment.

By being available and approachable, you are encouraging your people to talk to you, openly and honestly. This will ensure that your team feel listened to, which is vital. This will also ensure that you get real-time feedback on what it is like to be on the ground, which is incredibly important too.

It is a poor leader indeed who won't engage with their people on the ground, in favour of a nice comfortable life. They don't want the aggravation they perceive any feedback will create. In my view, this type of behaviour demonstrates that the wrong person has been promoted.

For a team to work effectively, the leader must work

effectively. If you want your people to go the extra mile, you will also have to go the extra mile too. Get the balance right and the results can be extraordinarily powerful. I will close this chapter with an example of just how powerful it can be.

I once met a lady from a big animal foods business. When we got talking she had no idea that I knew the CEO of her company very well. She told me that she'd recently been to a dinner where she had sat beside someone she knew to be a senior leader in her company, but was at that time unsure of his role. She said that he'd been unfailingly polite and very interested in her and the challenges she faced in the business. One of the words she used to described this person was he was 'normal,' which I thought was interesting.

She was, of course, as she later learned, sitting beside the CEO. Even in hindsight though, she noted that it was clear that he wasn't the same as other CEOs she had met in other big businesses. She particularly described the way he gave the people in his team credit for their incredible levels of success. While their industry had faced challenges from a market that they couldn't control, the CEO never once complained that these challenges existed. Instead, he focused on the way his people had fought back so well. He highlighted how they had still delivered when tens of millions of pounds of profit were being removed by circumstances outside their control. The CEO had no blame to apportion to anyone and showed no hint of taking any credit for himself.

The lady finished her story by telling me that the team were 'devoted' to this CEO. I know for a fact that that type of feedback would have embarrassed the CEO, but it is also incredibly empowering.

SUMMARY

1. Leadership should never be easy. It is not an excuse for self-aggrandisement.
2. Leaders should maintain a healthy presence at all times and never be over-bearing and critical for the sake of it.
3. It should always be a priority to give full support and recognition to the people on the ground.

PERSONAL DEVELOPMENT EXERCISES

EXERCISE ONE

Teams don't work unless you do

Business benefit

You will develop a set of principles the team will operate with

»

Resources

Time in a team meeting

Format

Create your team charter. A team charter exists to enable teams to operate as effectively as possible.

Allocate up to ninety minutes, at the beginning of a specific period, i.e. the start of a new business year. Ask the team to come up with ideas that will dictate how the team will interact, both with each other and with external stakeholders. Any boundaries or resources available should be stated clearly.

Next, define the rules and standards that the team will adhere to. As a minimum, the topics you should cover are how the team will:

- Celebrate good news for an individual within the team.
- Celebrate good news for the team.
- Manage bad news for an individual within the team.
- Manage bad news for the team.

- Represent the team when with people outside the team.
- Communicate with you, the leader.
- Expect you to communicate with them.

Include other topics that are relevant to your team in your own list.

Collate the results of this workshop and then distribute the charter to the team maintaining it as a working document.

PERSONAL DEVELOPMENT EXERCISES

EXERCISE TWO

Teams don't work unless you do

Business benefit

Your team will tell you how they think you can help them

Resources

Time

Format

Create a list of five skills that you think would add value to your own development and to the team. Explain to the team that you want to add more value to their development by developing a skill of your own.

Having signposted your objective, give them your list of five skills and manage a debate about the relative value of each of the skills. Gain the team's priority through debate or voting.

Agree when you will lead a development session on this topic.

Do it.

Ask for feedback from the session, measure the implementation of that new skill by the team.

Analyse results.

CHAPTER 4

CREATE A CULTURE THAT ENGAGES YOUR TEAM

In 1986, my first battalion commander left to be replaced by Lieutenant Colonel Alexander 'Sandy' McNeil. I had never met Sandy before, but he had a reputation for being a fit and aggressive commander who was well respected by the Gurkhas.

We were told that the whole battalion of 1000 men were to parade in the gymnasium to enable Sandy to address us on his first day in command. I was sitting on the floor at the back with my soldiers when I saw someone walk in to the gym at the far end. I vaguely heard the word 'ub' but didn't know what it meant. People started to stand up but the response was lethargic and disorganised. The man who had appeared at the front of the gym turned on his heel and walked out.

The senior Gurkha Officer intervened and told us that we were to stand up when Sandy came in. 'Ubhinu' is the Nepali verb to stand up and 'ub' is stand up as a command. We sat waiting for about five minutes. When Sandy reappeared, the Gurkha Officer shouted 'ub' and everyone leapt to their feet and stood to attention. Sandy McNeil had arrived. We had just been given an insight into what life was going to be like under his command.

Sandy was a man who walked the talk. Many people say that you shouldn't ask someone to do something you are not prepared to do yourself, but very few practise it. We all quickly recognised that Sandy would push himself harder than he would push us and we respected that. He was exceptionally fit on any level. The fact that he was sixteen years older than most of the young officers was never mentioned by him. He knew that to be an effective leader he had to be physically robust. This robustness would make a direct contribution to his ability to both think and lead the battalion in battle.

It is worth noting here that the one-thousand men that made up 2nd Battalion 2nd Gurkha Rifles didn't change. The only person who changed was the boss, Sandy. Within a week, we were being given an insight into the demands that Sandy was going to make on us as soldiers and officers.

'We are infantrymen,' Sandy told us in an early briefing to the officers. 'We need to be very fit and very good at carrying heavy loads over long distances and quickly, by day and by night. We must also all be extremely good shots. I expect everyone in the battalion to be excellent in these areas, and, as officers, we must be excellent at other skills as well. We will measure our progress and constantly push the boundaries further.'

We now had our mission. Sandy had set his vision for the battalion of 1000 soldiers. As subordinate commanders we had to pursue the mission with relentless focus. We were clearly going to be in a high-performance environment where all of the key activities were going to be measured. Within two weeks, we had all undertaken standard British Army fitness and shooting tests and the scores had been logged. We understood immediately that this must have been pre-planned. Gaining access to shooting ranges generally took months to arrange. Sandy had obviously put this plan into action long before he walked into the gym on his first day.

> Many people say that you shouldn't ask someone to do something you are not prepared to do yourself, but very few practise it.

When these initial assessments were complete, we received our performance targets for fitness and shooting. For fitness, we were to become the first battalion in the British Army where every single person could complete the standard fitness test at least one minute faster than the time allowed by the British Army. For Gurkhas this wasn't too big a challenge. However, we all knew that as soon as everyone in the battalion had completed the test at the stipulated one minute below the army time limit, Sandy would inevitably require us to complete the test more than *two minutes* faster than the standard time.

I was very aware that while some older soldiers in my platoon would be fine with the first time challenge, they might well struggle with the next stage, which we all knew was on its way. I had to focus on preparing them for the time when the bar would be lowered, even though it could possibly be a year away. Clearly this would make us all fitter, which was the aim.

It didn't take us long to achieve the first milestone. Within four months of arriving, we had all passed the test according to Sandy's rule and he was quick to congratulate us. Achieving this goal had a beneficial impact on the whole battalion. As soon as we had finished congratulating ourselves for this achievement we were told that the objective was now to break the two-minute barrier, just as I had anticipated. We now all had to be able to complete the test more than two minutes faster than the time allowed by the army. Fortunately, we had all quietly been working towards this objective because we knew it was coming. About 85 per cent of the one-thousand-man battalion had achieved this objective by the time Sandy's tour of duty finished. He left behind a fit and energetic group of soldiers.

We had to strive in other areas too, such as shooting. In the standard army shooting tests, the normal pass mark in the British Army was 70 per cent. The test involved firing seventy bullets at seventy targets from a variety of distances and positions. Fifty hits out of seventy was a pass under normal circumstances and we were well versed in how to accumulate fifty hits from the easier shooting positions of the shorter ranges. Sandy introduced a new target for all of us. We now had to score 95 per cent in this test. Please bear in mind that 95 per cent represented sixty-seven hits out of seventy, which meant we would have to include hits on targets from three-hundred metres and from difficult shooting positions. This was going to take some work.

When we analysed what we were going to have to do, it became apparent that we would have to use our practice time to get better at the longer ranges in the more difficult positions. It seemed Sandy was clear in his thinking about how we were going to progress.

What was good about this was that the performance targets were relevant, simple and measureable. Plus, the performance targets applied to everyone in the battalion and I liked that. I had long held the view there were too many middle-aged officers who returned to the battalion after a cushy staff job and weren't fit enough, literally, to lead fighting soldiers in a harsh environment. It was just a shame that it took Sandy's targets to encourage the right type of behaviour.

The impact on our culture was immense. Training exercises now involved groups of soldiers marching across long distances with heavy loads by day and night. This improved fitness and mental toughness and made us all better navigators in darkness. Previously this type of activity wouldn't have been incorporated or given the priority it had now.

People who were already fit and strong got even fitter and stronger. Shooting results started to get better. Very few people got to 95 per cent quickly, but we all improved and could see that we were improving. We started to develop a belief that if we were tested against the other four infantry battalions in our area of operations, we would march them off their feet. This mattered to us. Regimental pride is very important.

In the other skills and disciplines relevant to officers, Sandy introduced performance targets. Again the topics were relevant and measureable. We practised calling in heavy fire support on enemy positions. We developed the ability to do this quickly and accurately, often while we were being put under a lot of pressure. As we got better at this key battlefield skill, we became more confident and competitive with each other.

It was clear that Sandy was focusing on the skills we would need if we went to war. This appealed to all of us because we wanted to be ready if that opportunity came. While we were working damn hard, we also enjoyed some good social time with our men and their families. Sandy was involved in this too, without ever taking over the events. He was good at talking to the Gurkhas, not talking at them. The old cliché work hard, play hard was evident and we were doing it. It was starting to become part of our culture.

The lessons I took from all of this were several fold. If you want to create a culture that engages people, focus on things that are relevant. It sounds so simple but too many organisations layer on stuff that is irrelevant. Bureaucracy is a real issue and is always highly frustrating for everyone other than bureaucrats.

Sandy's focus on developing and measuring skills was also key. Success in any discipline comes from the relentless application of the correct skills by determined people. In sport, coaches know what they want their people to do and the skills they want them to execute. Business must be the same. Companies frequently don't spend enough time developing the skills their people need to be successful. They kid themselves that if they think there is enough activity the business will flourish. I don't agree. All activities must be clear and measureable if a business is going to be able to evaluate the quantity and quality of employee contribution.

I worked with one company that employed one-thousand salespeople and was an excellent case in point. This service business gave advice to clients and any sort of negativity was frowned upon. Everything was done to keep the ranks below believing the business was profitable, when it wasn't, but the management mistakenly believed the team would be motivated if they believed everything was OK. I was entrusted with the job of spending some time with the salespeople in a bid to understand how effective their client meetings actually were and whether there was a problem there that was eroding profitability.

I quickly found the sales meetings weren't effective at all because they were always rushed. Clients were fed into a pipeline of meetings, exposed to a sixty-minute process that defined the meetings and then moved out so that another client could appear. This wasn't great for the client but, interestingly, the client didn't really complain, because the experience was no worse than the clients' experiences with other companies who did the same thing. However, they didn't buy much either.

I wanted to know why the sales meetings were so rushed. Digging further, I discovered that one of the key measures in this business was how many sales people were at work each day. Figures were reported to the managing director daily, after a lengthy reporting process. It began with the first line managers phoning each of their people to see who was in work. This information had to be passed to a second line manager, who would then collate it and pass it to another manager. This would then be presented to the managing director, ideally by ten o'clock. If there were a lot of people clocked in, it was perceived to be good. This caused a huge amount of work, every day and completely distracted the entire management team for about two hours. If someone was off sick, this needed to be investigated, which took even more time. More significantly, the business also painstakingly measured how many client meetings were taking place each week. These were all clues to why everything was so out of balance.

This company was clearly on top of how many people were in the building and how many meetings they had, but, amazingly, it didn't seem bothered about what was actually happening when these people were working. When I asked the managing director what the people who were at work were doing, he couldn't seem to understand why I wanted to know. He couldn't connect to the fact that the management information coming out of the business was only really showing that sales people seemed to be seeing a lot of people, but it did not show why their customers weren't actually buying anything.

When this inefficiency was pointed out, the initial response from the management team was to tell their people to see even more potential customers. Even though the meeting process was flawed, the company concluded it should shove more clients into a flawed process. Incredible.

None of the managers saw how much pressure their salespeople were under because they never spent any time with their people. It was easier not to acknowledge what was going on because they didn't really know how to fix it. They preferred to stay in their offices in blissful ignorance.

The bottom line was that the culture was all wrong. While business measures were analysed, there was not enough honesty about the figures they got as a result. It wasn't one person who caused this, but collectively the people who could do something to fix it wouldn't acknowledge that it was wrong.

This situation required a leader to establish with clarity exactly what was happening, warts and all, and make this information available to the relevant people. This isn't an example of focusing on the negative. It is about establishing a starting point from which everyone can move forward together. I've known a couple of great leaders who will turn over every stone in order to be sure that they have established the root cause of an issue. It is not possible to fix something until you know what is wrong. Some leaders aren't too keen to turn over any stones in case they find something they don't like.

Of course, one problem many modern firms face is creating a culture among a team that can be in many different geographic locations. This can bring in a whole set of new challenges.

It is certainly a scenario I experienced in Angola where my team worked in six separate locations, up to forty kilometres apart. Communication was complex and was mainly via a central radio that was difficult to access because every other department at each location also needed to use it.

It was clear that, even if I wanted, it was going to be impossible to make all the decisions for the team. Decision-making authority had to be devolved to the senior person on the ground. While I had great confidence in my people and was happy to employ this as part of our culture, I was shocked to discover that some of the more senior men who were based out in the locations were uncomfortable with this. While their qualities as soldiers were without question, there was a real fear of making decisions. This surprised me. When I analysed the reason why, I realised that I, like the army, was placing too much emphasis on the time the men had been in the army, not their ability to adapt to a new environment like Angola. This was a challenge I hadn't been expecting.

In my initial team of fifteen men, I had a range of ranks from a Queens Gurkha Officer with thirty-two years' experience to a Staff Sergeant with 'only' eighteen years' experience. When I thought about the men who seemed to be most suited to leading smaller teams, it was often those who were less experienced that appeared to be more suitable. They were less fixed in their ways and therefore able to adapt, which is what I required. My challenge was that the system in the army encouraged the less experienced Gurkhas to defer to the older Gurkhas, whether they were right or otherwise. For my team to succeed in this hostile place, I was going to have to undo the old culture. This was a real challenge, but one that needed to be dealt with quickly and sensitively.

> Effective leaders pride themselves on good organisational skills, which help those around them to plan their objectives and strategies.

I spoke to the most experienced Gurkha there, a man on whom I had depended initially and he understood my dilemma immediately. He shared with me that the task in Angola was more demanding than a lot of the men had expected. He also told me that he thought his presence would hold us all back and surprised me by offering to leave.

After giving it some thought over the next twenty-four

hours, I realised that leaving Angola was the best thing for this man and for the team. If it all kicked-off, he could become a liability to us, as he was older than really appropriate for this task. While never saying so explicitly, I think we both knew that this was the case. His selfless act also meant that I would have the opportunity to promote a man who would pick the correct team leaders, with my support of course.

The point was that for our team to survive and deliver, we needed a culture that some of our existing and most senior people were not going to be able to operate in. This senior man made my first task easy for me and I respected him for that. After that I was able to promote a younger man who had a confidence we needed in that environment. Within two months I had replaced another senior person with a younger man too. While these decisions were both tough to make and tough to follow through, they paid dividends. When the mine was subsequently attacked, some of our young men displayed extraordinary courage and initiative in the days immediately after the attack.

For example, one man was stranded at a wash plant, thirty miles from Luzamba. He was on his own with Angolan security and Brazilian mine workers when his plant was attacked. He hid in the African bush overnight before walking along the riverbank for about eleven miles just before dawn. When he was opposite Luzamba he swam the Cuango River, correctly assuming that if he was quick the crocodiles would be asleep. They were. Another young Gurkha stranded forty miles from Luzamba hot-wired a sixteen-ton truck and drove into Luzamba, even though he had never previously driven a vehicle.

Being detained in Luzamba, there was no way we were going to be able to assist these men. We couldn't even communicate with them. I admired the fact that they got up off their backsides and did something about it, as opposed to waiting for other people to do something for them. This was the culture we had had sought to create because we knew this was the culture that the situation required.

This may sound like a simple culture to promote but it wasn't. We were fundamentally challenging the environment these men had grown up in, in some cases, for thirty years.

What is the key to an effective culture of engagement? The key to an effective culture of engagement is as follows:

1. **Communication:** Good quality verbal and written communication is essential to present options and expectations to the team in a way they can understand. During my time as a young officer in the British Army, I devoted a lot of time learning to speak Nepali. This was my choice and it certainly paid off in Angola.

   I was able to communicate with every member of my team and be sure that they could understand me. I've observed a lack of understanding between two people speaking the same language, never mind a foreign language.

2. **Organisation:** Effective leaders pride themselves on good organisational skills, which help those around them to plan their objectives and strategies. There are two military principles that have great value in the commercial world. Two that stand out in this context are: to give people as much notice as possible of forthcoming challenges; and to ensure they practice concurrent activity. Concurrent activity is the art of making sure that everyone in your team is doing something valuable at the same time. In other words, ensure that people aren't idle waiting for others to complete a task that they can then take on.

   I've seen too many leaders over-manage situations. This stops them from enabling the use of concurrent activity from their people and also inhibits their ability to oversee the entire operation. One of my main roles is building working relationships with people who could help us to execute our tasks effectively.

3. **Confidence:** A good leader is confident in his abilities (see chapter one) but he is also confident in what his team can do. When I make a decision, I am sure to show I am confident in that choice and in my team, plus utterly committed to what we are going to do together.

4. **Respect:** Respect of the team is an essential quality. Teams should be empowered to offer their ideas and

input about the decisions that directly affect them.

5. **Integrity:** Above all, a good, effective, team leader is always open and honest with those around him. Leaders with integrity always gain the trust of team members because they say what they will do and then do it.

At the beginning of the chapter I introduced Lieutenant Colonel Sandy McNeil. The reason I chose to focus on Sandy is because he showed me it is possible to radically alter the culture in a relatively large organisation, in our case one-thousand men. While his precise focus on our capabilities and the standards he required played a big part, for me, his entrance into the gymnasium told all of us that things had changed. From day one, there was a focus, energy and engagement I hadn't experienced before. The tone was set and then followed through.

Behind every great organisation is a great culture that engages and energises the team. In every case it is the leader who defines, shapes and personifies that culture. Shaping a culture is a formidable task, but that doesn't mean you can shy away from it, or hope it will come together in the end. It is a leader's job to shape their organisation behind their own beliefs and values to build a dynamic and distinctive culture.

SUMMARY

1. It is culture that shapes and energises a team and it is

up to a leader to set that culture.

2. If you want to engage the team, ensure the culture is relevant, not an exercise in bureaucracy.
3. Make sure all activities that contribute to the culture you are trying to achieve are clear and measurable.

PERSONAL DEVELOPMENT EXERCISES

EXERCISE ONE

The importance of culture

Business benefit

Define two key skills that can enhance exceptional performance

Resources

Time with the team

Format

Spend time with your people to establish two skills that will enable the team to deliver exceptional performance: your own company's version of Colonel Sandy's 'be fit and be good shots'. Allow the team to debate this until you have consensus on two key skills.

When you have identified two key skills, ask the team to identify up to six component skills that will make a direct contribution to the development of each of the two skills. For example, if being a great public speaker is the goal, identify six things that

»

contribute to being a great public speaker; one might be creating introductions that have impact.

Support the team as they decide how they can develop these skills. You can either coordinate the team's activities, or delegate that to one of the team.

Track progress.

PERSONAL DEVELOPMENT EXERCISES

EXERCISE TWO

The importance of culture

Business benefit

Your team will be able to develop the two key skills

Resources

Time with the team

Format

Having identified the two key skills and the component skills, allow the team to start the development process.

When the programme has been underway for half of the time allocated, ask the team to prepare a short presentation that describes:

- What they have learnt
- How they have applied it
- The success this has generated

»

- What they think they still need to develop – what they now plan to do and how they will be able to measure progress.

CHAPTER 5

PLAN TO MAKE YOURSELF REDUNDANT

A few years back I had some lengthy discussions on a turnaround position. It was a full-time role in a business that was having quite a few problems. I spent a lot of time talking to the company owner, as well as some of his key advisers and after many weeks I decided I would give it a go.

'I want to make myself redundant within three years though,' I said, when I told them of my decision.

They looked utterly dumfounded at what I was saying and the company founder demanded to know why I didn't want to stay.

'I fully expect to have finished the job and turned it around by then,' I said, confidently. 'In fact, if I haven't got a group of people in place by then that can run this place smoothly, then I would have failed and should leave anyway.'

I wasn't just grandstanding either. I honestly believe it is the job of every leader to make themselves redundant.

The idea of making oneself redundant is an anathema to most of the population. In fact, having been through a period of economic challenge at the end of the first decade of this millennium, most people are focused on hanging onto their jobs at all costs. While this attitude is understandable, when it becomes all-pervasive, the impact on business is profoundly negative. If a leader holds this attitude too, the effects can be even more damaging because, when people are unwilling to take any form of risk, they are often very unwilling to take any form of responsibility either.

Insecure and ineffective leaders who are preoccupied with holding onto their position will make poor decisions. Even if their team are forward-looking enough to turn up with good ideas, they are more than likely to be quashed because they are seen as 'too risky'. Yet, if good ideas are allowed to stagnate, the talented people who come up with them won't stay. They will feel suffocated by indecision and unwilling to tolerate the limiting approach. Ironically, by concentrating all their energies into holding onto the status quo, a bad leader will erode a company from within and produce the very effect they were trying to avoid. They will drive it into the ground and put everyone's jobs at risk.

To be a good leader, sometimes you do need to

'bet the farm' and empower those around you to be prepared to take the odd risk for the greater good. There is no way you can do this though, if you always have one eye on the potentially negative effects it might have on your career or lifestyle prospects.

Like I say, it seems counterintuitive to actively work towards making yourself redundant, but it is only once you accept this mindset that you will be able to make yourself incredibly valuable to the organisation.

How I can make myself redundant is always on my mind, whether I am working in a commercial situation, or in the military. I know when I am constantly looking ahead it keeps me on my toes and thinking innovatively. When I arrived in Angola, for example, my role was to ensure that the Gurkhas were deployed effectively and that they had the equipment they needed to fulfil their obligations. About four weeks into the contract I was happy that everything was running smoothly. We had men on rotation onto various tasks and the administrative side of things was fine. As soon as I felt myself to be at a loose end I spoke to my boss and told him that I had the time and energy to take on another role that would support the overall security objective. We agreed I would take over ensuring that the diamonds we were extracting made it to the bank in the capital city, Luanda. The first time I took part in the removal of diamonds from the mine to Luanda, I took one of my senior Gurkhas with me. I found I only needed to go once to understand the process; so on the next occasion I stayed in Luzamba and my former understudy took another member of the team. My understudy was now making himself redundant.

This may sound very simple, and it is. But, even then, I could see my approach was different to that of the Brazilians and Angolans who also worked in the mine. The Brazilians and Angolans viewed the trip to Luanda as a holiday, which is pretty much what it was. It often took the Mining Department four or five days to arrange to weigh and check the diamonds at the central bank in Luanda and this gave the couriers time to kick back and relax in the relative comfort of a hotel.

How I can make myself redundant is always on my mind, whether I am working in a commercial situation, or in the military.

Meanwhile, back in the mine, I assumed responsibility for what was known as the sort house, which is the final stage in the diamond extraction process. As the head of security for the sort house, I was responsible not just for the security of the diamonds during the extractive process, but also the cleaning of the diamonds, using acid and the process for passing them across to the Angolan Government representatives.

As I was being trained to understand the protocols and to fulfil the various duties that were the responsibilities of the head of the sort house, I was already thinking how I could make myself redundant. The episode in my first week when we had been shot and then chased by the illegal diamond miners had reminded me that the risks were high and the risks of losing people were real. Three members of the mining team were killed in accidents in six months and that didn't take into account the fact that me and my people were very often in an extremely hostile environment. Interestingly, I think the process of thinking about how I would make myself redundant helped me counter this challenge.

As soon as it became clear that the sort house could run very well without me, I was promoted and given responsibility for the four separating plants that were located out in the bush.

My aim out in Angola, and indeed in every other role since, was that every aspect of my role could be developed in one other person, who in turn then passed it on to someone else. By supporting the desire to make myself redundant and then requiring my colleagues to teach others, I was enabling the development of others on the team. It is a strategy that works in everyone's favour.

The true test of effective leadership is how a business or team runs when the leader is absent and/or when something goes wrong. If a team can excel when things don't go to plan and the leader is absent, this is evidence that you have made yourself redundant.

Making yourself redundant is not just about passing the knowledge of processes and the responsibility for those processes across to other people either. The objective isn't for them to learn how to mechanically perform a 'mirror image' strategy of your own. It is about building a team that can problem-solve in a timely and effective manner and lead the business onto newer and better things. As a leader, it is your responsibility to identify and train those who come behind you.

Of course, thanks to my experience in the military, I know only too well that being part of an army unit means there is a vast resource of highly experienced people who have been developed to the point that they can take additional responsibility competently and confidently. But, what if a leader doesn't have access to this type of resource? How do they go about identifying and developing the competence and confidence that they require so they can step back and let those below get on with the job?

There has to be an efficient, gradual and stepped process that enables the right type of person to step up to additional responsibility.

The process has a number of stages once you've identified the tasks that you want to delegate:

1. Identifying the person to whom you are going to

delegate the task

2. Engaging with that person so that they are prepared to start the process of taking on that responsibility
3. Essential training
4. The transitional process
5. Allowing them to take absolute control
6. Ongoing support.

As a consultant, I have seen a variety of versions of this process, ranging from the very poorly executed to a system that works perfectly. It might help to outline both ends of the scale here to help you identify the most appropriate process for your own business or team.

At the poor end of the process scale the sequence of events often goes something like this: people are accepted into a position of responsibility because they put their hands up and ask to be given more to do. They may not necessarily be the best person for the job and most of the time no effort is made to ascertain this either. This, of course, means the process is flawed from the beginning. As an aside, although I view volunteering as a good thing, I am always keen to know what is behind the desire to volunteer. Some people volunteer because it gives them an opportunity to get away from the front line and that attitude doesn't just apply to soldiering.

Likewise, people are often identified as potential leadership material on the basis they do their current job well. For example, I work with a lot of sales teams and the process for identifying a potential leader often focuses on sales performance. A good salesperson is deemed to be someone who will make a good leader. There is apparently an unshakeable belief that if someone is good at one thing, they will automatically be good at something else, regardless of the fact it might be a completely different discipline. Obviously, this isn't often the case and that is why this strategy is also flawed from the start.

Another common mistake at the identification stage comes in the form of opting to hire experienced leaders. I consistently see people being hired straight into leadership roles with little thought to their suitability, other than ascertaining they have done 'something similar' elsewhere. The thinking goes they'll naturally fit right into the next business as a leader. I don't agree with this train of thought. What this often means is that the experienced person has some knowledge of the sector or industry and may even have some knowledge of the processes that might be similar to yours. However, it doesn't necessarily mean that the culture they have come from will be similar to the culture in your business. This is the reason why, all too often, people join a new employer, stay for six months and then leave. It is because the culture they came into wasn't what they were expecting and they found it impossible to fit in. That's bad news for everyone.

Even if the identification process isn't flawed and somehow you get the right people on board, the poor version of the development track is dominated by insufficient training, coaching and mentoring. That's if you're lucky too. In the worst-case scenario, the business in question offers almost no guidance, bar some ineffective, generalised training that ticks a few boxes, but doesn't go anywhere close into building the confidence and competence required to do the job properly.

Unfortunately, the situation where potential successors are given inadequate or badly thought through development opportunities is one I encounter far too frequently. As a result, those who are being asked to take more responsibility won't benefit to the extent they ideally need. Unless they are exceptional people, this type of unprofessional handover will result in anxiety and hesitancy on all sides. It may even encourage the leader to revert to doing it all themselves, which means the whole process was a bit of a waste of time.

Coaching and mentoring are fundamental to building your people. Coaching is about supporting them through the development process, while allowing them to take calculated risks and learning from them. Mentoring is about giving advice, because you've been there yourself and you can help the mentee bypass mistakes that most people make.

Ideally, the coach and the mentor should be different people. This will allow the mentor to focus on giving advice and the coach the opportunity to develop the individual. The mentor can be someone from the business who has been trained in basic mentoring skills development, while a coach needs to be someone who is skilled in the art of coaching.

In recent years there has been an explosion in the number of coaches advertising their services, and life coaches in particular. Just to be clear, in my view, a coach is someone who is highly qualified in the discipline, or skill, they are coaching and adds to that credibility by being a highly skilled and practised coach. An individual who has completed a five-day coaching course, who now puts themselves out there as a coach is probably someone to avoid.

So, what does the 'good' end of the scale look like? In the course of my military career I attended a six-week leadership programme, during which sixty men were subjected to both rigorous development and evaluation. This is an incredibly resource-intensive strategy, but it wasn't just an evaluation process, it was a development one too. The sixty men who participated didn't go through any form of initial vetting, they were simply men who were the correct age and who had the right amount of experience to be exposed to the rigours of this process.

The men were trained in the classroom, shown the application of the new skills in a realistic environment and then allowed to practise, while being observed by experienced practitioners, all of whom had been through this process themselves. Opportunities for demonstrating ability were fairly shared and evaluation was incredibly objective.

At the end of the six-week programme, the participants were classified from one to sixty, based on their overall performance. There were only vacancies for about twenty men to be promoted immediately. These twenty men were promoted to lance corporal and were given immediate responsibility, while being mentored by an experienced corporal who had been in the role previously. Once the newly promoted recruits were trained in all of the skills, they then had the opportunity to observe them 'in the real world' and put them into practice.

> The hardest part for most leaders is judging exactly the right moment to make yourself redundant and walk away.

Although undoubtedly intensive, there are a number of benefits to this approach which would have real merit in the business environment. Previously hidden leadership talent can be identified, adding value to the entire organisation. The sheer number of potential recruits is important too. In an infantry unit there is a risk that the new leaders will be killed or injured, while in a commercial organisation, people leave. The benefit of both developing and evaluating all of your potential leaders is that if people leave, there will be a pool of talent that is ready to step up with the minimum of time needed for preparation.

It would be a mistake to do what so many companies do, which is identify the talent and then develop only that talent. It may appear to be more commercially sensible at first glance, but turnover of staff doesn't necessarily mean this is always the case.

Similarly, the people an organisation uses for development and evaluation varies. In the six-week scenario described here, the staff were picked from the ranks of the most capable people in the unit. It was a feather in your cap to be chosen to participate as a member of the staff.

Although it takes hard work and dedication to identify and develop the right people on the team, perhaps the hardest part for most leaders is judging exactly the right moment to make yourself redundant and walk away. This doesn't just mean when your three years is up, or however long you judge it needs to take to complete the job, either. I mean every single day. A big part of making yourself redundant is quelling the urge to micromanage the team every step of the way. Just as I did in Angola, where I made the trip to Luanda once, learned the ropes and then immediately handed it over to one of my senior Gurkhas, you must be prepared to let go and move on once you are satisfied things will run smoothly.

Too many leaders attempt to create their worth through micromanaging issues. They can't bear to be perceived to be on the sidelines when there is an issue to be addressed, even when they are clearly not the right person to be dealing with whatever is going on.

There was a perfect example of this one time when I was serving in an operational theatre, which is a slightly less alarming expression for a war zone. I was attempting to get into the operations centre, to receive my next tasking when I was barred from gaining access by a soldier.

'Sorry Sir, you can't come in,' said the soldier, who I knew in passing.

'Why not Rifleman Smith?' I asked.

'Incident. On going Sir. A bomb has been found.' He said.

While a risk, this wasn't unusual.

'Who's in the Operations Centre?' I said, feeling a rising sense of annoyance.

'Who isn't Sir? The commanding officer, the second in command, your company commander, the operations officer, the operations warrant officer and three watch keepers.'

Then, for good measure, he added, with an apologetic shrug: 'It's a bit crowded.'

'It seems so.' I agreed, drily.

While a bomb being found was relatively routine, to me the real issue was that this group of leaders hadn't empowered their people to deal with it. Every minute that I wasn't able to get into the operations centre, our progress stalled. To be honest, the overkill of people getting involved was very uninspiring too. In reality, it was only the operations warrant officer who should have been dealing with it. Even though he was theoretically the most junior decision maker in there, he was the most capable by a 'country mile'.

This type of incident is not unusual in any walk of life. It happens all the time in business, where senior managers can't wait to be at the centre of things, even when their presence can actually hamper, or even prevent, the right people doing their job. Obviously, this is not ideal and can and will have serious long-term negative effects on company growth. In a military situation, it can even put lives at risk.

Happily, following the incident above, my faith was restored a few days later when I came across a really good example of making yourself redundant. By then, I was in a different operations centre, in a different city, with a different unit. When I walked in to be given my orders, the warrant officer told me to be aware of six ongoing incidents in one part of the city. He was the only decision maker in that operations centre and seemed very calm and assured. It transpired all the senior officers were somewhere else doing other things. While I was planning my tasking, I heard him on the radio to the soldiers who were dealing with the incidents on the ground. He was in control and confident about what he had to do.

I guarantee that this warrant officer wasn't just put into this position of responsibility without any form of preparation. After all, there was a risk involved and bad decisions could lead to injury and death. However, once the senior offices were satisfied of his skills, they were content to let him get on with the job and gave him complete authority to manage the operations centre. This, in turn, freed them up to do other things, while also demonstrating how much they thought of this man. It was hugely inspiring.

When you give people responsibility and trust you are saying that you believe in them and their ability to complete the task in line with your standards. As we've seen, you will need the right development track to build both their competence and confidence, but the underlying message from the leader is very inspiring. In my experience in the military and with some of the biggest brands in the world, when people are given this type of trust it is repaid many times over, both by how hard people work and by their determination to deliver great results.

People like being given responsibility, especially in an environment where they believe that their endeavours will be valued. Plus, of course, you have to step away and let them get on with it. Hanging around to look over their shoulders isn't going to help anyone.

To be effective, a good leader should be continually improving performance and moving forward. Sure, it is nice to stick around to see the fruits of your success, but once you have done what you need to do, either move on, or find something else that needs fixing. Don't let your ego keep you in one place, treading water, or constantly interfering in your team's decisions. It is no good for anyone, especially you.

The art of making yourself redundant as a leader is based on the idea that leadership can be shared and passed on to the team as a whole. Everyone around you has a role to play in decision-making and the more you hone this skill the more effective both you and your organisation will be. In the early days, this may well take huge amounts of trust, patience and organisational skills, but it will be worth it.

Get it right and you will not only prove to yourself what you are made of. You'll also be able to prove to a whole bunch of other people just what they are made of too.

That really would be something to be proud of.

SUMMARY

1. Every good leader should plan their strategy with one eye on making themselves redundant.
2. It is your responsibility to identify, train and develop those who will take your place and fully empower

them to do their jobs.

3. Once you've given your people responsibility, stand back and let them get on with it.

PERSONAL DEVELOPMENT EXERCISES

EXERCISE ONE

Plan to make yourself redundant

Business benefit
You will build your team and create more time for yourself

Resources
Planning and meeting time

Format
Look at your diary for the last two weeks. Make a list of all of the activities that have taken up your time.

Prioritise the activities in two ways; i.e. those which:

a. take up most of your time
b. you can delegate with the least risk.

Evaluate how you can delegate tasks that will save you time and make a contribution to the professional development of your people. For example, if you have a monthly team meeting, create an opportunity for professional development by delegating the management of these sessions.

»

Give them clarity on the topics to be covered, but also provide them with control over what they do and how they do it.

Match low-risk activities to appropriate members of your team, ensuring that successful completion of the task will enhance the professional development of each person.

Now delegate.

PERSONAL DEVELOPMENT EXERCISES

EXERCISE TWO

Plan to make yourself redundant

Business benefit

You will build your team and create more time for yourself

Resources

Planning and meeting time

Format

Allocate time with each member of your team.

Use the time to analyse which parts of their role they might be able to delegate to other members of the team/business. For example, if you manage relationships with clients, analyse which clients or which aspects of the relationship your people could delegate to someone else.

If possible, you should coach your people through the delegation of one task to their people. »

This coaching should involve helping them formulate the initial conversation with the person to whom they will delegate and guidelines on how they will ensure the delegated task is conducted effectively.

Where possible, the tasks delegated should develop the person who is assigned to do them. This will enhance engagement, leading to personal development for the person to whom the delegation is being made and creating more time for the person who is delegating.

Be available to support the person who has done the delegating.

This should be an ongoing process to ensure development of additional capabilities across the team.

CHAPTER 6

KEEP IT SIMPLE

The company I worked for in Angola was Brazilian and, without a doubt, our Brazilian employers liked a party, or a fiesta, as they called it, and they liked to do it a lot. It was pretty understandable that they liked to unwind. In those early days, life on the mine was tough. Drinking water had to be collected from a purifying centre, the diet was monotonous and it was extremely hot and humid. Plus, as we were in the process of establishing the mine in a hostile place, everyone had to work very hard. So, every Saturday evening was fiesta time.

The challenge for the security team and me was these fiestas created a lot of interest and had the potential to be a focal point for trouble. Everyone in the area wanted to attend, while the Brazilians wanted to restrict access to just Brazilians so they could have a bit of time to let their hair down together. It was a very reasonable request, but it didn't go down well with the local people whose core objective seemed to be to agitate.

They wanted to be involved and if they weren't invited, you could count on them to cause trouble.

Having discussed this challenge with my team, we agreed that the wrong approach was to deploy lots of our team in the fiesta, or in the area of the fiesta. This type of heavy presence could actually aggravate the situation, rather than help us to manage it.

We also agreed that if we put a small team into the area of the fiesta, we ran the risk of being outnumbered and therefore being assaulted, or even worse. Some of the local people had an ability to lose their tempers very quickly and easily. This often led to an outbreak of violence when we weren't expecting it, which had the ability to escalate into a big problem unless it was contained very quickly.

We opted to have a presence at the fiesta that I would lead, but we would also have a team of ten men close-by but completely out of view. This team of ten would be able to react at very short notice, which in military terms is a quick reaction force. The commanders of this team needed to know when I wanted them to deploy. We decided that any signal that might need to be given should not alert any potential troublemakers to the fact that we were in the process of calling for back-up. That would only inflame the situation.

How were we going to do this? The one asset that

we had were hand-held walkie-talkies; yet if I were to speak into my walkie-talkie while in the middle of a confrontation, this could make me vulnerable and antagonise the people we were trying to manage.

We opted to use what is known as the Prestel switch as the signal that I wanted the reaction force to deploy. The Prestel switch is the one the user presses down when they want to speak on a walkie-talkie. When pressed, it creates a clicking sound at the receiving walkie-talkie, before the user says anything. We could use this as our signal for help.

If I wanted the team to come out and support me, I would continually press the Prestel switch, creating a very obvious series of clicks on all of the other radios. It wouldn't be apparent to anyone standing near me that I was doing this, which would give my team a head start. I would stand with my hands on my hips, as I often did, with my hands close to the walkie-talkie, while I chatted to people. I would therefore be able to alert my team about potential troublemakers and easily deploy them before any issue escalated.

The reason we chose the continuous pressing of the Prestel switch over, say, a distress signal that involved three presses, was simplicity. Clearly, the code had to be as simple as possible. You couldn't have the guys on the receiving end scrabbling about asking: were those five clicks or four? Should we fire, or hang on? But, used properly, it was hugely effective through its sheer simplicity.

There is an important lesson here for modern leaders. As leaders, we are called upon to do a variety of often complex things for our organisations. We've got to articulate strategies and visions, inspire our teams and constantly drive everyone towards our objectives. It would be very easy to tie yourself in knots with everything that needs to be done.

Except, the best leaders don't do that; they simplify everything. They:

- Simplify the mission. What is the company trying to do? If you can't explain it in one sentence, you don't have it yet.
- Simplify the values. What are the core beliefs that drive your company? Again, if it takes more than a sentence, forget it.
- Simplify processes. It is no coincidence that most of the best-known leaders have a reputation for being a bit of a maverick when it comes to bureaucracy. All they want to know is how to make things easier, faster, and more manageable.
- Simplify the next step. Smart leaders are very clear about who will do what next, and when.

If you want to add value, keep it simple.

The place simplicity really comes into its own is in the field of communication, just as it did in the Prestel example above. No matter which field you work in, if you get this side of things right it will have wide-reaching benefits. Indeed, take a tip from the Prestel next time you are about to present an hour-long strategy session. If you want people to do it, make it brief, understandable and doable.

Simplicity in communications was something I once saw demonstrated very well by an incredibly successful care home business, which is at the cutting edge of dementia care. This business employs a thousand people in different locations and many of them work on shifts. In addition, the firm often has to engage temporary staff to meet the ever-changing numbers of residents that they look after.

If you want to add value, keep it simple.

The prime objective of the directors can be distilled into one word: occupancy. Having care homes that are full of residents is what they want and there are many great reasons why occupancy is so important.

A full home means staff have job security, which gives them confidence in their futures and this, in turn, benefits the residents. It means the home is a vibrant place too. The atmosphere in the home is far better when rooms are full. Plus, there is more money available to invest in extra trips, or shows, for the residents, so everyone benefits.

Even one or two empty rooms massively impacts the financial side of the business because costs don't change, but revenues clearly do.

However, while it is fine for directors to focus on occupancy, the question is this: Does every member of every team in every home understand the importance of occupancy? A team must know what the business is trying to achieve and why it is important. If this is going to be known, it has to be simple, like the Prestel switch example.

To get buy-in from the whole team, the care home business began by bringing a group of people together to establish what four things made the biggest contribution to occupancy. After brainstorming it, they suggested that the business would achieve 100 per cent occupancy and possibly even a waiting list if the following four things were done extremely well:

1. Food
2. Physical environment
3. Resident entertainment
4. Communication with the families of the residents

The next step was to communicate these four things to the teams, which were spread across a variety of locations. Management/leadership teams were given authority and responsibility for communicating this information. Competitions were run to see which of the locations could get to a position where every member of staff on the premises, including temporary staff, knew and understood the focus on occupancy and the four things that would most help achieve that aim.

Teams made up of people from across the business were then tasked with coming up with ideas for enhancing the 'big four,' as they started to be known. These teams were given three months to come up with their ideas and had to present them to a team made up of directors and health care professionals. They had to present their ideas in the priority order they thought would make the greatest contribution to occupancy. They also had to present a detailed explanation of the cost and the potential benefits.

All of the ideas were presented using just one word. For example, with food, the first recommendation was variety. The team who had done the thinking had to present exactly what they meant by the expression variety. This approach continued across each of the big four. Ideas were implemented, reviewed and adjusted on an ongoing basis.

As a result of this innovative programme, the underlying requirement for simplicity now pervades that business. There is even an unexpected by-product of this approach. Every member of the staff has become an active marketeer for the business, at work and when they are out and about in their communities. When people ask them why the homes they work for are so good, they automatically come back and say: 'We have a great environment, the food is excellent, the residents have lots of different things to do and we look after the families as well.'

If someone who was interested in possibly recommending the home to a friend were to ask, 'what's so great about your food,' they would immediately get one of four responses that are a reflection of the priorities in the delivery of great food across all of the homes.

'There is great variety. It is nutritious, locally sourced, fresh food with a carvery every Sunday, which the families can join as well.'

This business has a simple approach to delivering their simple, one word, occupancy strategy. Everyone in the business knows how and why occupancy is important. They all know the big four. They all also know the four things that contribute to the achievement of the big four. They know their business and they are ambassadors.

Interestingly, the families of the residents also know about the strategy and why it is important. A lot of family members know the big four and some of them even know the four words that contribute to the big four. This means many of the families of the residents have also become ambassadors.

That's pretty special.

This simplification has made a huge impact on what was already a great company with great leadership. The directors of the business have provided clear simple understanding of what they want and enabled their people to create the solutions.

Of course, as we all know, keeping things simple isn't

always, well, that simple. There is an art to making sure communications are straightforward and clear-cut and it is easy to get things very wrong. Let me give you an example of how simplifying things can backfire. This comes from my time as a platoon commander of 2nd Battalion, 2nd Gurkha Rifles and training on Dartmoor.

We had all been given orders for an overnight march, after which we would launch a dawn attack as the grand finale to a two-week training exercise. My immediate boss told me to take 100 men, referred to as a company, to a position where they would then form in preparation for the attack. His precise instructions appeared straightforward:

'Bryan, you lead the company to the rendezvous with the rest of the battalion. Go west for about 600 metres, until you reach the river and then go down the river to the rendezvous.'

That seemed simple enough.

Off I set at the head of 100 men heading west. I had a compass to keep me right and I was counting my steps (known as pacing) because I knew how many steps I roughly took per 100 metres. When I got to my equivalent of about 600 metres, the distance to the river, I was relieved and quietly proud that I hadn't messed it up. It was pretty simple after all.

Now, all I had to do was to 'go down the river to the rendezvous' as my boss instructed.

I started following the river downstream, in the same

direction the river was flowing. I had spent time in boats, so I was well aware of the difference between upstream and downstream. By this time, I stopped counting my steps as all I needed to do was follow the river.

After what seemed quite a long time, I still hadn't come across a large group of men which would indicate I had reached the rendezvous. This seemed odd, because we had covered a reasonable distance. Still, I pressed on.

All of a sudden, I received a call on my radio. I recognised my boss by his radio call sign and could tell by his tone of voice that he was slightly agitated.

As an aside here, let me tell you this was 1986 and the enemy could still easily listen into radios back then. Radios today are equipped with special encryption that stops anyone listening in being able to interpret what is being said. This lack of security on that day meant that my boss couldn't refer to anything which could potentially be interpreted by the enemy. That means he couldn't refer to the river, which is clearly a landmark on a map an enemy could use. This complicated an already fraught situation.

'Are you on the way to where we are due to meet?' he began cautiously avoiding the word 'rendezvous' as well as 'river'.

'Yes I am,' was my response.

'ETA?' He asked testily.

'Not sure, I thought we'd be there by now,' I replied, feeling increasingly anxious.

'Where are you?' he asked.

'Heading along beside the prominent feature,' I said, somewhat awkwardly, avoiding the word river.

'Which direction is the prominent feature travelling in?' he asked.

'It is heading in the same direction as I am,' I explained.

'Ahh, you should be heading in the other direction,' he said; now the penny had finally dropped.

I had to tell the Sergeant Major we were going the wrong way and we all had to change direction and head upstream. What else could I say? We had to get a move on too, or we'd hold everybody else back.

I was now annoyed and frustrated. I had done what I thought was correct but it was clearly wrong. What had happened? My boss had said 'go to the river and go down the river to the rendezvous,' but clearly what he had meant was 'go to the river and go down (south) the river to the rendezvous'.

I had gone down the river, in other words, downstream but was actually heading north. By going downstream I was going away from the rendezvous. Something that should have been simple ended up being a disaster. Fortunately, this wasn't a real war scenario and it is precisely for this reason that armies practise and rehearse. A command that had seemed to be simple had been misinterpreted and caused a problem for eight-hundred men. By my being late to the battalion rendezvous with my company of one-hundred men, the whole battalion would now have to move more quickly than expected, carrying very heavy loads.

As a direct result of this experience and others, I am fastidious when I am giving, or being given, instructions. It is a lesson I have carried over into my commercial career too. In the modern business arena we are all too ready to rely on the spoken or, more likely, typed word, to impart instructions. These instructions often look, on face value, to be simple, but are very open to misinterpretation.

A technique that I rely on to avoid misunderstandings is called briefback; this is an effective tool to manage that ambiguity. A briefback, sometimes called 'brief back' with two words, or 'backbrief' is exactly what it sounds like. The person(s) receiving the instructions gives a synopsis of what they've just received. This enables the person who originally gave the instructions to determine whether the message was received properly. Obviously, if the repeated version is not the same as the original intent, the directions should be clarified.

A technique that I rely on to avoid misunderstandings is called briefback.

Briefbacks serve a few, very important, purposes:

- If people know they may be called on to provide

a synopsis of the plan, they are more likely to pay attention and take notes.

- Everyone will walk away with the same understanding of the plan.
- It makes the team hear the plan at least twice. Repetition helps retention.
- It reduces waste by preventing rework when a plan is misinterpreted.
- It provides leaders with a chance to hear their plan out loud. This opens up an effective opportunity to critique their own ideas in a way that is sometimes difficult to do in their head.

With briefback, a leader is able to refine any plan as required because problems can be identified and raised during the process.

The other area where simplicity always comes into its own is in any sort of planning process. As the US author and strategic thinker Joel Barker once said: plans with action are dreams, while dreams without action are nightmares.

There are too many people who dream big, but do nothing to turn the dream into reality. Leaders are in the perfect position to help their people to dream about creating stretching goals and then help them to define the plan that will take them to the goal. When the plan is in place, the leader can further support their people in taking the action needed to take them to that goal.

When there is any sort of plan, it is imperative that

simple, clearly defined tasks are allocated to individual members of the team. This is the bit many leaders fail to do effectively. Most people in managerial or leadership positions are familiar with the acronym SMART. By 'familiar,' I mean that they know what it stands for even if they don't necessarily apply it. I am a huge fan of giving people responsibility with accountability; SMART delivers that.

SMART means that any task allocated should be:

Specific – clear and without ambiguity

Measureable – you will know when it has been achieved

Achievable – not impossible

Relevant – the person being given the task can see its value

Timebound – there must be a deadline

Success is about relentless application, evaluation and learning. While you may think that applying SMART is the antithesis of empowering your people, it isn't. SMART is about clarifying boundaries within which you want your people to apply themselves.

When we have new people join our business, we apply SMART to everything that they do. For example, all of our people are qualified to use three psychometric tools that provide information for people such as their impact as a leader. We use SMART to create the plans within which goals must be achieved. This is known by the new joiner and their coach. We apply SMART so that progress towards the achievement of the final goal can be measured. This enables our new joiner to be supported as they stay on top of their progress.

When SMART doesn't exist, you lose clarity and you lose simplicity. This leads to confusion, frustration and poor results. When SMART is applied you have clarity, simplicity and great results. Leaders who apply SMART consistently and conscientiously develop a reputation for detail and 'follow through'.

Effective leaders don't just implement plans simply, they consistently evaluate any aspect of their business to see how what they do can be simplified. I was fortunate enough to sell for a company who consistently reviewed the rules imposed by the regulator in our sector. As a direct result, our processes were well honed, without ambiguity and, most importantly, without unnecessary bureaucracy. At the opposite end of the scale, when I started consulting I worked with a well-known Scottish financial services company that tied itself in knots with bureaucracy. The sales people were subjected to the most complex policies and procedures I had ever come across. All management information was gathered by telephone, requiring managers to make a minimum of thirty-six telephone calls twice a day. Each salesperson had to demonstrate that they had filled in a client questionnaire that was 72 pages long. This meant filling, on average, 216 pages of information per week. Recommendation letters to support sales were often 55 pages long and took up to twelve hours of work to produce. The business was being strangled by bureaucracy. Then, just as the managers and sales people were getting to grips with these procedures, they changed and then they changed again. To make matters worse, I found that so many executives were jumping in and trying to influence the processes, they too were adding layer after layer of their own processes too. It was quite amazing and, of course, enormously damaging to the business.

Fortunately, the boss of the financial services company wanted simplicity and had the foresight to make it happen. We sat down and compared the business practices within his team with my experience of the same sector. When we analysed the layers of bureaucracy his team were dealing with and compared them to the rest of the sector, we were able to devise a plan to take back to his boss. Then, when we had developed buy-in from his boss, we were able to take this back to the business and challenge the perceived wisdom that had created so much complexity in that business.

This wasn't an easy task. We had to devote a lot of time to influencing six important stakeholders including the head of compliance, head of marketing and three sales directors, who had been entrenched in their working practices for over five years. Armed with solid evidence that simplifying processes would lead to better results for clients and for the business was at the heart of our case and we were able to simplify every single step of the process.

Sales people now had a questionnaire that was twelve pages long and not seventy-two. The letter of recommendation was reduced to fourteen pages and now only took two hours to complete, not twelve, and managers were required to collate management information once a week, not every seven days.

The direct result of simplifying their client-facing process is that the time needed to complete a sale dropped from a staggering twenty-two hours to a more appropriate six hours. This trebled their efficiency. This trebling of efficiency was achieved by challenging the status quo and by demonstrating that simplification could make a direct contribution to a better result for the client and for the business.

Even highly successful businesses and teams need leaders who will continually challenge everything to find simpler and more effective ways of doing things. With considerable developments in the technology available to everyone, bureaucracy, in particular, has to be evaluated to make sure that the bureaucracy that does exist is there for a reason.

Simplicity is everything.

SUMMARY

1. Although all leaders are called upon to do complex tasks for their organisations, the most successful ones simplify everything.
2. Simplification in communication is a core skill and, when perfected, will pay huge dividends.
3. When allocating tasks to members of the team, pay attention to the SMART acronym, which will ensure simplicity and effectiveness.

PERSONAL DEVELOPMENT EXERCISES

EXERCISE ONE
Simplify

Business benefit
Develop clear business focus

Resources
Time with the team

Format
This exercise can be done with your team. You will need about sixty minutes for the initial step. Get the team to work as individuals for the first part of the exercise.

The idea is to impart your strategic intent – your version of the expression 'occupancy' from the care home business. Explain your strategic

»

intent and ensure the team understands what it is and why it is so important. Tell them they must come up with four things that contribute to the achievement of the strategic intent.

When the team have finished, take feedback and facilitate a conversation that leads to agreement on the big four.

Next, create four teams, giving each team one of the big four. Challenge them to come up with a prioritised list of four elements that will enable the achievement of the big four.

When this stage has been completed, take feedback and create a development plan to enable the teams to work on the detail that underpins each of their ideas.

Use these ideas as part of the development strategy.

PERSONAL DEVELOPMENT EXERCISES

EXERCISE TWO
Simplify

Business benefit
The team will develop precise focus on a key performance area

Resources
Time with the team/one to one

»

Format

Ask the team to think about one aspect of the business which they think can be simplified and give them some time to come up with their idea. When they have come up with one, take time to meet them to discuss it. Ask them to explain what they would simplify, why they have chosen that one issue and how they think simplifying it would add value to the business. Ask them to quantify the business benefit. If they are unclear on how to quantify business benefit, focus on the amount of time their idea will save, or the additional revenue the new approach can deliver.

When the team have all come up with an idea, and you are happy that the potential reward outweighs the risk, give them an opportunity to implement their ideas. Stay close to the initial stages of implementation to ensure that the concept is unfolding as expected and any potential risk is being managed.

CHAPTER 7

QUESTION EVERYTHING

My working career has been punctuated by dramatic changes of direction and decisions that may have seemed pretty crazy at the time to anyone on the outside; most of the time though, they worked out just fine.

The one example I draw upon most is the time I dropped everything to go and guard the diamond mine in Angola. At the time I made that decision, I was about to work for an upmarket adventure company, guiding mature and wealthy clients to notable tourist spots around the world. When I got the call, I hadn't even realised I wasn't particularly stimulated by the idea of being a travel babysitter, but as soon as the seed was sown, I realised it wasn't me at all. It wasn't that Angola was the proverbial better offer, because in many ways it wasn't. It just suited me, my abilities and aspirations far better.

I had a similar light bulb moment when I chose to leave the army. I'd been bored for some time because

I wasn't seeing any action, so I decided to go and start a business in Nepal. Of course, a few weeks after I left army life behind, the Gulf War began. As I said earlier, *most* of the time these snap decisions worked out fine, but there is always the exception.

There are a lot of reasons behind my restless spirit and I'm sure a psychologist would have a field day, but on a purely basic level, the thought of being bored, or stuck in a rut, horrifies me. So, why am I mentioning this here? Well, I think the most important part of these scenarios was that I was fully prepared to regularly question my position and leave my comfortable perch when necessary to fully stretch myself.

This is not to say you should consider chucking in your job and trying a new career (unless you want to), but only that you should be prepared to regularly disrupt yourself during your leadership career. It is once you allow yourself to become too comfortable with anything that everything starts going downhill. Innovation ultimately begins on the inside and if you don't give it room to flourish you'll never know what you could achieve.

If you are not about to change your job, how might this work in practice? How could you truly stretch yourself by trying something utterly new with no idea whatsoever what could happen next?

To begin with, you should throw out all the

performance metrics so beloved by large corporations and consultants. By this I mean, the measures you currently use to gauge how well you are doing by grading factors such as sales growth, markets opened, staff retained, or whatever specifically applies to your industry. These statistics are useful, but it is easy to become too reliant on them, so much so that you fail to look behind them and really question what is going on.

Give some thought as to how you should really be measuring success. If nothing was standing in your way, what could you be doing to really transform things? If you thought the unthinkable, what would it be? What are the completely new market opportunities that no one in your firm has ever considered before?

Virgin is a great example of a company that consistently questions and challenges the 'market leaders' in markets where they don't have a presence. Starting with mail order records, we know that Virgin have an airline, a cola business, run trains and offer banking services, amongst others.

Sir Richard Branson's approach is not necessarily to invent new products, or services, but to challenge the established providers and ask questions to establish how Virgin can deliver better products and services than the ones that already exist. The Branson/Virgin brand is built on being unconventional, on challenging the big players, like British Airways and looking out for customers. That's why people like and trust the brand, because they know they will constantly question things. If Virgin believes that something needs to be changed to make it a market leader, they will change.

One of the reasons people are often reticent to embrace big changes (so don't even bother thinking about them) is because it is well known that such action will lead to a temporary dip in performance. The famous example of this is when world class golfers Nick Faldo and Tiger Woods reviewed their grips. The change did indeed result in a short-term dip in their competitive rankings and it must have been pretty troubling for them both. However, they both realised it was a necessary step to get their game onto a higher plane, so they persisted. Their fortitude paid off because after a short time their game improved significantly.

These golfers' willingness to step out of their comfort zone really was a game changer, which is why it is well worth looking more deeply at this notion of a 'comfort zone' here.

A comfort zone is, as everyone knows, the familiar place where we are, well, comfortable. We say to ourselves that this or that works well enough, so there is no need to change it. To be an inspirational leader though, you need to be prepared to step out of your comfort zone and constantly disrupt yourself.

We weren't always so wedded to our comfort zone,

so perhaps it is prudent to draw lessons from our past. As children, we all liked nothing better than pushing the boundaries and seeing how far we could go. We questioned everything. 'Why not?' we'd demand petulantly and nine times out of ten would try whatever we'd been cautioned against anyhow. Sometimes it worked out and sometimes it didn't, but that is how we learned.

Then, as we grow up a subtle changes begin to occur. Through our process of trial and error we become used to one of two outcomes: success or failure. Inevitably, our younger selves begin to link self-esteem with these outcomes. Getting something right is good and widely applauded and it therefore brings a positive boost to self-esteem. Meanwhile, getting it wrong is seen as bad and can lead to ridicule, disapproval or even punishment, which is obviously pretty negative on the self-esteem scale.

> To be an inspirational leader, you need to be prepared to step out of your comfort zone and constantly disrupt yourself.

Gradually, we learn to avoid situations that will impact negatively on our self-esteem. We cease to question, or try new ways to do things. Instead we develop fears. Even a faint suggestion of trying something outside our comfort zone will conjure up unwelcome visions of rejection, humiliation and embarrassment. It is little wonder most of us seek out the comfort and familiarity of the status quo.

Of course, if we were all like this, nothing would ever change, great inventions would never be invented and things would be pretty boring. Luckily, there have been one or two leaders in history who don't think like this – such as Steve Jobs, Richard Branson and Marissa Meyer, to name but a few – and that is how things change.

What leaders like this have in common is they always question everything, all the time. Often, even when it feels uncomfortable, they will push to try something new because if there is a slight chance it might work, then it is worth doing. Sure, every time they try something new, they don't necessarily get the outcome they are looking for, but what makes them different (and ultimately successful) is they will learn from the process, see it as a step forward and then they'll try again. They'll keep on trying too until they get it right, or prove definitively they were wrong. Even then, they won't give up, because they'll already be trying something else.

The digital revolution means that today, perhaps more than any other era in history, there are new opportunities at every turn for every leader. All your assumptions about the best way to do things need to be re-thought, re-aligned and re-imagined. Every day. As a leader you have to be prepared to boldly go where no man, or woman, has gone before and to take your team along on that exciting journey. This means you should be asking the questions no one else is asking and taking a completely new approach.

Of course, if you begin to question the unquestionable, you will always come up with some resistance. You may have overcome your own affinity to your comfort zone, but it is often quite difficult to break the attachment held by those around you. Many people will dig in their heels at any suggestion of a completely new direction.

This was certainly the experience of Sir Steve Redgrave, five-time Olympic rowing champion. In 2010, I had the opportunity to host and speak at a conference with Sir Steve. He and I are the same age and we both rowed at Henley Royal Regatta in 1980, although our rowing careers went in vastly different directions after that. He gave me a remarkable insight into the concept of disruptive, questioning, leadership and just how effective it can be.

Sir Steve started rowing at Marlow Rowing Club when he was 16 and very quickly achieved success as a junior international rower. He got into the Olympic Squad for the 1984 Los Angeles Games. During training in 1982/3, while only a relatively inexperienced member of the squad, he quickly developed the view that the approach to training, which hadn't been challenged or changed for a very long time, was unlikely to enable them to achieve the success they desired.

His basis for forming this view was pretty straightforward. The training programme was the same one that had been used for years. So far it hadn't delivered the success that he, and others, aspired to so there was no reason to believe it would now.

Previously, winning a silver or bronze medal had been deemed to be success for the GB rowing squad. Steve Redgrave wanted more than silver or bronze, but to win gold he knew something had to change. While he didn't initially know what, he did know they couldn't afford to do the same thing again. Please remember, while these thoughts were bubbling away in Steve's brain, he was still a relatively new and inexperienced member of the sqaud despite his success as a junior international rower.

When he voiced his opinion that something needed to change, his view was met with resistance by those who had presided over the training for the previous Olympics. It is quite likley they didn't like the fact that their methods were being challenged, particularly by someone who was so new to the squad.

Sir Steve Redgrave is a determined, persistant and straight-talking man. When the people he was challenging said there was no good reason for changing, his response was that they had nothing to lose. When the establishment said that big change, relatively close to an Olympics, was bound to end in failure, Sir Steve declared that in his view, any result other than gold was failure.

This commitment to excellence was new. At that moment in history, East Germany had dominated international rowing for a number of years. If a non-East German crew won a gold medal, it was truly remarkable. But, it still did happen now and again and in Sir Steve's eyes if there were crews who were competing against and beating the East Germans, this meant that it could be done. It was equally clear to Sir Steve, that Great Britiain's rowing squad didn't yet have the winning formula. He pushed hard for a new training programme and his persistence paid off.

In the summer of 1984, a boat with four rowers and a steersman, a boat with Sir Steve Redgrave in the crew, won Great Britain's first Olympic rowing gold medal since 1948.

The rest, as they say, is history and Sir Steve went on to win gold medals at the next four Olympic Games. Despite his success, he never once considered he'd gone far enough. Throughout his rowing career, and beyond, he has retained the firmly held view that it was vital to continue to strive for excellence. He firmly believes it is necessary to consistently challenge and question the plans and methods that people use, *even when* they were winning.

What is remarkable about this story is that a person like Sir Steve Redgrave, who was new to the national rowing squad, was confident enough to challenge the perceived wisdom at that time. To be successful in such a challenge, you usually require credibility.

It is undoubtedly easier to question things when you have a track record of success and are therefore, credible. It isntantly puts you at an advantage because credibility can encourage others to make decisions and undertake activities that they otherwise might not. However, whether you are at the beginning of your leadership career, or have a good few years under your belt, the same rule applies. Question everything.

I have often been described as a challenging person, which I take as a compliment. This word challenging means that I do not say what I think people want to hear. I challenge what my clients are doing and why they are doing it so that the solutions we build together are appropriate and effective.

I have to confess I learned this lesson the hard way. Remember the ill-fated decision to go to Nepal, to work in adventure travel? The one which took me out of my humdrum army life a few weeks before the Gulf War? Well, it wasn't the best decision on many other levels either, although, on a positive note I did learn some valuable lessons.

I'd gone into the Nepalese venture with a colleague of mine from 2nd Gurkha Rifles. He too was serving in this theatre, in a different area and had made up his mind to leave the Army. His suggestion was that we build a travel lodge in the hills of west Nepal. We would build it from scratch and live there, offering treks and white water rafting for foreign visitors.

The third partner in our business venture was to be my colleague's father. I had met this man on two or three occasions and had liked him from day one. One of the reasons I thought my colleague's father was a good potential business partner was that he had a demonstrable track record of having successfully established businesses. Back then in 1990, I viewed myself as an inexperienced businessman and thought this would hold me back. It made sense to seek the guidance of someone who had been successful in several business ventures.

Due to my dates for leaving the army, my colleague went to Nepal about six weeks ahead of me. His plan was to see what types of opportunity were available for us in Nepal. I vividly remember one lengthy telephone conversation with him. He was in an office in Nepal and I was in the operations room on my final operational posting.

The news was not what I had been hoping to hear. It seemed that it was impossible to establish a company in Nepal without having a Nepali person as the controlling director. Without a company we could not own land. If we did not own land, we couldn't build a lodge. In short, the plans and dreams we had discussed for months were going up in smoke. When I finished speaking to him, I telephoned his father in England. We discussed the implications of this new-found information. My colleague's father suggested the Nepal venture was now in jeopardy and we should reconsider alternative business options in the adventure travel industry.

A small voice in my head probably agreed with my colleague's father. I did not, however, choose to listen to the little voice. I had obviously decided to take a chance, a big one at that. A subjective and rather naive evaluation of the situation told me that it would still be possible to achieve something in our chosen field. For that reason I went ahead with my plans to leave the Army and I joined my colleague in Kathmandu six weeks later.

I started to focus on trying to make our new business venture a success, although I was becoming a little concerned, both with the lack of real progress and with the speed with which money was being spent. Despite speaking to my colleague's dad in England regularly, there didn't seem to be any evidence of future bookings building up. Neither my colleague nor his dad seemed concerned. In general, there seemed to be a lack of energy or focus on sales activities.

By this stage we had identified that the only way to do business in Nepal was to establish a joint venture with a local Nepali adventure travel company. My colleague had identified a guy who was keen to do business with us. In hindsight, it was obvious why. He perceived a steady stream of visitors, who he would then take on trekking and rafting expeditions. For a

Kathmandu-based business, marketing in the States and Europe is the key to their success.

He gave us the use of an office within his office just off Durbar Marg. My colleague and I used to wander down there each morning and sit in the office. With hindsight, I am not sure what we were really expecting. We certainly weren't doing anything that would make something happen.

While looking through various documents that were in the main office, I discovered a Ministry of Tourism report. The report included a summary of the destinations from which most travellers arrived in Nepal. I decided to have a closer look. Until that point I had assumed that they came from Europe, the United States and Australia. I was surprised to learn that most visitors to Nepal came from India and that only a small proportion came from the United States or England.

It was also clear that the percentage of people who arrived in Nepal with pre-booked expeditions was very high. In this case, 'very high' meant that about 98 per cent of visitors had pre-booked treks and expeditions. This obviously meant that any walk-in business, never mind substantial walk-in business, was very unlikely to come our way.

When I started to question the amount of time potential clients were going to devote to making their decision, I discovered that it usually took between a year and eighteen months from someone deciding to come to Nepal and actually arriving. Looking at how this impacted on the financial aspect of the business, I discovered that the company would receive a deposit of 10 per cent at the time of booking. The balance would be paid two months before the party arrived in Kathmandu. This meant that even if we were able to attract a party to Nepal, we wouldn't get any type of income for about 16 months.

It is testament to our collective naivety and lack of questioning that we hadn't worked this out before we set up a base in Kathmandu. In January 1991, two months after I had arrived in Nepal, it became very obvious to me that the best place for us to be was in London. Someone needed to be there, walking the streets, telling all of the travel agents that we had this fabulous trekking business where the lead guides were Irish/English and spoke Nepalese.

What concerned me most was that it was me, the novice business person, who had identified this particular issue. I was the person who had done the questioning, albeit belatedly. None of these issues had been identified by my colleagues, yet I had gone into business with them because of their business expertise. Not unsurprisingly, I was starting to get alarmed.

Then, we encountered another unexpected challenge, which was that a foreigner could actually only gain access to Nepal for four months in any one calendar year. There were ways around this particular restriction but they involved paying bribes to officials, which was something we were against.

My, by now, rapidly developing understanding of the adventure travel industry was telling me that it would take at least eighteen months, from the creation of a brochure through to greeting our first paying guests in Kathmandu. It became quite clear to me that, on this occasion, we had failed. We didn't have the funds to see us through those eighteen months. I had probably known that this was the case for some time.

There were some real lessons here. For too long it was easier not to question this and accept what was really the unacceptable. The reason the business venture failed was naivety. None of us questioned the facts that we had in front of us. I was naïve throughout the planning stage and the initial start-up in Kathmandu. While I take full responsibility for placing my future success in the hands of others, I could kick myself for not questioning the information I was being given.

I have no doubt that there was space for us in the already crowded adventure travel industry in Nepal. If both of us had honestly questioned our value to our business, we'd have established that:

- We weren't going to be any use while we were based in Kathmandu. We didn't have the expertise that the established companies had and we didn't have the money needed to build that expertise.

- We weren't going to be much use when our clients were out on trek. There were plenty of guides who could do a much better job than we could.
- We weren't any good at selling.

If we had really questioned our value, we'd have seen that it was in marketing our business in England, where the expression 'Gurkha' has so many inspiring connotations. We could have created marketing material and I could have attended a sales and marketing course. This would have enabled me to sell the trekking and climbing trips we could access through the established companies. By questioning our value to the business, we'd have taken a very different path to the one we did take. But we didn't question it, not honestly anyway.

Looking back on this period now, the factor that is most galling is questioning things should have been instinctive for me. Questioning information was a key behaviour drummed into us at the officer's Academy at Sandhurst. When we were required to plan and execute any form of field-based activity, we would look at the facts and constantly ask the question: 'So what?'. This wasn't rudeness, or insubordination, it is an army term for delving into the detail of a plan and checking all possible avenues of what may go wrong, or send it off course.

For example, if I were planning to attack an enemy

camp, the plan would involve crawling into a position from where I would be able to see the camp and look at the ground between where I was and the enemy camp. We were trained to look at the ground in a very systematic way; this approach can help to ensure that you don't take shortcuts. In other words, no opportunity is missed to question every aspect of what you are seeing. While I was observing the ground between me and the enemy camp, in order to try and establish the best way to attack, I would start by looking at the ground on my left-hand side and the bit of ground nearest my position. Let's say there was a small wood close by. I'd question the value or otherwise of that small wood by asking myself the 'so what?' question. The process would go something like this:

- Ground, left, near. A small wood. So what? The trees would give us some cover from enemy view when we are preparing to attack.
- So what? Cover is good; it means we wouldn't have to rely on darkness to prepare out of sight of the enemy.
- So what? We could attack the enemy in daylight.
- So what? We would have options for the start time of the attack.
- So what? If there was fire support available, we could have that fire support because we could adjust our start time to coincide with the availability of the fire support.
- So what? That fire support could help us get on the

enemy position while the enemy were sheltering from it.

Deduction – ground left gives me cover and options – ground right is good.

The next step would be to have a look at the ground left – middle, in other words the piece of ground between the small wood and the final piece of ground leading to the enemy position.

- Ground left, middle – open ground, not much cover.
- So what? Couldn't attack over this ground in daylight without fire support – it's too open.
- So what? If we don't get fire support, ground left is dangerous in the middle.

This questioning approach would continue as we assessed each part of the ground around us so we could build up a complete picture. When we were choosing an attack route, there would often have to be compromise. It wouldn't have been possible to compromise effectively if we hadn't questioned every aspect of the situation.

The 'So what?' question is used relentlessly in the military to make sure that facts weren't overlooked for any reason, even down to the personal prejudices that people might have. The questioning was designed to ensure decisions were made objectively. Of course, initially this approach does take time. However, as we developed our ability to question effectively, we became more adept at using it. Looking back, I often wish I used the question everything approach for my Nepal venture. I certainly haven't made that same mistake twice and I make sure that my clients don't either.

There is one very vivid example of this that sticks in my mind. At a consulting session with one of my clients, the managing director told me that he was planning to build the business he was running, and then buy it from the owner.

'Why would you want to do that?' was my question.

'What do you mean?' he said.

'Why would you want to invest your time and energy in building it up to then buy it?' I asked. Privately, I thought this was a question he should have asked himself.

'Fair point' he said.

Six weeks later I received an email from him. I still have it. In the title bar it said 'Look what you made me do'.

When I opened the email I was really pleased to see that he'd gone off to a bank, secured the funding he needed to buy the business, approached the owner and agreed to buy it. I played no part in the actions he took. He did that. However, my one, fairly obvious, question had played a part in his changing strategy.

When he bought the business it had 22 employees. The business now has 115 employees and is doing very well. That business owner will tell anyone who listens that being asked one question changed his life forever.

I am delighted to have been the person who asked that question.

SUMMARY

- Effective leaders don't allow themselves to become comfortable with the status quo.
- Even if it is uncomfortable to do so, you should always push to try something differently, if there is a possibility there might be a better way of doing things.
- It is easier to question when you've got credibility behind you, but even if you are relatively new to a leadership role, you should never be afraid to stick your neck out.

PERSONAL DEVELOPMENT EXERCISES

EXERCISE ONE

Disrupt yourself/question everything

Business benefit

You will develop new ideas for operating more effectively

Resources

Time with the team

Format

Use a team meeting for this exercise. Tell the team

that they are going to be challenged to think about new ideas to increase business efficiency.

Spilt your team into two smaller groups and allow both groups the thinking time they need to address these two questions:

1. If they could only work for four hours a day, what would they change?
2. If they could only work for two hours a day, what would they change?

Allow the teams twenty minutes to come up with their ideas.

Take feedback.

Look for ideas that can be implemented immediately. Implement the ideas and analyse the results.

PERSONAL DEVELOPMENT EXERCISES

EXERCISE TWO

Disrupt yourself/question everything

Business benefit

You will develop new ideas for operating more effectively

Resources

Time with the team

Format

Allocate sixty minutes for this exercise and appoint

»

a facilitator for the team. Tell the team that you, the leader, will not be available for three days a week. You can dictate which days you won't be available and they can be consistent, i.e. every Tuesday, Wednesday, Thursday, or just three days that are inconsistent.

Explain to the team they must come up with ideas and practices that will enable them to continue to operate the business effectively. Ask them what changes they would make.

Take feedback.

Prioritise the ideas for perceived value.

Implement the highest priorities.

Analyse and measure the results.

Deliver feedback to the team.

CHAPTER 8
SPEAK TO INSPIRE

I have observed lots of leaders speaking to their people. One early experience that really stands out was as a young trainee rifleman in 1982. Our military training had been suspended so that we could devote all of our time to cleaning an old army barracks in time for an inspection. Even though we were new recruits we were annoyed at having to spend three long days washing windows, cleaning lavatories and shining floors. We wanted to be doing military training. My fellow trainees were starting to mutter that this was what the army was really about. Everyone was unhappy.

On the second evening of cleaning, just as we started cleaning yet another shower block, we were told to meet in a training room. We weren't to smarten up; we were to go there directly. When we arrived, our instructor told us that our platoon commander Lieutenant Henry Worsley was going to come and speak to us. As was customary, our instructor bellowed a command when

Henry walked in. We all jumped to our feet and stood to attention. He told us to sit down.

He sat on the edge of a table and began to talk about our training being set aside to prepare the old barracks for an inspection. He acknowledged that we were unhappy and he said that he understood why. However, he explained that, as we were the only platoon in training at that time, the full responsibility had fallen on us. He agreed this was unlucky, but that there was nothing we or anyone could do about it. He certainly didn't apologise for the state of affairs. He assured us that as soon as the inspection was over we would get back to full military training.

His final point was that because we were the only platoon in the barracks at the time of the inspection, the quality of the inspection would reflect directly on us, adding that soldiering as an infantryman was often about doing the unpleasant, mundane stuff really well.

When I think of great leaders, I think of people who can inspire others by how they communicate.

'Platoons that pass through this barracks build a reputation, whether they know it or not,' he said. 'You may think that getting a reputation for being good at cleaning is a bad thing for people who want to be fighting men. I can assure you that that isn't the case. If you do this well, you'll build a reputation for being people who can do a crappy task really well. It's easy to do the exciting stuff well, not so easy to do this type of thing. That will send a message to the rest of the training staff.'

We then went back to cleaning the shower blocks. The difference was that we now had a determination to do the job well. After all, we now had an opportunity to build a reputation for ourselves and for our platoon.

Over thirty years later, I can clearly remember how Henry Worsley spoke to us.

Henry didn't apologise for the fact that we had to do what we had to do. He made good sense and most all he spoke from the heart. What he said had a galvanising effect on us that was borne out in the results of the inspection. We had done a very good job and were awarded the highest score attainable. Military training then started in earnest.

When I think of great leaders, I think of people who can inspire others by how they communicate. Some people think being an inspiring orator is a gift of some kind, a capability that you are born with. I don't accept this because I believe that it is possible to develop the ability to do anything with a bit of hard work and practice. In fact, when I consider this, I always think of a quote from one of the most famous orators of the last century: Sir Winston Churchill. When the Prime Minister was interrupted in a side room of the House of Commons before one of his important war time speeches and was asked what he was doing, Sir Winston replied: 'Why, practising my impromptu remarks of course.'

I once worked with a HR Director of an IT services company to help him be more confident about speaking in public. Public speaking was something he didn't enjoy, which isn't unusual. Most people don't enjoy it. I had asked the man, Peter, to prepare a three-minute presentation before we met.

I'd arranged that he would deliver his talk to me and three of his colleagues. Speaking in front of colleagues is usually particularly difficult because your success or otherwise is going to be known by them and the concerns are two-fold. Firstly, you are not going to be very good and secondly, no one wants to be poor at something in front of their colleagues. If a colleague who is good at public speaking is in the audience, this is worse. The accomplished colleague isn't often seen as someone to be learnt from, but more as someone who can show you up.

From the moment Peter started speaking, we were all entranced. He spoke without notes or slides for three minutes. His only prop was an empty two-litre plastic bottle, which he revealed to us after about ninety seconds. His presentation focused on a man from South America called Alfredo Moser who devised a rudimentary light bulb from plastic bottles. We were fascinated from start to finish.

The presentation was videoed. When we replayed the video we were able to find one or two improvements, but overall Peter had made a great presentation, delivered with fluency and passion. When I asked Peter how the presentation he had just given compared to the presentations he usually delivered in his professional career, he told me that most of the other ones he had to deliver were different. When I asked how, his response was that the content of his presentations was generally dull and boring. I pressed him for an example.

He told me that he often had to present in front of sixteen-year-old boys and girls and their parents at recruitment seminars the business ran during the school holidays.

'It's all the HR stuff,' he said.

'How is HR stuff boring?' I pressed.

'It's all terms and conditions,' he said. 'I have to tell them what working with us will mean to them, as far as their contract is concerned'.

I still didn't understand. It seemed to me it was not a problem with the content itself, but in the way it was being delivered. The focus of my development work with Peter focused on the three Ss:

- substance
- structure
- style.

SUBSTANCE

This is the message you want to get across. This is most frequently the starting point in the speaker's preparation where they will write some form of script, or worse still will open up a programme like PowerPoint and go straight to a slide show.

In actual fact, the speaker should start by asking themselves what they want to achieve in their presentation. What are their objectives? If they don't know, they may like to think in terms of general objectives which should be to inform, inspire and possibly entertain. In reality the objectives are usually a combination of all three.

The speaker then has to establish:

- What they want to inform the audience
- How they are going to inspire the audience
- When and how they are going to entertain the audience

Bear in mind, this is still a conversation about substance. The structure will follow later. Something that works well is to use Post-it notes, or something similar, perhaps in three different colours, one for inform, one for inspire and another for entertain. The benefit of this will become apparent later.

The amount of substance will be driven by the time the speaker has available. If they are the only person speaking, you can assume that if they are told that they have thirty minutes that they will get thirty minutes. If the person is speaking at a conference with other speakers, there will usually be a requirement to be adaptable with the allotted time.

If a speaker tells me that they have forty-five minutes, I suggest they aim for sufficient substance to speak for thirty minutes, or roughly two-thirds of the time they have been allotted. Most speakers underestimate how long they will need so overrun, and there is nothing worse than hearing someone skipping through their last slides, so the audience can go for coffee.

While defining the substance, it is important to think about the words that will be used. It is helpful to write the words out on a piece of paper and then attach them to the appropriate Post-it note. If a speaker intends to tell a story, I always advise they write it out in full so they can start to evaluate the structure of the key components.

As far as substance is concerned, there is no short cut in this initial stage. True stories that support the key points you are trying to make are excellent value. It is impossible to hold an audience's full attention for forty-five minutes and that's not necessarily the objective. People's minds wander. One way to get a wandering mind's attention is to use story. As stories can both entertain and inspire, for that reason you have to make sure you don't overdo using them. When we begin to think about the structure of the presentation, we can start to evaluate the balance of the different type of substance.

It is really useful at this point to check for words that appear too often and for jargon. Jargon is fine if the audience all come from the same business, otherwise it should be explained, or possibly avoided completely. Likewise, if certain words are overused they lose their impact and the audience will drift off.

I once watched a sales director of a European company speak for forty-five minutes at a national sales conference which was attended by more than 250 people. If he said the word 'important' once, he said it fifteen times. Everything was qualified with the statement 'this is important' or 'this is very important'. At the end of his speech, his reliance on the word important was commented on by several people, in a less than positive way. The sales director, however, was completely oblivious to what had happened. This smacked to me of a lack of preparation.

Many senior leaders will think or say that they don't have time to devote to preparation. My view is that the leader who thinks that the opportunity to speak is important will find the time to prepare. Of course, the more public speaking you do, the more confident you will become, but you have to have some form of plan to follow to ensure that you maximise the opportunity.

STRUCTURE

The next step is to put a structure on your substance.

There are three basic components to a presentation:

the introduction, the middle and the summary or finale.

The introduction is often referred to as the point where you tell the audience what you are going to tell them. I recommend that you devote no more than 10 per cent of your allotted speaking time to the introduction.

The middle is where you tell them what you are going to tell them. This is usually the biggest chunk of your presentation. This will be between 75 per cent and 80 per cent of your speaking time, depending on the summary and finale.

The summary and finale is where you summarise and bring your presentation to a close. I recommend about 10 per cent to 15 per cent of your time be devoted to your summary and finale.

If you are asked to speak for forty-five minutes and follow the rule above of allotting two thirds of that time to deliver your talk, you now have twenty minutes for the middle of your presentation.

How do you go about applying your substance to the structure? I'd recommend using something like the format shown in Table 1.

Table 1. Example of applying substance to structure.

Stage	Time	Objective	Substance (for example)	Visual
Introduction	3	ENT INSP	Ice breaker Thank you	Holding slide Picture
Middle	22	INFO INFO INSP ENT INFO INFO INSP	Key point #1 Key point #2 Impact – story Light hearted introduction to Key point # 3 Key point #4 Impact – short story	Slide Slide Picture/ holding slide Nothing Slide Slide Picture/ holding slide
Summary/ finale	5	INFO INSP	Summary Thank you – keep at it	Slide Picture

The Stage column is self explanatory. The Time column is the amount of time you have. You can rehearse against this. The Objective column is designed to allow you to analyse the balance between the three objectives of inform, inspire and entertain. I would put the text for inspire (INSP), inform (INFO) and entertain (ENT) in a different colour to further help with balance.[1]

Be a little creative with the title of your presentation, but don't hoodwink. Depending on the objective of the presentation, consider focusing on the possible result of what you are imparting as opposed to the concept. For example, a sales skills presentation might be called 'Increase your results and no cold calling'. The skills being imparted here were those needed to be an effective networker, therefore the title was designed to encourage people to think about the results, not just the topic.

Break down other key areas you may like to include in the substance as follows.

KEY POINTS

As the name implies a key point is something drawn from the analysis of the substance that needs to be got across. This could be anything from business performance against target, to an analysis of the competition, or the plan for the year ahead.

A common mistake made here is to use key point slides as a store for all of the information the speaker wants to impart. People who are unfamiliar with the presentation then divert their attention and spend all of their time looking at the slides for prompts, or reading from a paper printout of the slides. If you write

1. For a planner template, email bryan@bryandunlop.com

information onto a slide, your audience will read it. It is far more effective to acknowledge there will be additional information imparted to the audience that will be supported with some form of handout they can take away. The amount of detail on the slides can then be reduced and the speaker can stick to the key points. If you are using PowerPoint, or a similar type of presentation creator, remember to use the 'animations' capability to reveal information in line with your presentation, but do keep the animations as simple as you can.

When you have imparted a key point, support it and break up the presentation by adding a short anecdote or story. The anecdote must be linked to the key point and must be relevant. If you support a key point with a story, use a light-hearted link to take you into your next key point.

One good example of using key points effectively was demonstrated to me by a senior leader who talked about his business being on a journey. He began with a very short and entertaining ice breaker along these lines and it was immediately clear that the concept of the business being on a journey was what he wanted people to remember. He used one basic slide, representative of a journey and he systematically added his key points to this slide. He spoke for twenty minutes without reference to notes, based on this linear development of his story. He had clearly thought about what he wanted the audience to remember and created his key points to support it.

If you start to build your presentation through the identification of relevant objectives, good substance and a clear structure, you will deliver a great presentation. Visual aids can be used, but remember, if you are a speaker, the audience want to hear you.

SUMMARY AND FINALE

As with any good comedian, timing is everything and a good speaker should leave an audience wanting more. Avoid, at all costs, the rushed conclusion to your presentation. If you do, what do you think the audience will remember? Besides, finish within time and the conference organiser will be your best friend for life. Planning the ending to your talk is fundamental.

> When you have imparted a key point, support it and break up the presentation by adding a short anecdote or story. The anecdote must be linked to the key point and must be relevant.

A good summary and finale will inform and inspire. Leaders have got to be able to inspire so take the opportunity. The three-stage structure and, most specifically, the summary afford the opportunity to really focus on the messages that need to come across.

My recommendation is that the summary contains just three points. Two is too few and four is too many, unless you have had more time to present.

The summary points should be linked to the key points that formed the majority of the presentation and delivered in the same order as they were delivered originally.

Always introduce your summary by saying: 'so in summary' and use a slide to emphasise the summary points. Be very concise in the words you use on your slide. Don't say, 'It's all about activity,' just put the word 'activity' on the slide. You can embellish the points in the words you use. Again use the animation capability to reveal the summary words. You must know these off by heart.

When you have summarised, you have an opportunity to close your presentation with something that the audience will remember and something that inspires them. We all like leaders who say thank you and mean it. Thank you is one of the most important expressions a leader can use and it isn't used often enough. At this stage the audience must be fixed on the presenter, there can be no distractions. Consider a slide that simply says 'thank you'.

Speak from the heart and mean it. Then walk off the stage.

Your objective is to get the audience to remember your summary words and the sentiment of your finale. Don't get bogged down in explaining how the coffee break works, the conference organiser can do that. Just make sure the organiser has some idea about how your presentation will close so that they are ready to take over from you.

STYLE

There are some further skills that are well worth developing and which will prove invaluable in delivering speeches effectively; these are to do with your demeanour and speaking style. After all, once a leader has stopped speaking, the audience will remember some of what was said, but they will focus on exactly how it was said. Whenever I ask an audience to remind me of the people they classify as great speakers or presenters, they will often mimic the style of the speaker more than the substance. That doesn't mean that substance is not important; of course not. There are some expressions that will continue to have impact forever and a great deal of that is to do with the delivery. When Churchill described RAF Fighter Command at the Battle of Britain as 'the few' that expression went down in history. Some people are even able to repeat that quotation verbatim with a Churchillian accent.

I break style down into two components: Voice and physiology – in other words, how you use your body.

VOICE

Voice can be further broken down into five components:

1. Volume: can you be heard? There are occasions when lowering your voice will have as much impact as raising your voice.
2. Speed: do you speak too quickly, or are you slow? You'll need feedback on this.
3. Tone: be wary of sounding bored. Stories are a good way to inject additional tone.
4. Emphasis : choose certain words or expressions to emphasise.
5. Pauses: very important. Most speakers don't pause enough. This can be linked to a desire to bring the presentation to a conclusion. Using a combination of key points, stories and humour can break the presentation up.

PHYSIOLOGY

There are many aspects of physiology. The main ones are:

- Eye contact: can you get and hold eye contact? If the audience is big, break it down into four chunks: front, left and right; and rear, left and right. Remember to engage with someone in each chunk on a consistent basis.
- Movement: do you stand behind a lectern, do you sit on a stool, or do you move about the stage? The answer may be that you do a bit of all three. Speakers who stay behind the lectern are missing an opportunity to engage.

- Hands: don't overdo the use of hands. If you are moving around, you can anchor one hand in your pocket, if you have pockets. Make sure pockets are empty. If you are using a remote control to move through your visual aids carry it with you to help control your hands.
- Appearance: you will make an impression whether you want to or not. Your audience and the context may dictate this, i.e. black tie or business casual. The aim is not to alienate through your dress code. Some speakers make a point of making a statement through their appearance. In my experience, immaculate professional business dress is ideal. Grey suit/white or blue shirt or blue suit and a white shirt.
- Gestures: be sure to avoid gestures that could cause offence, especially if you are abroad.
- Orientation: meaning how you face the audience. If the audience is big, you may need to face people full on to truly engage. The orientation of your body will create better engagement if you stand and face them. As with sharing eye contact, don't forget to change your orientation to make sure that every member of the audience gets the same treatment.

Although most leaders fear public speaking more than anything else, failure to master this communication skill will severely limit their opportunity to get across their thoughts and ideas and may even stifle their personal and professional growth.

Speaking well is not a natural gift. Even the greatest orators have to work at it and practise. Given time and persistence though, it is a natural progression. When mastered, speaking well will improve your outlook. It is, however, surprising just how quickly progress can be made. It can take just a handful of speeches to become an effective public speaker and the knock-on boost to those around you will be phenomenal.

I still remember listening to my platoon commander Henry Worsley, all those years ago, when we were doing that mundane cleaning. I can recall exactly what he said and how he said it. Despite the fact that the topic was dull, he inspired us all in a very short period of time.

His substance was good, his structure was good, but most of all he spoke from the heart. That's what leaders do.

SUMMARY

1. There are tremendous personal and professional advantages to be gained by conquering a fear of public speaking, not least that it is an essential leadership skill.
2. Public speaking is not a gift. It requires planning, practice and persistence to hone speaking skills to perfection.
3. When planning speeches, consider the three Ss: substance, structure, style

PERSONAL DEVELOPMENT EXERCISES

EXERCISE ONE

Communicate with groups

Business benefit

You will be able to speak in public with confidence

Resources

Time for preparation

Format

Use the template and formula described in this chapter to create the next presentation in your business or personal life. When you have completed the presentation, rehearse it at least five times.

Ideally, video the entire presentation so that you can review it. If this isn't possible, video at least the introduction and the summary and close. Review it and ask someone you respect to review it as well. Listen to their feedback and ensure that:

The key points in the summary and close are clear

The introduction catches the audience's attention

If this is the case, use the presentation in its current form; if not, make adjustments and undertake the review again.

PERSONAL DEVELOPMENT EXERCISES

EXERCISE TWO

Communicate with groups

Business benefit

Your team will develop their presentation skills

Resources

Time for preparation and time to present

Format

Give each member of your team a business-related topic to present on. Ensure that the length of the presentation is kept quite short – certainly no more than fifteen minutes.

Provide team members with the template outlined in this chapter and coach them through the process, emphasising the need to start with the summary and close, as well as an engaging introduction.

Be prepared to give the team some of your time in the preparation stage.

Create a forum for the members of the team to present and ask their colleagues to give feedback on the structure of the summary, close and introductions, in particular. Once they have developed the ability to do this effectively, move on to helping them develop their delivery of the key points.

CHAPTER 9

STAND FIRM – HAVE THE COURAGE OF YOUR CONVICTION

When I was an officer cadet at Sandhurst we often travelled away from the Academy to practise war skills in training areas elsewhere, such as Salisbury. When we were on exercise, as it was known, the cadets would be given the opportunity to take up leadership appointments we might subsequently have when our training was over. Those asked to command part of the team were given an armband displaying the rank of the officer, or non-commissioned officer, whose role was being played. Normally, rank badges are worn on the shoulder, not the upper arm and most soldiers know this.

On one occasion, I took the part of platoon commander and was given an armband with one star on it. This star was designed to remind other cadets I had authority and, of course, responsibility. We were all sorting out our equipment before travelling back to the academy, when a soldier walked up to me and asked me how to get to the armoury. I stood up and pointed out the way I thought he ought to go. He thanked me and then saw the star on my armband.

Straightening up, he saluted me and said 'thank you, Sir,' before marching off.

For a moment I didn't know what to do. As a cadet I wasn't entitled to be saluted as I hadn't been granted my commission. I felt like running after him and saying, 'you don't have to salute me. I'm not a real officer'. To tell the truth, I was embarrassed. I found the experience very odd. It wasn't the saluting part, per se. The problem was that, in my mind, I shouldn't have been saluted, because it is the commission bestowed on an officer by the Queen that warrants being saluted.

Of course, when I applied for officer training I'd always known that I would be given responsibility, but for some reason this incident brought this into sharp focus. That soldier didn't know that I was a cadet. He was so used to seeing a badge of rank that he would respond to the badge not the person. I realised that I was on the brink of being treated very differently to the way I had been treated as a soldier. Experienced soldiers would assume that I was a real leader. This unsettled me, but it also made me more determined than ever to get the most value from the training and my time at the academy. If people were prepared to give me respect without my earning it then I was determined to be as capable as I could be. The responsibility weighed very heavily on my young shoulders.

When I eventually left Sandhurst and exchanged my blue beret of the academy for the rifle green beret of the 2nd Gurkhas, I looked at the Sandhurst cap badge for the final time. 'Serve to lead' is the Sandhurst motto and we had been reminded of this every day during our training. Everything we did was measured against the standards required of a leader. Our appearance was inspected daily, even when we left the academy to go out on leave. When we played rugby, we were expected to play very hard but fairly and win or lose, and be gracious to our opponents.

Today, when I work with leaders outside the army, I am always keen to see how they behave when not officially in role. I often see leaders when they are socialising with their people and, in particular, at conferences. To my surprise they don't always demonstrate the rigorous standards of leadership I've seen in the corporate environment. This inconsistency does not go unnoticed elsewhere either.

Let me give you an example. I once observed a senior leader in a financial services company speak passionately and compellingly at a launch event for a major change initiative. He took time to explain what was required and the reasons why it was so imperative. It so happened that the change he was signposting did mean that there was the likelihood of short-term pain for long-term pleasure, as many change programmes do, but he was clear in his reasoning that the objective was serious and that the team needed to get behind it. He also told them that it wasn't a case of opting in, or choosing to opt out; if people didn't adhere to the goals being set, they would have to find a different place to work. As I listened, I was very impressed and slightly surprised at his level of conviction. I had worked with him on previous occasions and he had often seemed too easily influenced by others in the businesses he had led. Perhaps things had changed. His balance of the carrot and the stick, incentive and consequence, was just right and started the event on exactly the correct footing.

I was involved with the company on a consultancy basis, so I found myself being quizzed by various people on several occasions during the day about just how serious the organisation were about these changes.

'You heard it from the boss,' was my response. 'He's absolutely behind this and meant every word he said.'

People within that company had a reputation for staying up late and enjoying bar room chat. I joined in for a while at the end of the day and then excused myself at an appropriate hour and headed off to bed. The next morning I was in the conference centre in good time. One of the people I knew from that company joined me unexpectedly.

'You ought to know that a good few of them were late to bed last night,' he told me. 'The boss stayed until about two and was very drunk. One of the senior guys asked him if the company would really sanction people who didn't hit the key performance indicators.'

'What was his response?' I asked, with a rising sense of dread. I already sensed the answer.

'He paused for long enough for people to make their own deductions,' replied my informant. 'He certainly didn't reiterate what he had said when he opened the conference yesterday morning.'

From that moment I knew that no matter what this director said in the future, he had shown a lack of conviction. Instead of reiterating the need for the change, he had taken the easy option and that is the message his managers passed on to their teams.

This leader clearly had no moral courage and was prepared to flex and bend to the whim of those below him. This is not an isolated example either. I've seen other examples of this in companies I've worked with elsewhere. But, why would any leader choose to pursue a course of action that they knew to be wrong, or publicly change tack? I think there are a number of reasons for this:

1. Popularity. Everyone wants to be liked. Some leaders want to be liked more than anything else. This is not to say that a desire to be liked is a bad trait, but when

it comes at the expense of the goal and a leader's responsibilities, it is definitely bad.

2. Self-preservation. There are occasions when telling it as it is brings the bearer of that news into a spotlight, and many people like to avoid this exposure. People can't help but think about how a situation is going to affect them, their spouses or partners and their families. While this is a natural concern, it does not justify fudging the facts and is certainly not leadership behaviour.
3. Lack of integrity. Inconsistency is the most obvious sign of a lack of integrity. Sometimes the signs are subtle, such as slight shifts in opinions of exchanging loyalty; other times it is obvious and dramatic. This style may give the appearance of affability, but what it actually says is this leader can't be trusted to do what he or she says they'll do.
4. Unwilling to say no. There are occasions when some ideas being put forward are clearly not good ones. They may be driven by one or two people who have their careers attached to the success of the idea. A weak leader may attempt a half-hearted implementation to satisfy the people who are driving the idea. He or she might do this in the hope the idea might shrivel and die without anyone ever having to take full responsibility for kicking it into the long grass. This way they avoid saying 'no'.

If the leader doesn't think it will work after giving it a full analysis, they should say 'no' right up front, together with the reasons why they are saying 'no'. Culturally this would be a challenge for a lot of companies because a 'no' to an idea can have negative implications for the person who suggested it. However, if skilfully managed, it is possible to find the right balance between encouraging people to come up with ideas and also helping them understand that a 'no' isn't a bad thing.

Standing firm behind an idea, goal or belief is a vital characteristic of strong leadership. Yet, strong leadership should never be confused with being dogmatic in the face of changing landscape. While leaders must have the courage of their convictions and a determination to see things through, they must also have the ability to put their ego to one side when the course of action they are championing is no longer the best way forward. This will be difficult for all leaders.

It is not easy to say the course of action that they once supported must now be changed. In an ideal world, everyone would recognise that the ability to park one's ego and adapt is actually a great strength, and it is. One of the main barriers to this happening is those with different agendas will often attempt to use this adaptability to their own advantage. You may judge that it is easy to snipe at others when the ultimate responsibility for results is not your own, but the damage is done. It makes leaders reluctant to stick their necks out.

I see this too often. Politically motivated people will bend and distort facts to present any change in direction as weakness. It takes a strong leader to stand firm and the boards behind those leaders should support them.

A leader will learn a lot about their people when they seek to make adjustments to a plan they have previously supported. Great leaders and great teams meet changes and respond constantly. Those people who habitually moan and complain will make themselves known. But what does a leader do if it goes beyond sniping from the side-lines. What if, for example, senior members of the leadership team use this type of situation to try and unseat the leader?

I worked with one team in banking which had a new leader from outside the business. The company was in a challenging place and needed firm leadership and some fresh ideas. I knew this leader would take some time to establish a plan, but he also wanted to start the implementation process without too much delay. His view was that his and his team's ability to respond to an ever-changing landscape is what would make them successful. I don't know how many times he told his senior team they were going to have to be adaptable, but he told them often. This didn't dilute the strength of his desire to get the best outcome, but what he was saying was that he had a plan. It was the best plan for the circumstances, but they might need to adapt along the way.

This isn't to say that he flexed with every challenge they met, far from it. There were many circumstances when he and his team decided that they would stick to the plan that they had and forge on with the commitment they needed to get the job done. There were also occasions when it became apparent that they needed to adapt. These were times when the challenges they had met were so significant that to maintain the current course of action would have been very damaging.

> Standing firm behind an idea, goal or belief is a vital characteristic of strong leadership.

This leader expected a full and frank analysis of each challenge, followed by detailed planning, extensive communication with the teams and implementation. He also expected people to park their own agendas and get behind the new plan. It became clear quite early on that one member of his senior team was unwilling to do this. He had a close relationship with the previous leader and had been quite influential in the past. As a result this person constantly sought to undermine these demonstrations of adaptability, often in quite devious and underhand ways. His behaviour caused immense frustration among other senior members of the team who couldn't afford the time or energy for this activity. The boss confronted the agitator and told him the planning stage would benefit from his slightly contrary views, but he needed him to get behind the implementation of the plan that was agreed by the entire team. However, while the agitator appeared agreeable to this, it was obvious his true support would never be forthcoming. Reluctantly the senior leader decided that the cons of having this leader in his business outweighed the pros. For that reason, it was deemed necessary to move the agitator into another part of the business.

The new leader was prepared to park his ego to enable changes to the plan. Yet, one of his key people wasn't prepared to take the same approach.

Everyone must be prepared to analyse results being achieved and change when necessary. This will occasionally mean some degree of self-sacrifice on behalf of a leader. There is nothing worse than seeing people in positions of power being unwilling to make personal sacrifices. This is the type of mindset that usually goes hand in hand with the attitude among weaker leaders that when they are promoted into a position of responsibility, they should be treated differently. Or, more importantly to them, they can certainly expect to receive additional perks. The perks quickly become seen as an entitlement.

It is worth noting here that in the military the opposite applies. An officer or a non-commissioned officer will be exposed to far more dangerous situations than their men. In all phases of war, where the danger levels are high, officers are expected to be right in front of the danger and leading from the front. Any leader who is not prepared to do this, won't last long. If there is pain to be had, a military leader is expected to be (and to want to be) out in the front. The only time this doesn't apply is when there is something good to be had, such as for example, when everyone is being fed when out in the field. In this case, leadership is expected to be at the back of the queue. The most junior soldiers eat first. If there isn't enough, the officers go without.

Contrast this military model with typical leadership behaviour in the commercial world. If there is some pain to be had, a lot of leaders will do what they can to avoid being involved and make sure that their people deal with it. Yet, when there is something nice to be had, the leaders appear. I have witnessed leaders in countless companies that have put the front-line team under a lot of pressure, giving them a very hard time, day in and day out, while ensuring they are comfortable and under no discernable stress. One regional manager, in particular, behaved in an appalling way. Although he could and should have been on the front line with his people, he was always found in head office, miles away from his dejected and motivated team and the angry customers that couldn't understand why they weren't getting great service. Sadly, this leader was more concerned with the perks of being in his comfortable office, rather than thinking he should go out into the field and make the right personal sacrifice to lead from the front. His behaviour was reflected in the lack of success of this business, all the way down the line.

When I encounter leaders for whom a position of leadership is something that is taken for granted, a right, I always recall the military academy motto 'Serve to lead' because I find it hard to fathom this attitude. It is inconceivable that there might be people who think their leadership responsibility can be switched on and off, but sadly there are. They are happy to stand up and tell people to work a bit harder, take personal responsibility and commit themselves to the company and the cause, when they do anything but that.

The very worst examples of this occur when leaders use their position to place younger members of staff into very awkward situations. Sadly, it does happen. I have observed some senior leaders behave in an appalling way on one or two occasions, when a single instance would be one to many. These 'leaders' may argue that they were just having a good time and are as entitled to relax as much as anyone else, but if they cross the line of common decency it is abhorrent on any level.

There are a great many leaders who do take the leadership mantel very seriously. They spend time with their people and are even able to have a good time with their teams, although they never lose sight of the fact that they set the standards of behaviour. They don't seek the limelight, but allow their people to occupy it, often by way of reward. They certainly never misbehave and will very frequently disappear with very little fuss when the rest of the audience are starting to really let their hair down.

The leadership role must be the first priority though. Leadership involves sacrifice and if you're not prepared to sacrifice yourself for others you shouldn't be in the role. All leaders have to take positions and make decisions that are unpopular. It works all the way down the line too. Senior leaders depend on junior leaders to know what is right and what needs to be done as a result.

Moral courage, the courage to do the right thing even though it may have adverse consequences, is a huge part of leadership. As Theodore Roosevelt said, 'knowing what's right doesn't mean much unless you do what's right'. This attitude is hugely important in training and appointing successors. Skilled and confident junior leaders can and do have a huge and direct impact on a business. A lot of that will be a reflection of the man or woman who has brought them on.

Selecting people for roles and promotion is taken very seriously in the military. To gain entry to the military academy, recruits have to pass a rigorous three-day selection board in Wiltshire. This event involves about fourteen different procedures, including public speaking, practical problem-solving, writing essays on current political issues and physical fitness. The behaviour of the candidates is also measured in their time off.

Allowing time for selection is a privilege that most big companies don't have. In my experience, managers watch their people and attempt to see who might be management material. Unfortunately, the definition of 'management material' is often very unclear. In sales teams, for example, management material often means a very good salesperson. Yet, just because someone is a great salesperson doesn't mean to say they'll be a good leader. Indeed, I've found that the opposite often applies. The same applies in many other industries.

> Capable, confident leaders ... have no concerns about being marginalised by someone who is more effective than they are.

If someone is deemed to be management material they are often given responsibility very quickly. Responsibility in this instance might take the form of a leadership candidate being asked to understudy for their boss, for example, when the boss goes off on holiday. However, this is sometimes as far as it goes. Weak leaders won't develop those below them in case they turn out to be more effective than they are. There is the potential double whammy of a weak candidate being promoted and then not being given any help whatsoever to develop their skills. This perspective appals me.

In the chapter entitled 'Plan to make yourself redundant' the point is very clearly made that one key aspect of leadership is developing people. Capable, confident leaders give this priority. They have no concerns about being marginalised by someone who is more effective than they are. In fact, they welcome such occurrences. They know that if they consistently demonstrate an ability to identify and develop talent that they will become even more valuable to the organisation. Contrast this with some leaders who are less capable and confident. Their prime objective is the retention of their role. With this goal they are unlikely to seek out and develop their more talented junior colleagues. This is short-sighted on so many levels.

The traits of leaders have had much analysis. When I was a young cadet about to be commissioned, the Queen said: 'I am sure you will be faced by many challenges, many of which will be very dangerous. You may not know what to do. If you do the right thing and you lead by example you will uphold everything that makes our armed services the envy of the world.'

I have often thought about this since, and I also frequently cast my mind back to the Academy motto, 'Serve to lead'. A leader must lead and should never shy away from that duty, or put their personal interests first. It is what their people want and it is often what their people need. A leader owes it to his or her team to deliver it.

SUMMARY

1. While a leader should relax with his team and have a good relationship with all members, they should also always stand firm and be consistent.
2. Leadership does occasionally require personal sacrifice. You can't shy away from that.
3. Moral courage is important when bringing on successors and developing strengths within the team. A leader should do what needs to be done because it is the right thing to do, not because it is the right thing for them.

PERSONAL DEVELOPMENT EXERCISES

EXERCISE ONE

Stand firm - have the courage of your conviction

Business benefit
Strengthen your leadership impact

Resources
Thinking time by yourself

»

Format

Think of a leader that you really respect. Identify one aspect of their character that contributes to your high level of respect for them. This should be one aspect of their leadership style that you want to demonstrate more frequently, or with greater conviction. When you have identified the trait you admire, you should think about five different types of occasion when displaying this trait would strengthen your impact as a leader. For each occasion, you should identify the type of behaviour that will contribute to enhancing your impact in that situation. For example; if your objective is to enhance your impact at team social events, you should understand how the leader you admire would behave at this type of event, what they would do and how they would do it.

Don't attempt to make such a drastic change that you compromise any aspect of the type of person that you are; instead start with small adjustments and build over time. This stepped approach will enable you to analyse what works well and what might need to be adjusted as you go.

PERSONAL DEVELOPMENT EXERCISES

EXERCISE TWO

Stand firm - have the courage of your conviction

Business benefit

Strengthen the leadership impact of your team

Resources

Time with each member of your team

Format

Create an opportunity for each member of the team to think about the five leaders they admire and the specific traits that contribute to this level of admiration. Agree which trait each of your people wants to develop and identify what behaviour will inform both you and them of the adjusted behaviour.

Agree a timeframe within which you expect to see the behaviour demonstrated consistently.

Analyse the extent to which the behaviour is being demonstrated – both in frequency and consistency. Provide feedback to each individual. When the first habit has been adjusted, move on to the second habit they have identified as being of value to them and start the process again.

This exercise should form part of a 'formal' development programme.

CHAPTER 10

WITH TRUST YOU CAN DO EXTRAORDINARY THINGS TOGETHER

There are a lot of clichés and sound bites banded about describing the importance of teamwork, but how many of us really look at how it works in practice? What qualities do you need, as a leader, to encourage the people around you to follow, even when the path ahead isn't exactly smooth? How can you inspire the trust and respect of those you lead? I have been in teams, I have influenced teams and I have led teams. My views on how a leader can work with its team to help everyone perform at their best, even when under almost unbearable pressure, are very simple and are probably best encapsulated in the following story from my rowing days.

We usually rowed in a boat containing eight oarsmen, very similar to the boats you see on TV in the annual

Oxford and Cambridge boat race. I rowed in the seat nearest the back of the boat, called the stroke seat. All of the rowers in front of me faced the back of the boat and the steersman, or cox as he is known, faced the front of the boat.

My role as stroke was to put into practice the tactics that had been devised by our rowing coach Robert Northridge, who I referred to earlier in his role as a maths master. Robert was as good at coaching rowing as he was at teaching maths. He was very considered and inspiring.

The race that epitomised the need to work together occurred at Henley Royal Regatta in 1980. We were due to race Emanuel School from London on the first-day heats. During practice Robert made sure that he had seen all of the crews that we might encounter in our competition, including Emanuel School. Before we got in our boat to go out and race Emanuel, Robert took me to one side, away from the rest of the crew.

'Bryan, it is highly likely that Emanuel will be faster away from the start than you are,' he said. 'Don't mention this to the crew, but be prepared for this and be ready to attack them about two minutes into the race. You'll probably only have one chance to overtake them, so it had better be a good one.'

This was important to know. When we raced in Ireland, we tended to be the fastest starters and, as a result, we were used to leading, not being led. I thought about what Robert had told me. He was right; we didn't have much experience of overtaking, which is very difficult to do. I found the steersman, Alistair and asked for a quiet word.

'Between you and me, Robert Northridge has spoken to me about Emanuel,' I told him. 'Apparently, they are fast off the start and we are very likely to go behind as a result. I am not going to tell the others, but they all know that Emanuel are good. There is every chance that they will pull away to about half to three quarters of a boat length. If they go further away than that, you'll have to tell me because if they get that far away that quickly we'll have to attack them fast. If they go out to about a half to three quarters of a boat length but go no further, we'll sit behind them for thirty seconds, or so. When you think it is right, you call for a big ten, OK?'

A big ten is ten of the hardest strokes you can pull. It is designed to accelerate your boat when you fall behind, so that you start to draw level. The key to a successful attack is the quality of the big ten. If you don't succeed with the first big ten, you will probably be too exhausted to succeed with another one.

'Alistair. When you call the big ten I want you to count out the strokes,' I directed. 'When you get to the sixth or the seventh stroke I want you to tell the guys that we are going up.'

'What if we're not actually going up?' asked Alistair.

'It doesn't matter; just tell them that we're going up,' I insisted.

We got into the boat and rowed up to the start of the course on which we would race. We started well. Emanuel were beside us for the first ten strokes, but then they started to pull away. Suddenly, I could only see the end of their boat. Robert had been correct.

'They're not going away completely,' Alistair said as we continued to row. 'In fact, they've settled about three quarters of a length ahead.'

This was important information. If we had been the crew that was three quarters of a length ahead, our strategy would have been to put in a big ten, to make sure that we got away completely. Emanuel were sitting in front of us, but not going away.

'Big ten,' I gasped. Breathing was hard enough while rowing flat out, without trying to talk.

Alistair called the big ten and started to count out loud as each stroke was completed.

'One, two three, four, five, six, seven, YOU'RE GOING UP!' he screamed, as per our plan.

It did actually feel as if we were going a bit faster and despite the fact that this strategy had been agreed with Alistair, however, I couldn't help but be intensely curious as to whether we really were gaining on Emanuel.

'Are we really going up?' I hissed.

Ireland Junior VIII extreme right

Australia 83 - outback

Western Nepal – dawn attestation parade

Panmunjom Truce Village Korea

Haircut in Luzamba

Prize giving – Marathon on the day of Peace – Luzamba, Angola May 1992 – I came first much to the Gurkhas delight.

One of the Angolan security guards – tensions were heightening

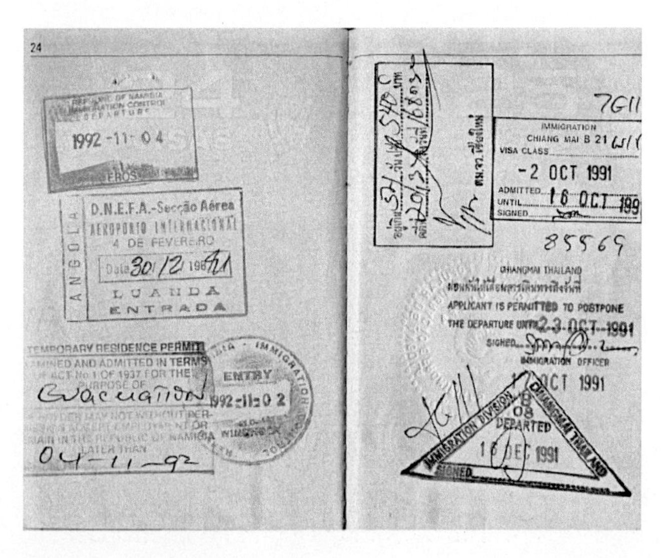

My passport – evacuation stamp

'Yes, we're really catching them; well done lads; we're catching them,' said Alistair confidently.

I instantly felt a surge in our boat and I certainly gave the next six or seven strokes all that I could. We were all already exhausted, but we'd found a bit more.

'You're going up, you're going up,' roared Alistair repeatedly.

Sure enough, the end of their boat had receded and I could now clearly see the man in their boat that would have been sitting opposite me if we'd been level. We were level!

'Another big ten,' I gasped, every muscle burning.

'Take it for ten,' screamed Alistair.

Again the boat surged.

'We're going past them,' bawled Alistair.

So we were. I was now ahead of about four of their eight oarsmen. We were definitely ahead. As the big ten finished, Alistair called for longer strokes and we deployed various other techniques that keep our team of rowers focused on boat speed.

We could all see the Emanuel crew as we pulled away from them. Very soon there was a clear space of water between the two crews. We pushed on even though there was very little chance of their coming back at us now. By the time we crossed the finish line we were a whole three boat lengths ahead of a very good Emanuel crew. Everyone was ecstatic.

When the initial celebrations were over, I took Alistair to one side.

'During the first big ten, when I asked you if we were going up, were we really?' I asked.

Alistair looked at me.

'No,' he said frankly. 'We weren't going up.'

'So why did you say we were?' I pressed.

'Because I knew that if I said that we were going up that you would really go for it and if you and the crew really did go for it that we would overtake them,' said Alistair.

'So you double bluffed me?' I said, laughing.

'I did what I thought was the right thing for all of us,' Alistair said, simply. 'And, it worked, didn't it?'

It did work. My plan had been to build a very inspiring belief in the rest of the crew, because I knew that if they thought that Emanuel weren't able to respond to our attack the momentum would shift to us. This is vital in a race, especially at this stage. While our lads were definitely adding more power to each stroke during the big ten, we were all able to double our efforts when we started to believe that we had them in our sights. As we overhauled the opposition, our self-belief and confidence soared and we flew past them. When we got out to a boat length lead, our momentum took us even further ahead. They were a very good crew but, our self-belief made the difference at a vital time in the race.

While I was in a leadership position as the stroke of the boat, Alistair also had a leadership role to fulfil, which he did very well. It was critical the guys in our boat trusted Alistair and me enough to believe the white lie we were using. The other oarsmen in our crew couldn't see it for themselves, because you're not allowed to look out of the boat, it upsets the balance. This had been the case for the five years we had rowed and raced together, so the trust had been forged. The crew had no reason to doubt us now. It worked for me on a personal basis too. I trusted Alistair, which is what encouraged me to lift the rate of strokes and power during the race. If we hadn't had that trust, the doubt would have inhibited our attack.

It is worth pointing out that although we didn't tell the absolute truth to the crew (either before or after the race), in our view the end justified the means and maintaining the strong bond of trust between us was key to our success. In the relationship between the leader and the team, trust is vital. When trust is lost, everything is lost.

Of course, in the example above, no one was exposed to any risk. There are plenty of other instances in history where leaders have to weigh up whether it is prudent to expose their people to lots of risk in order to achieve a given aim. The power and responsibility of leadership in such an environment shouldn't be taken lightly.

I certainly felt this weight of responsibility strongly when I made my decision to go back to Angola, hours after I had escaped the bloody conflict there. Even making the decision to re-enter Angola, was tough, but after that I had many more life-or-death choices to make too. This was clearly an immediate consideration for all of us on the team, not just me, but as leader I bore the burden of what might happen next. It was up to me to find a way to motivate them to get through what lay ahead and ensure they were in the right frame of mind to do their job, however daunting the environment we all had to work in.

The flight back to Luanda was three hours long in the back of a C-130 Hercules plane, which could normally carry 130 fully equipped paratroopers. There were only twenty-four of us, which meant that we had plenty of space to move around, but the engines were so noisy that we couldn't really talk to each other. This didn't help because it gave us all an opportunity to think about the dangerous situation we were about to face.

I needed some way to distract the team.

One of the engineers on the C130 asked me if I wanted a cup of tea, motioning me to follow him onto the flight deck. When I got there, I was able to look over the pilot's shoulder and see Africa from 22,000 feet, which was amazing. I noticed that the pilot was writing post cards, which I thought was interesting. The plane was obviously on autopilot as we flew back towards a war zone. I knew that this pilot had flown helicopters in Vietnam and had seen a lot of war service. In relative terms, flying a C130 into Luanda, even during a civil war, was much easier than flying a helicopter into a landing zone while being fired at by an enemy from less than one-hundred metres away.

I asked the engineer if I could send the men up in groups of six to have a cup of tea and see the view from the cockpit. He agreed and I went back into the main hold of the aircraft and sent the first group up. I really wanted them to see how nonchalant the pilot appeared to be. Seeing the pilot had made me a bit less apprehensive than earlier and I thought this might have the same effect on the men. About ten minutes later the first group reappeared and I sent then next group up. I watched how the first group communicated with the rest of the team. In a complete change from before they were now chatting animatedly, albeit battling with the engine noise. I even saw one or two mimicking the act of writing. The pilot must still have been writing his postcards.

By the time the C-130 Hercules had landed we were in a much better frame of mind. The flight was behind us and we now had a job to do. As we watched the C-130 turnaround and take off, we knew we were committed, we were the people who had responsibility for our own safety and that felt good. We wouldn't be exposed to the risks that come when you are dependent on people who aren't as capable as you are, as we had been. To be in control of our own destiny felt great.

While most of us who have commercial careers won't have to return to a country at civil war, we are all frequently faced with the prospect of change of some kind within the business setting. Whether that change is big, or small, it is enough to make people feel unsettled and anxious. In my experience of working with lots of big companies as they approach and implement change, this is an area where leaders can play a vital role.

The leaders are not always privy to the actual detail involved in a change. Sometimes, as in the case of my return to Angola, the only precise detail is that change of some kind is coming. The unknown scares some people and leads to their naturally assuming the change is going to mean pain of some kind for them. The first job of the person at the top is to help them confront uncertainty, even if they themselves are feeling nervous about the future.

The position I take when I am working with leaders is slightly at odds with the traditional perspective on change. Because of a number of experiences I've had, my view is that any form of stability is the exception. Uncertainty is ever present and life can and does change in an instant, due to circumstances beyond anyone's control. When you accept that this is the case, and begin to think about change in this way, it should make the challenges we all meet easier to cope with. Test pilots, for example, are conditioned to expect the unexpected. Their role is to fly prototype planes that are designed to fly but have never actually been flown. When these planes take off, the pilots expect things to go wrong. When they do, they start to fix them immediately. They certainly don't waste time moaning that something unexpected has occurred.

I encourage the leaders I work with to be constantly prepared for unexpected change, even if the view is that there is nothing imminent on the horizon. Too many leaders become complacent when life is easy. They stop focusing on investing in and developing their people, or preparing them for the unexpected. To me, this is akin to soldiers not training in the time between wars. There is no room for complacency here and there shouldn't be in your business.

I believe that the best way to address this challenge is to devote sufficient time to defining and executing an appropriate development plan for each member of the team. When each member is being invested in appropriately, they will not only develop the capabilities both you and they need, they will stay engaged to you as their leader because you are offering them the development they will really benefit from.

When change comes, you and your people should

be ready. The leader can then allow a short period of time to be devoted to allowing the team to react to the initial issue before refocusing and moving on. And this brings me back to Angola. While we had been a tight team in Luzamba, the events surrounding the attack, the four days as captives and the return to Luanda had further strengthened the bond between the team. I was determined that we would control our own destiny. In Luzamba we operated as civilians who had been in the military, because that was what the situation demanded. The situation in Luanda required us to behave as soldiers in a hostile environment, a context that we all knew very well.

I implemented the working practices that replicated those of a military unit on operations; in other words, in an environment where full combat could kick off at any time. The team were able to adapt to this very easily because of their training. In no time we were operating as a well-tuned unit, ready to counter any challenge we were faced with. This approach energised and motivated us all. We were now on the front foot.

We were assigned to the villa complex on the outskirts of Luanda. The villa had always needed to be secure so it did have a fence and two points of entry and exit. We were told that there hadn't been any direct attacks against the villa, but that people in the city would assume we had food, petrol and alcohol so it was still a target. We were also asked to provide cover for the company store in the centre of Luanda, which contained a lot of food, beer and cigarettes and was also a prime target. So, yet again, when we broke off to patrol areas like this I was leading a team into intense danger.

It was after a fairly eventful evening with a company of eight Gurkhas at the company store, when I returned to the main villa to discover that some of the Brazilian security officers who had been with us in Luzamba, but who had left Namibia to go home, had returned. My team had already been there for a few weeks by then, occasionally in some quite intense situations, and I immediately knew the arrival of this other group would change the dynamic completely. Although we needed as much help as we could get and the Brazilians were undoubtedly capable, they'd lost whatever respect the Gurkhas had for them when they fled earlier on.

> I encourage the leaders I work with to be constantly prepared for unexpected change, even if the view is that there is nothing imminent on the horizon.

As I weighed up the situation, I could see one of my men from the corner of my eye, who was wearing denim jeans that had bullet holes in them. The jeans had been on the line drying when the attack had taken place at Luzamba. For me that was the difference between my men and the Brazilians; a bit of grit.

For the good of us all, I had to find a way to integrate the Brazilians into my battle-worn team, which I knew would be no mean feat, and then build some kind of team spirit between my Gurkhas and the Brazilians. My men clearly didn't respect the Brazilians and were a little irked that there had been virtually no recognition of what they had done to date. The Brazilians, on the other hand, seemed utterly unrepentant about the fact they had gone straight home at the first sign of danger and then only returned when another group had taken all the big risks. In fact, they acted as though it wasn't a big deal at all. Everyone on my team, including me, was annoyed and it needed sorting out if we were going to work together at all.

I was about ten years younger than most of the leaders of the Brazilian team. I was less experienced in general, but I had spent more time on operations than any of them. While using this experience to counter their perception of my youthfulness wouldn't have been my natural approach, I was damned if I was going to be preached at by them. I still needed to build the team.

I arranged to meet their leaders and took one of my senior Gurkhas with me. He had spent six years fighting as an Indian Army Gurkha and was a fierce and impressive man. I started by telling the Brazilian contingent that the trust we had built up in Luzamba had been badly damaged by their decision to go home from Windhoek. I didn't criticise them, far from it; I just told them, very objectively that we had been surprised and disappointed with their response. It had, after all, heaped more responsibility onto us.

I said I thought we could rebuild the trust, but that it would take time and would be achieved by demonstrations of brave action and not words. On a couple of occasions, one or two of the Brazilian leaders tried to interrupt and shout me down.

'Have you ever been on operations?' my senior Gurkha asked them very directly. 'Have you ever been in a proper theatre of operations where the enemy have real bullets and bombs and are trying to kill you?'

They clearly couldn't bring themselves to say no, so they looked away.

'We have, we all have,' my senior Gurkha said passionately, warming to his theme. 'Captain Paddy (the Gurkha's name for me) has commanded soldiers on operations; you should start by listening to him. Our men know that you have never been on ops and then you went home. If you expect them to trust your people immediately, you are mistaken. We know that the bigger the team the better, but we've always gone for quality over quantity.'

The Brazilians were a little stunned by the approach,

but we'd made our feelings clear. This opened the way for an honest discussion of the situation and we agreed that the integration would take time. A strategy we thought might work was to build relationships in an environment where my Gurkhas didn't feel that the inclusion of some Brazilians into their team was going to create additional risk. We proposed to integrate the Brazilians by adding them to the existing teams, while ensuring the Gurkhas were in the majority. My Gurkhas had to feel confident that if they got into a difficult situation and the Brazilians didn't step up again, they would be strong enough to prevail.

I stipulated that my Gurkhas would give me feedback on the performance of the Brazilians and if the Gurkhas thought that any Brazilian was going to be a liability, then he'd be removed from that team. I wanted control with my men, because they were the experienced soldiers.

After that, I got my team together and I made the case to them for integrating the Brazilians. I reiterated that while they hadn't performed well in Namibia, we didn't actually know how capable the individuals were. The Brazilian team was very hierarchical in its decision-making; it was therefore possible that the older members of their team had overruled some good guys while we were in Namibia. I emphasised the benefits of creating bigger teams who had the right skills and teamwork, adding that we had the power of veto over any underperformer. If they wanted a Brazilian out of their teams, they just had to say so. There would be no requirement to justify anything.

This direct approach worked. There were, as I suspected, some really good guys in the Brazilian team and they respected my people. The Gurkhas I chose to lead my smaller teams were outstanding soldiers and commanders. I made sure that once a team had settled, it didn't change. Quite quickly we got to a point where it was possible to have five Brazilians with three of my Gurkhas. The eight-man unit is at the heart of the British Army team structure and we replicated it here to ensure we could use the tactics we understood so well.

From my own point of view, I found it difficult to build relationships with all of the senior Brazilians, although I did identify two men with whom I was able to create a good working relationship. I kept at it though, because it was important to demonstrate to my own people that I was prepared and able to build the relationships. After all that is what I was expecting them to do.

The impact of this effective integration is that we were able to build from a team of twenty-four men to a team of seventy-two. Having seventy-two men enabled us to undertake a lot of tasks, safe in the knowledge that we had the all-important reserves we needed if things kicked off. Not only did we have the reserves, because we had Gurkhas in the leadership positions, we also had widespread understanding of the standard operating procedures that were at the heart of how we did things. This gave us all confidence and me in particular. I was determined that I wouldn't expose my Gurkhas to the additional risk of operating in a very hostile place while having incompetent people in their teams.

The best thing I did towards integration was allow it to happen between my men and the Brazilians at an operational level. By giving my men control over who they had in their teams, I gave them the authority they needed to lead and to develop willing, but inexperienced, people. In turn, the Brazilians knew that they were being led by people who had been in war zones and had thrived. This combination gave us a strength we couldn't have had on our own.

Building a great team needn't be a very lengthy process.

Some people assume that it is the actions of the leader, alone, that galvanises the rest of the team. While I believe this is certainly possible, I would say that, as I've shown in these two cases, the confidence I needed to lead these people came from my belief in them. Once you have that belief, leading a great team is easy. All that is needed next is to employ the correct strategies to enable everyone to harness their belief and skills.

Building a great team needn't be a very lengthy process. If the leader has confidence in the people, regardless of their starting point, and sets a meaningful direction and is consistently supportive, it will go a long way to creating the team they want.

This may seem like a very simple recipe and, to be honest, it is; but it can't be achieved unless a leader puts their people first.

SUMMARY

1. Trust is at the core of effective teamwork.
2. Fear of change can be debilitating for any team. A good leader helps those below him or her to see change as inevitable and not necessarily such a bad thing.
3. Integrating new members into a strong and established team must be handled sensitively and with careful planning.

PERSONAL DEVELOPMENT EXERCISES

EXERCISE ONE

With trust you can do extraordinary things together

Business benefit
Build team spirit

Resources
Time

Format
Ask the team to come up with a team activity that requires sponsorship. You may choose to limit the target for sponsorship to, say, £50 per person, to pitch it at a level that is attainable for the team. Similarly, you could cap the amount of sponsorship to ensure that everyone feels they have made the same effort.

Choose a challenge that everyone can complete, and agree a date and a time when this event can take place.

PERSONAL DEVELOPMENT EXERCISES

EXERCISE TWO

With trust you can do extraordinary things together

Business benefit

Your team will have a template for integrating new colleagues

Resources

Time at a team meeting

Format

The team are to create a template for successfully integrating a new colleague into the team. Allow them to workshop the activities they would like to see happen in the following timeframes:

a. On the new colleague's first day in the business
b. At the first team meeting
c. In the first ninety days.

Take feedback and document for application.

CHAPTER 11

STRONG LEADERS ARE GREAT LISTENERS

I once had an interesting conversation with the CEO and the senior leadership team of a high-profile security services provider. We were chatting about one of the senior directors of the business, who had recently left to pursue other interests.

'We liked James, he was a really good guy,' the CEO said. 'He was the type of person that would talk to you and not at you.'

I knew the James in question and wasn't surprised to get this feedback from people he had worked with. James came from a solid upper-middle class background, but was adept at working with a varied collection of people, from often very different social classes. His approachable attitude had helped him to build very strong professional and personal relationships across the business and across a number of geographical regions.

'Why do you think he was so good at building relationships?' I asked.

'He was a very good listener,' was the response.

'You think that's important?' I pressed. While I have long felt that listening is a key leadership strategy, I hardly ever come across good listeners, so I wanted to check.

The boss considered my question for a moment and then said: 'If you know you're going to be listened to, you'll contribute, but if you know you're not going to be listened to then you don't bother. Why should you?'

Good summary. He was spot on. The strongest leaders are all great listeners.

We know that the ability to communicate is a key leadership skill. If you can't talk to your people, you can't build relationships with them. Yet, to be able to communicate effectively, you first have to develop the ability to listen. The problem is that most people *think* they are listening, when actually all they are doing is just hearing. There is a major difference between the two. You can hear without much effort. To listen, you must participate actively. Listening is a skill; it can be learnt. The easiest way to become a good listener is to want to be a good listener.

When I joined 2nd Gurkhas in 1985, one of the first officers I met, a major, said: 'If I can give you some advice, learn to speak the Nepali language well.'

When I reflected on his words of wisdom, which I had listened to carefully, one word really stood out for me and that was 'well'. I started to wonder what he meant by 'well'.

The battalion was based in England as part of 5th Airborne Brigade. The relevance of this was that the Queen's Gurkha Officers (QGOs) and the British Officers (BOs) shared the same dining and socialising accommodation, known as a mess. If I had joined the battalion in the Far East, which is where the Gurkhas are based most of the time, I'd have been separated from my men in a BO only mess. This, as you will see, would have removed a great learning opportunity.

I was in awe of many of the QGOs, as they were old enough to have fought in what was an undeclared war against Indonesia from 1963 to 1966 in Malaya and some of them had won awards for bravery in the face of the enemy. I could clearly learn a lot from them. My early observations of the QGOs in the mess showed me that there were some QGOs who were fluent English speakers and some who didn't speak English that well at all.

As far as the BOs were concerned, they too were split into a number of camps. There were BOs who clearly spoke Nepali fluently and some who didn't. The division in capability didn't necessarily just depend on age and length of service. There were some young BOs who obviously spoke Nepali very well, though they were very much in the minority.There were one or two senior BOs who were excellent Nepali speakers too, and their ability to communicate in a foreign language was very impressive.

The reason some officers placed so much importance on learning to speak Nepali well was that there was a message contained in their actions. It told the soldiers that they were important. It told them that their officers were prepared to invest their own time in developing a skill that they could probably live without. At that time, in the Brigade of Gurkhas, senior people were stressing that it was important for Gurkhas to learn to speak English. While this was true, I thought that it was just as important for me for me to speak Nepali well as to teach my men to speak in English.

Once I had an insight into what the officer had meant when he said 'learn to speak the language well', I made up my mind; if I was going to be able to communicate, specifically, to listen, I was going to have to learn to speak the language well.

Although we were based in England, the ten-week language course I was entitled to attend took place in Hong Kong. I knew that the battalion's forthcoming two-year tour would be very busy. We were due to spend four months in the Falkland Islands in 1986 and six weeks in Belize, in Central America in 1987, just before we all moved back to a base in Hong Kong. I had a couple of options. I could wait until I was sent to Hong Kong, or I could get on with it myself. I decided that I'd get on with it myself.

I took every opportunity to learn to speak Nepali. There were some QGOs in the mess who had previously been seconded into the education department in the battalion, so I asked them if they would help me to learn. They graciously agreed and, to their credit, were very good about helping me to learn vocabulary and verbs. In fact, they layered the vocabulary on and I was soon learning fifteen words a day. They reason I say layer was that at the end of each week I was tested on seven days' worth of words at fifteen a day. They expected high standards. Within three weeks my tutors told me that I had learnt all the words I would need to speak the language to a good standard. They advised me to listen out for words or expressions that I didn't understand, make a note of them and raise them at our next learning session.

It became obvious that the Nepali numbering system was very important. Each soldier is given an eight-digit army number. When I was a rifleman in the Royal Green Jackets, my number was 24625511. I will remember it forever. I was duty officer one weekend and although I had many duties to fulfil I had plenty of free time. I set myself the task of learning the numbers perfectly by Sunday lunchtime. I made flash cards of the numbers and consistently tested myself against them. One of my soldiers volunteered to test me. For every one I got wrong I had to give him a can of beer, which would be shared by the platoon. By Sunday lunchtime, I had memorised all of the numbers and could recall them instantly.

That day I took the roll call, which meant repeating110 numbers that were each eight digits long. I got to the end with no mistakes and received a round of applause from the 110 men in front of me, who were smiling.

'Well done Dunlop sahib,' said the second in command of the company. 'You did that very well.'

However much time I had devoted to learning the numbers, and whatever volume of beer I had had to hand over, was repaid in an instant. Most BOs actually weren't that great at the language and even poorer at the numbers. I had made a statement of intent and it created an instant bond with my troop.

In the following months I had the opportunity to see how important this endeavour was. By speaking to my soldiers fluently in their language, I really got to know and understand them. I could see how effective this was, when I observed colleagues who based their relationship with their men on everyone's ability to speak English. A lot of young Gurkha riflemen couldn't speak English that well. The relationship suffered as a direct result.

In 1987, I did finally go to Hong Kong to attend my

language course. Although I could already speak Nepali very well, I had to take the course in order to sit the exam that would officially qualify me. At the end of the course, I scored 193 out of 200 and was pleased to gain a distinguished grading, which had been my objective.

This score and my capability wasn't the output of ten weeks of learning though. It was the result of 18 months of intense learning in my own time, in the evenings and weekends. I did it because I was inspired by that first officer who had said 'learn to speak the language well' and because of my desire to become the complete Gurkha officer. I wanted to win the respect of my peers and my men and I could only do that if I could listen to them properly.

The obvious question is: how did this skill and all of the energy that I expended to learn to listen to my men effectively actually make a contribution to my success as a leader? The short answer is: considerably.

Being able to understand what was being said to me and then make myself understood very concisely and quickly was essential in high-pressure situations. When I was involved with a helicopter crash in the Falklands Islands, which I will talk about more fully in chapter seventeen, I am convinced that my ability to assimilate a huge amount of information quickly enabled me to make better decisions. Those decisions made a contribution to saving people's lives. In that situation we were operating in a freezing cold and very windy place, where communication was extremely difficult. If I had had to consistently keep asking for people to repeat what they had told me or, worse, translate it into English, this would have directly hampered their ability to act quickly.

In my later career in Angola, I made similar efforts to learn Portuguese. While working in the sort house in Luzamba, I found ways of developing my understanding of Portuguese by consistently focusing on what people were saying and making a note to establish what that was. In addition to this, when I was driving across the mine site, I took the opportunity to travel with a Portuguese speaker, as opposed to travelling with an English speaker.

The desire and ability to listen is a key leadership trait and skill. If you can't understand your people, you will never gain their full respect and, as a result, you can't be sure that they will follow when they need to.

Although the drive to learn to communicate effectively with those around me may have come from the fact that I knew these listening skills might be used in a life or death situation, this doesn't mean the lessons can't be applied elsewhere. Don't fall into the trap of believing that just because you don't necessarily have the same motivations for developing skills beyond your core skills that listening is any less important. That is simply not true

Listening is a skill. Skills can be learned; therefore this means that you can learn to listen.

Of course, it helps if you actually want to listen and a lot of leaders don't want to, or, perhaps more accurately, they only want to listen to what they want to hear. There is less appetite for the things that they don't want to hear.

Ineffective leaders shy away from listening intently because they know if they hear something they don't like and other people know they know it, it means they have to do something about it. That often means more work or responsibility.

Leaving aside the subject of lazy leadership though, how do people develop the ability to listen? It isn't enough to just tell them they need to listen. There is a requirement to actually learn how. I have developed some simple ideas to learn and apply that could also be easily evaluated as part of the coaching process.

The components are:

1. **Create the opportunity.** When most people listen, they are actually in the process of preparing to respond, as opposed to seeking to understand what has been said before they create their response. The evidence of this is that conversations often occur without any significant pauses. This must mean that the response was being prepared while the other person was still talking, so one party wasn't really listening.

2. **Give someone your full attention.** I had one boss who was very approachable. If you asked him for the opportunity to ask him a question, he would always say 'let's find a seat for a couple of minutes'. If the timing was poor, he'd ask how important it was then schedule accordingly. I always felt that he was taking me seriously, which is what I wanted. I didn't approach him with trivial issues, so I welcomed the fact that he was giving me both his time and his complete attention. This approach was reflected in the way he engaged with all of the team and it made an impact with everyone.
3. **Use audible flags.** An audible flag is a word or expression about which the listener could ask additional questions, as long as it is relevant. For example, I was coaching a senior executive undertaking a recruiting meeting. He asked the potential recruit what she did.

   'I'm a housewife now,' she said 'Now' is an example of an audible flag. If you are listening for audible flags, you'll pick them up in every sentence and you will often hear more than one. We then have to consciously identify which audible flag we choose to explore further and then create the correct question.
4. **Use 'response driven questioning'.** This is simply the act of using the information you have heard,

including audible flags, to enable you to act a pertinent supplementary question. In the case of the housewife above, the response driven question should be:

'What did you do before that?'

'I was a war correspondent (she was!).'

At this point the interviewer became really interested. The challenge was that he was so interested that he stayed on that subject for too long and ran out of the time. The key point here is that we have to consciously choose the audible flags that are most relevant, not necessarily the audible flags that stand out to us. In other words, we have to listen, think about what we've learnt and then chose the topic to explore. This is listening to understand as opposed to listening to respond, which is what most people practice.'

5. **Use open questions.** I actually recommend that you use what I call 'openopen' questions. Open questions usually start with one of 'What?' 'Where?' 'When?' 'Why?' 'Who?' and 'How?' When I quote the need to ask open questions to gather knowledge and build understanding, most people think I am too focused on what should be a basic skill. People often know what an open question is, though can't necessarily use them effectively. I often have to prove this inability before I am able to help them develop.

   An openopen question is one that starts with an open question, but is consciously designed to be very open. 'What's the plan?', for example, is so open that it allows the respondee to prioritise and feed back on their most burning issue or priority. When we allow respondees to give us this insight, we can then use response-driven questioning to delve into their issues in order to develop the understanding that we need.

> Listening is a skill. Skills can be learned; therefore this means that you can learn to listen.

6. **Don't tailgate.** Tailgating is finishing people's sentences for them. This is done verbally by actually cutting people off in mid-sentence. When you tailgate, you are effectively saying 'speed up,' 'I know what you're about to say' and, at worst, 'you are boring me'. Tailgating is incredibly rude.
7. **Maintain eye contact when you are listening.** It's simple. Keep eye contact in a natural way when someone is speaking to you. Even if you sense there is something that you'd like to look at in your peripheral vision, keep the eye contact. If you attempt to glance away, this will be very obvious to the person you are talking to. Don't stare though.
8. **Use the 'Why?' question carefully.** 'Why?' is a great question, as it allows us to understand a number of things, motivations in particular. If a member of

your team has a specific goal, it is good to know why that goal is relevant to them. Generally, if you ask five 'Why?' questions in succession, you will get to the bottom of the true underlying reason behind your discussion. I also recommend that the listener listens out for the word 'because' and the expression 'so that,' as these warn us that we are about to be given insight into the reasons that something is important.

These are a number of skills that will help you to develop your ability to listen. They will also help you to help other people to develop their own listening skills. Leaders are, or should be, teachers too. Listening is such an important skill that leaders should be able to teach it.

I saw many good examples of excellent listening skills when I was starting my career in financial services. Lots of people told me that I needed to understand my clients before I could start to give advice and one manager I worked with, in particular, stood out in respect of this skill. I'll give you an example of how he worked from a meeting I sat in on between the manager, Alan, and a client, who I will call Geoff. It emerged very quickly that although Geoff had more than £100,000 in a pension fund, he was reluctant to use the sum.

Geoff was fifty-six-years old and had retired following a heart attack. While we were gathering the facts, Alan focused on one life assurance policy that Geoff owned. He was curious why Geoff hadn't cashed it in. Geoff explained that since his heart attack, he would probably find it difficult to get another policy if he needed one. Alan was still not satisfied, so he pressed the client.

'Why do you keep paying for this one?' he asked.

Geoff said: 'I need it because our youngest daughter will be at university for another four years. If something happens to me, my wife Sheila would need the money.'

'You're paying £300 a month though; why that much?'

Geoff agreed it was too much but again felt helpless to do anything about it, because he was unable to change his policy owing to his health issues. Alan pressed on, asking Geoff what he intended to do once his daughter had finished her education. Geoff said he and his wife were intending to go to the theatre a bit more often, stay in London, and have dinner and all the usual stuff.

'Having a heart attack does focus the mind on enjoying life,' joked Geoff.

'I am sure it does,' responded Alan. 'If you had the £300 per month now, what would you do?'

By now it was clear he had got Geoff's (and my) interest. Geoff agreed that if he had the cash now, he would immediately begin enjoying his life to the full.

Alan began his summary: 'Well Geoff, it strikes me that you have to keep paying the premium on the policy in case something happens to you. Equally, the £3600 every year is a drain and at over £12,000 over the four years it does mount up. You can't reduce what you're paying because your medical history is against you and you wouldn't be able to cancel and start again for lower cover and a lower premium. Finally, the £300 per month could definitely be used for a variety of other purposes.

'I have an idea. Why not use the £100,000 in your pension fund to pay the premium? You could access as much of the fund as you needed to pay the premium, freeing up your own £300 so that you can start to go to London now. It wouldn't take long to organise either.'

Geoff signed the paperwork that afternoon and he and his wife received more than £300 per month, which made a huge contribution to their enjoyment of life. They were incredibly grateful.

Why had this gone so well? In very simple terms, Alan was curious. During the preparation that took place ahead of the meeting, Alan established with me that while Geoff and his wife had a good income, they didn't have a huge amount. Alan immediately questioned why they were still paying for life assurance.

Having had the opportunity to observe Alan, I could see that the primary skill he was using was listening. This was interesting. Alan asked one question about a life assurance policy and then he just listened. What stood out as a difference between him and most other people was that he listened very carefully. When the client responded, Alan thought about it and then asked another question.

He did not start talking until he understood the whole picture. It was only when he was sure he understood that he started to reveal his idea. This was a perfect example of listening leading to deep understanding and I was very impressed, and so, clearly, were the clients. I resolved then to develop the same capability.

Our ability to understand our people is a key leadership trait and skill. If you are able to understand your people, and you take the time to do so, your people will feel as if you are interested in them. This doesn't always come naturally to everyone and, if this is you, you may need to make the effort to learn some listening skills. It is well worth making the time available to do this and to subsequently put the skills into practice.

If you are ever in doubt about how effective listening can be, remind yourself of the following quote:

'Managers talk at you, leaders talk to you'.

SUMMARY

1. To communicate effectively you have to develop the skill of listening.
2. Listening is a skill that can be learned – but you need to want to listen and to take the time to learn the skills required.
4. If you listen well, your team will know you are interested in them and will respond positively.

PERSONAL DEVELOPMENT EXERCISES

EXERCISE ONE
Listen

Business benefit
You will be able to understand your people

Resources
Time with the team

Format
Use a short, formal training session to develop your team's understanding of response-driven questioning, openopen questions and audible indicators. Add to these concepts an understanding of the need and benefits of listening in three timeframes:

- past
- present
- future

It is beneficial to consciously listen across all three timeframes because it enables us to build full understanding of the person we are with. Too often people chat about the past and the present and miss the future. As leaders, we have to understand how our people have developed and what matters to them now, but we absolutely must understand what they want from the future.

When you have completed the formal session, bring two people to the front of the room. Make

»

one of them the listener and the other the responder. Reassure the responder they do not have to divulge any confidential information if they don't want to. Meanwhile, instruct the rest of the audience that they are to listen out for response-driven questioning, openopen questions™, audible indicators and use of the three timeframes.

Give your listener and responder five minutes to engage in conversation with each other before facilitating a conversation about the successful application of the above skills.

Allow two other members of the team to undertake the same practice.

Continue to reinforce the implementation of these skills by using additional listening exercises.

PERSONAL DEVELOPMENT EXERCISES

EXERCISE TWO
Listen

Business benefit

Your team will understand the power of active listening

Resources

Time with the team

»

Format

Split the group into pairs, A and B. Ask the B group to wait outside the room. Inform the A group that their partner will speak to them for two minutes but that they are not allowed to interact with them. They can, however, put up their hand for five seconds every time their partner says something that makes them want to ask a question. They should also act out losing focus by staring out of the window, or looking at a detail on their partner's jacket, for instance.

Inform the B group they are to speak to their partner about something of interest to them, for instance their last holiday or anything positive that has happened to them within the last six months.

At the end of the three minutes ask the B group how they felt while talking to their partner. Answers will probably include 'didn't feel listened to,' 'didn't understand why they were putting their hand up,' and 'lost my train of thought because they obviously weren't listening'.

Then run the exercise again, allowing the A group partner to interact this time by asking questions and becoming involved in the conversation. Compare the two versions to see which was the most satisfying experience

CHAPTER 12

A LITTLE DISSENT AND TENSION IS GOOD

In the run up to the 1997 British and Irish Lions rugby tour in South Africa, the coaches agreed that one of the biggest threats to their success was the pressure the Lions team would most likely come under in the scrum. To the uninitiated, the scrum is a contest between eight men on either side and requires strength, aggression and technique. When the two scrums meet, you have three men from one team engaging with three men from the other team. The two groups of three men are known as the front rows and the rest of the teams fill in behind them. In certain countries, the men love scrimmaging and their ability to do it well and enjoy it is often seen as a reflection of their masculinity.

The Lions were acutely aware they were going to be confronted by eight very big South Africans who would be determined to bulldoze them in the scrum. With this in mind, the team coach, a tough Scotsman called Jim Telfer, devoted a lot of time to practising this aspect of the game. Most teams practise scrummaging by pushing against a special machine, which is a bit like a heavy roller. While Telfer also used the machine, he was a big fan of practising scrummaging by using two full groups of eight men in a 'live' exercise. Telfer wanted to replicate exactly the challenge his eight men would face when they played matches against the South Africans. Telfer had sound reasons for doing so too. While it is often difficult for a referee to see what goes on between the two front rows, there is a lot of verbal niggle and physical intimidation. The two front rows do everything they can to head butt each other, pinch, even bite and punch. This is seen as part of life in the front row and most of the people who play there accept this type of behaviour as normal.

During the Lions tour training sessions, two teams of eight men from the same squad began to regularly scrummage against each other. These were men who could and would play on the same team against various South African teams. After about an hour's scrummaging practice both sets of eight men would be tired and bruised from the repetitive nature of the highly physical contact. Most interestingly, on a number of occasions, the two men in the middle of each of the front rows started fighting with each other once the scrum was over and all the men had stood up. While the fights were brief, they were intense and both men clearly wanted to hurt each other. The coaches and their colleagues always broke up the fight but, sure enough, the same thing happened again after the next scrum and the men squared up to each other once again.

When the two British Lions who had been involved in the fighting were questioned about it, they were both unrepentant.

'Scrummaging is a physical contest,' they said. 'When we practice scrummaging we practice it as if we are both playing against another team, not as if we are playing with friends and team mates. There's bound to be a bit of fisty cuffs, it's all part of the fun.'

Naturally, the Lions team managers became concerned that the South African press would hear about this. The last thing they wanted was for the press either at home, or in South Africa to use this information to demonstrate a lack of unity in the squad The men did, after all, come from Ireland, England, Scotland and Wales, which are four countries that have an intense rugby rivalry.

As it was, they needn't have worried. In South Africa, where highly competitive scrummaging is seen as a strength, these brief but important fights were viewed as a very positive thing. When the South African public discovered that this was happening, they wanted to know if this type of activity was happening in their own team's training. When they discovered that this wasn't the case, there were a number of people who wanted to know if the South Africans were training with the right amount of intensity.

The intense scrimmaging was, therefore, a bit of a PR coup. There is, however, a very important leadership lesson tied up in here too. In my opinion, Jim Telfer used this type of eight men versus eight men training to facilitate a degree of tension between the people competing for places on his team. It wasn't just because they had to prove their worth to gain places in the starting team, it was also preparing them for the fact they would almost certainly have to stand shoulder to shoulder in the face of some very physical intimidation from the opposing sides too.

By choosing that training method, Telfer was undoubtedly taking a risk. If his players had used the scrimmage machine, they would never have got to a point where they fought one another. Yet, while international rugby is not about fighting, the scrum is an important part of the game and if you're going to prepare effectively for the scrum, you have to replicate what is going to happen on the pitch. Telfer had to take the risk of dissent, even fighting in the ranks, for the greater good of the whole team. As the leader in charge of preparing his team for their experience in South Africa, Telfer sought to replicate the tension they would undoubtedly face on the pitch.

Modern leadership gurus talk much about alignment. The view is that to get anything done, you've have to get everyone paddling in the right direction, hopefully with some degree of synchronisation. If the team is aligned, it is happy and if it is happy, it will be productive. That is all well and good as far as it goes, but, as we can see here, a truly innovative leader sometimes needs to go a step further.

> One way dissent can prove very powerful is when you empower the team to conduct healthy debates so they can contribute and kick around ideas of their own.

Contrary to popular thought, your time might be better spent fostering a little dissent in the ranks now and again. Old-fashioned parlance might call it picking a fight, and in the case of the Lions team that was undoubtedly so, but occasionally the easier path is not always the best way forward.

I should add a single word caveat here when it comes to picking a fight and that word is 'right,' as in always pick the *right* fights. Dissent is not always the right way forward, and the last thing you want is for your team to be distracted by bitter, energy sapping scraps. The strategy does need careful thought and to be used in the right circumstances.

One way dissent can prove very powerful is when you empower the team to conduct healthy debates so they can contribute and kick around ideas of their own, because one single person will never hold all the answers. Dissent is the key to getting maximum innovation and will guarantee to produce some unexpected results. As a leader, it is your job to control the debate and, of course, you have to find the best way to take it forward and have the power of the final decision.

The trick is not to let destructive tensions take over and destroy the whole process. If your teams see it as a license to unleash age-old power struggles, that's clearly not the right fight. Likewise, you need to assure everyone that the idea is to change things for the better. You won't be playing the blame game because you are looking for open debate. As well as only choosing the 'right' fights, timing is crucial here.

In the military, dissent is often at its most powerful when used in the planning stage. It begins when the mission, in other words the objective that must be achieved, is given with great clarity. Then, in what is known as a 'Chinese parliament,' everyone regardless of seniority, has the opportunity to debate the components of the plan. All ideas are considered and usually worked through via a series of headings. For example, if a team is thinking about what type of transport they will need, the transport planning issues will be considered in three interdependent phases:

1. Insertion: How does the team get to the objective?

2. On the objective: What needs to happen to the transport when the team is engaged in delivering the objective?
3. Extraction: How do they get away from the objective?

There are many options. If, for example, the team is inserted by parachute, this means that they'll probably be without any type of vehicle for the other two phases, unless they plan to commandeer some transport. This is an important consideration because vehicles enable troops to carry a lot more vital equipment, ammunition, rockets and water, which are all very heavy. By the same token, vehicles can give a squad away when they are trying to approach the objective without being seen or heard. The decision that needs to be made is do they go in on foot, in which case they may well escape detection, but will be limited in what they can carry? They would also be limited if they had to get out fast, possibly being pursued by the enemy.

A Chinese parliament is very democratic. Everyone is encouraged to participate. This can include officers and soldiers from within the regiment who may not even be part of the actual patrol. Decisions are made by consensus as far as possible, although the person who is going to lead the team on the ground has ultimate responsibility for the outcomes and so has decision-making authority.

Transport is obviously just one consideration in a

military planning scenario, but it is a useful example of how it works and dissent can be very effective indeed at this stage. However, this is as far as it goes. While dissent is fully encouraged at the planning stage, when the plan has been formulated and finalised and the team move into implementation, dissent is no longer tolerated. Everyone must now get behind the implementation of the plan, *even if none of their ideas have been incorporated into the plan.*

In my own, direct experience of this, the military are very good at parking their individual egos and implementing the plan with 100 per cent focus and energy. There may be a bit of moaning to begin with, but when the plan is implemented there is invariably full commitment. In chapter eighteen, we will see how a team survives, adapts and changes, as a plan gets put into action, because no plan ever survives first contact with the enemy, but for now, let's stick with the planning stage and the importance of dissent at this time.

How might this work in business? Well, it may be easier to begin by showing what happens when no dissent is encouraged, or even allowed. This is, in my experience, the norm in most companies, where what the person at the top says is usually seen as the final word. Thanks to the culture created by these autocratic leaders, there is no dissent in the planning phase. The leader delivers the objective and the plan, or pretty much most of the key components of the plan. He, or she, is so thorough and specific in their direction that any team-led changes are incidental.

In a scenario like this, there appears (on the surface at least) to be some form of tacit agreement that the team now has a workable plan and everyone will be engaged in the implementation of the plan. Where it all starts to go wrong is when everyone on the team disperses to start implementation, because this is often when the dissent begins. And in this case, it is the 'wrong' sort of dissent.

If people aren't fully engaged to the plan in its early stages, they will inevitably start to remove some of the aspects of the plan that they don't agree with. They may even insert their own ideas, because they believe that their own strategy is better. The result, as you can imagine, isn't what anyone expected and certainly not what the leader initially planned. What happens then? Well, clearly when the plan doesn't go as expected (as it is unlikely to because everyone has chipped in with their own versions), it carries on being watered down and adapted in a desperate bid to get it done. Pretty soon, it all falls apart and is a complete dogs dinner. It may even get discarded altogether.

The root cause of the plan's collapse is down to the leader on the ground, who didn't encourage dissent during the planning phase. As a result, everyone on the team ran off in their own direction and the original idea didn't stand a chance.

Let me give you a real life example of just how destructive this can be. A while back, I sat in on a team dinner with the managing director of a business and six of his direct reports. Each of this six reports led teams of about eight additional managers, who in turn oversaw teams of about ten people. The MD had, therefore, about 480 people in his business. The reason I had been called in was because the MD was dissatisfied with his team's progress and it was easy to see why. The average performance across the entire business equated to about 60 per cent of target.

During a quiet moment at the dinner, the MD leaned over and said to me: 'Are you familiar with the four principles I have told the guys that I want them to adhere to?'

I confirmed that I was and repeated them back to him, verbatim.

'Do you think that my people, those on the ground, know what the principles are?' he asked me.

'I haven't been out with them so I don't know,' I answered. 'Why don't we ask your regional managers? They're here. If they don't know then that will probably start to answer your question.'

At that, the MD turned to the regional manager who was sitting nearest to us.

'Paul, do you remember the four business principles

we discussed at our last strategy day?' he asked.

I could tell by the look on the regional manager's face that he didn't have a clue what his boss was talking about.

'The ones at the last strategy day?' he repeated slowly, clearly trying to buy some time. I also noticed he had said it just loud enough for one of the other regional managers, sitting beside him, to start to engage in the conversation. This tactic wasn't lost on the boss.

'Can I take it from that response that you don't know?' the MD pressed, sounding a little irritated.

There was a mumbled response to the affirmative from Paul. The second regional manager, who had been alerted to the conversation by Paul, clearly sensed there was some type of opportunity for a bit of one-upmanship.

He said confidently: 'Was is that we were to have the diary commitments for the following week agreed by Wednesday?'

'That was one of them,' nodded the boss, 'But, what were the other three?'

The conversation continued and very quickly all six regional managers became involved. The upshot of this debate was that the leadership team was able to identify only one principle in its complete form and about half of one of the other principles. Even this was only achieved after a lot of debate.

The MD turned to me and said: 'I think we're going to have to come up with a strategy for ensuring that the guys have a plan that they think will work for them.'

However, despite this, he still clung to his original plan and suggested that we implement a communication strategy to make sure that the teams knew his four principles. I said that as this hadn't worked in the first place, it might be better to empower each of the regional managers to work with their teams to create measures that actually meant something to them. The objective would be to inspire the teams to create and then implement some measureable actions that would demonstrate they were in control of the planning of their business.

The MD looked at me.

'Are you saying that we totally disregard the principles I issued?' he asked, sounding surprised. 'What will people think of such a turnaround in a very short time?'

'My view is that they will respect you for being flexible,' I replied. 'It seems that not too many of the teams knew that principles had been created anyway. What is there to lose?'

'Fine,' he said, at long last. 'I am willing to try it, but I am sceptical.'

The result of this change was that each of the teams came up with four principles that would demonstrate they had control of their businesses. A lot of the principles were very similar to the original ones, but the point was that they hadn't been imposed upon the team. They had come to the principles themselves and were, therefore, far more closely aligned with them.

It was easy for me to challenge the MD, because in many respects that was my role. Although encouraging dissent from his regional managers was a major departure away from the way he had managed his business before, to his credit, he let it happen and as a result he got the buy-in he originally sought.

In another case, I had the opportunity to work on a project which saw the collaboration between the staff of a community high school in Belfast and the management team of a local manufacturer. The two parties were engaged in a highly worthwhile mentoring scheme, whereby the sixteen-year-old children from the community school were assigned a mentor from the manufacturer. The relationship between both organisations was great and both leadership teams used to get together every six months for a leadership development session. I had the privilege of running this session on one occasion, working with a team of twenty-four people from both the school and the manufacturer and I set the group a challenge:

I asked them to pass three juggling balls around a circle of people, one after another, in a fixed pattern. The objective of the exercise was to encourage the group to problem solve in a leaderless environment. With twenty-four people in the group, there was going to have to be some collaboration and debate.

Both the head teacher and the managing director were the types of people who encouraged their teams to get involved. Both men were actively engaged, but neither of them took control of the exercise.

Every time the team undertook the exercise, I would tell them how long it had taken to complete. I would then challenge them to improve on their time by making true statements like: 'the last team I worked with was able to compete this in half the time'. While this group of people knew each other quite well, there was healthy dissent during the discussions. Everyone was very polite, but they were also very direct.

One result of this was that ideas on how to improve on their 'work rate,' which were suggested by one person, were often picked up and challenged by other people. The result of this dissent was that the initial idea was refined, improved and ultimately implemented. I was able to measure the value of each idea as their time got better and then feed back to the team by how much they had improved.

The one idea that had the greatest single impact on their improvement in performance came from a lady who worked part-time in the domestic department of the school. Her suggestion was slightly adjusted by a colleague and then implemented with enthusiasm. In percentage terms, the improvement was spectacular. They more than halved the amount of time it took to pass the three juggling balls around the circle. As the facilitator, I was able to use dissent to enhance their performance.

Having run the exercise a number of times with different groups, I knew fairly well how quickly it was possible to complete the task. Yet, when we got to that point, I didn't tell the team. Indeed, I kept challenging them to try and improve. They didn't know that they were close to what might have been a record, so they continued to debate and strive for improvement. They did make progress although the improvements got smaller and smaller. In reality though, the improvements were still spectacular when expressed in percentage terms.

At the conclusion of the exercise, I asked the team what they thought had most contributed to their success, 'dissent,' or in their words 'debate,' was one of the first things they said. On further discussion, they said that they were prepared to challenge the plan, but then implemented the plan with total commitment. This simple, but highly effective, formula enabled them to improve their performance by an incredible 500 per cent. When I asked the entire group what they would now do differently as a result, the head teacher said that he would create the opportunity for all members of his team to participate in the formulation of the school's strategy.

He said; 'Due to some preconceived ideas, I've not

been taking advantage of all of the experience and wisdom contained in my entire team. I am going to change this so that we are all involved in helping our children have better futures'.

I know this man and that this type of leadership is a big part of who he is and why his team are so engaged to the very challenging objective of helping children gain qualifications without minimal parental support. The team feel as if they are listened to and they know that their ideas will be listened to, adjusted and, if they have the potential to add value, will be implemented. The team also knows that if the idea is implemented and doesn't work the way they were expecting it to work that there will never be any blame. They will adjust the idea, make it better and implement again, with total commitment.

> Dissent is healthy. Part of a leader's role is to create the opportunity and environment to allow it to happen, without any concerns from the team.

SUMMARY

1. Dissent is healthy. It should be encouraged. Part of a leader's role is to create the opportunity and environment to allow it to happen, without any concerns from the team.
2. Dissent is most effective at the planning stage, then,

once a plan is set it should be implemented with absolute commitment.

3. No plan will please everyone, but if team members have been given their say they are more likely to get behind it with focus and energy.

PERSONAL DEVELOPMENT EXERCISES

EXERCISE ONE

Dissent and tension is good exercise one

Business benefit

Develop new ideas

Resources

Time with the team – sixty minutes should be sufficient

Format

Explain to the team the aim of the exercise is to evaluate how dissent can add value to the business. Depending on the size of your team, split them into smaller groups and give members the objective of dissenting, i.e. they have authority to challenge the topic you are about to give them.

Brief everyone that the dissenters are allowed to make any challenge they wish, but the challenge must be related to the topic provided and must be handled in a professional manner.

Give the dissenters a business topic and allow

»

them twenty minutes to prepare their challenge. For example, I have seen one team use dissent to challenge the start times and duration of team meetings. If the team are to challenge a topic, they are obliged to identify alternative ideas. All teams should know that when they present their alternative ideas that they will be subjected to rigorous challenge from you and their colleagues.

Make sure to give them parameters such as time and resources available.

Follow the format:

1. Their challenge to the topic – i.e. why they think it is less effective than it could be
2. Their alternative
3. How they think their alternative will benefit the team.

When the time is over, allow each group to present their plan in turn. Be prepared to facilitate a challenge from the other team and document the good ideas that arise with a view to implementing them.

PERSONAL DEVELOPMENT EXERCISES

EXERCISE TWO

Dissent and tension is good

Business benefit
You will develop engagement by encouraging idea-generation from the entire team

Resources
Time with the team

Format
Acting as the facilitator, your first step is to explain the rules that you will enforce. In this exercise you will give the team a challenge to solve. When the team understand the challenge, everyone will have up to ninety seconds to give their initial views, based on the order they are sitting in the room. Interrupting is not allowed and it is up to you to enforce this. Remind them there will be further opportunities to contribute.

After this initial round, everyone will be asked to make one more contribution. Again, these contributions will be managed by you, should be no longer than sixty seconds and cannot be interrupted.

Finally, give individuals the opportunity to make contributions at random. Take control over who speaks and do not allow interruptions.

When the team have come up with some ideas, document them and agree actions.

CHAPTER 13

MANAGE YOUR TIME AFFECTIVELY

In business, much is made of the 80/20 rule. For those who have been living on a desert island and never heard of it, I will give a brief explanation. It was devised in 1906 by Italian economist Vilfredo Pareto after he noticed that 20 per cent of the pea pods in the garden produced 80 per cent of the peas. This was extrapolated into the corporate world where he found 80 per cent of production often came from the most productive 20 per cent. The Pareto Principle or 80/20 rule as it became known has since been applied to many other situations, such as 20 per cent of customers usually account for 80 per cent of sales, 20 per cent of sales reps close 80 per cent of sales, and so on.

This one-in-four ratio does seem to pop-up constantly. However, very few companies seem to consider its significance in team management. Yet, all too often leadership focuses on just 20 per cent of the team, leaving the remaining 80 per cent to sink or swim.

Many times this can be down to simple geography. This was certainly a major contributing factor when I once worked with a director, who had six managers working for him as well as about forty-eight sales people in a sales business. I had been called in because, while the performance of the team was OK, it was very patchy. The business had two measures. The director was eighth out of sixteen in one of the measures, which was the quality of the record keeping across his team and tenth out of sixteen in the other, which looked at sales performance. In summary, there were small pockets of excellence and quite a high proportion of mediocrity.

I noticed that this director spent a lot of time in one office that was located quite conveniently close to his home. My immediate observation was this man was happy to allow his people to fight their way through some pretty horrendous commutes while he managed his own working experience carefully. I didn't approve of this.

After electing to spend a Monday with him to see how he used his time, I found the day was very full with a number of conference calls scheduled to speak to his boss and his direct reports. The content of the calls was largely focused on data collection, although the occasional bollocking was handed downwards when the numbers were particularly bad.

Closer scrutiny revealed this director didn't allocate the time he had for his direct reports on a proportionate basis. Curious, I asked what drove his allocation of time.

Picking up his telephone list of reports he went through it, jabbing a finger at each name as he mentioned them: 'Well, he's in London and is a bit of a lost cause. She's about a ninety-minute drive away and he's in north east London, which is murder to get to.'

I was amazed. I had never heard anything quite like it and resolved to dig still deeper.

As a regional director, he did have a number of calls on his time. He was deputising for his boss when he was away and he also had regional meetings to attend with his boss, which often involved travelling around his home country and abroad. Plus, he had his own managers' meetings which he held, guess where? At his own office. As a matter of course, everyone was required to travel to his office at least once every month for their team meeting. For some of the team this meant a regular five-hour round trip.

As we continued our discussions, I discovered that he had a son who was a very accomplished sportsman. His priority was to spend time with his son and specifically on certain days when he was competing. This meant he never wanted to be too far from his office. It also emerged that Friday was traditionally set aside as an admin day. He would schedule a few conference calls, get his paperwork squared away and be out of the office by four o'clock. He did, however, often find time for a quick glass of wine with his PA, to celebrate the end of week.

By this stage, I was utterly dumfounded. This director was happy to allocate the time he had for his people on the basis of his own convenience and the affection he had for them. If he didn't like someone, he tended not to spend time with them, or would only speak to them by phone. The managers he did like he would visit and, coincidentally, those people were without exception quite close to his office. He was definitely spending 80 per cent of his time with 20 per cent of his people. In his mind though, he was allocating his time fairly, I didn't share this perspective and, more importantly, neither did the people on the team.

There is another leadership-related issue in his approach too. A leader should never ask anyone to do anything they are not prepared to do themselves, regardless of how senior they are, or how tired and possibly bored they are with their role. That includes a needless one-day-a-month commute for no other reason than they like to stick close to home. If you accept that a key objective of leadership is to inspire the team, then one sure-fire way of demotivating them is for the person in charge to ask them to do things they are not prepared to do themselves.

This was a classic example of this type of flawed behaviour and needed to be fixed.

I agreed with the sales director that we would travel to meet each of his managers on their own patches. On the first visit, he undertook not to interrupt his manager on a whim, which a lot of regional managers apparently see as a big part of their role. The meeting, which was quite formal and followed a prescribed meeting agenda, seemed to go quite well and some good outcomes were achieved. It was what happened afterwards though that was the most interesting.

Once we'd finished, the director offered to take his manager out for a bite to eat and I tagged along. It was a pleasant enough lunch and I got on well with the manager. It emerged that she really wanted to retire to France with her husband, who was quite a bit older than her and had many compelling reasons for wanting to do so. We were both humbled by her openness with us.

Later on we reflected on how little the regional director had known about this manager and what she wanted to achieve. I suspected that this low level of understanding would be replicated across the other managers in his team. I was right.

By the time we'd met all of the managers, both formally and informally, we had discovered a great deal more about them. We found that one of them really didn't want to be a sales manager but wanted to run an online business selling drums. Another one wanted to run a pub when he got to fifty-five. Each person had a story to tell. The regional director had previously thought that he knew his people, but clearly this wasn't the case.

The most interesting meeting was the one with the manager the regional director had previously said he didn't like. We agreed beforehand that the regional director's objective was to listen and if he heard something that he didn't like, he wasn't allowed to challenge it. His objective was to ask more probing questions in order to understand his manager. This worked quite well, even though I could see that the regional director had to restrain himself from time to time, which he clearly didn't find easy.

We got to a point where the regional director discovered his manager wanted to become a teacher and this was a turning point in their relationship. When the regional director asked his manager what he could do to help him achieve his goal, the manager visibly began to engage on a level that hadn't existed before. From that point on, their conversation was 100 per cent more focused. A new relationship was born.

The next step in this director's transformation was to address the issue of convenience. It was decided the monthly meeting could be held on rotation at each one of the manager's offices and the manager in question would take responsibility for running the meeting. More progress.

The final challenge to address was the issue of his need to be in the office on Mondays and Fridays at the same time that his people were fighting their way into work, or home, through the rush hour. He suggested that heading into the London office from time to time on a Monday or Friday would be a start. I reluctantly agreed, although this did sound a bit like a poor interpretation of the original 80/20 challenge. As a further concession, the regional director opted to go to outlying offices from time to time on a Monday or Friday, especially when he hadn't been there recently on his manager meetings tour. This seemed slightly more promising, particularly now he seemed to understand the key point, which was that he had to allocate his time fairly, regardless of the depth of his relationship with the manager and the inconvenience to him personally.

To his credit, despite having to do some explaining at home, the regional director implemented the plan as he said he would. It bore fruit too. Not only were the team more relaxed, but they were also more productive. By the end of that calendar year, his team were first in record keeping and third in sales performance and showing continued growth in both.

I am convinced that this success had a lot to do

with his allocating a significant proportion of his time to his people and spreading that time fairly. His people genuinely enjoyed having him around, even if it was just to have a quick informal coffee.

I often challenge business leaders on why they spend so much time in their offices and not with their people. If the prime reason isn't geographic, they usually respond that they 'don't want to be a distraction'; yet, as this sales director proved, this is simply not the case. Another reason that leaders cite, and this is perhaps a more worrying one, is they don't really know what to do when they get out into the front line. They are not in their comfort zone and therefore unsure of what is expected of them.

The obvious answer is to get out there and find out what the people on the ground want to talk about; but as I have discovered in my consultancy work, leaders who do this are usually the exception to the rule.

One executive I worked with who did get it right led over 12,000 people working in nine geographical locations in a fast-moving consumer goods business. Whenever I phoned him, he'd be in a different European location. He was fastidious about allocating his time fairly. His leadership team would hold their monthly leadership meetings in each location in turn. This required him to travel extensively, even though it came at a personal cost. He was prepared to make this sacrifice though, because he believed that the travel was an investment.

While visiting the various locations, he always made time to go and speak to the people in the industrial units that made up his business. The majority of the workforce were in manual jobs and not very well paid. Again, this CEO was fastidious in making sure that he visited each department so that he had an opportunity to speak to everyone through the course of a year.

'What do you say to them?' I asked, when I finally caught up with him for a face-to-face meeting.

'Mostly I just thank them for everything they do for the business and for me,' the CEO told me. 'I tell them that our results are good, which means the long term is as secure as it can be and I ensure they know that they are responsible for that.'

'I also make sure to tell them that it is easy to overlook the value that people create when they are working day after day, but I reinforce how important their contribution is.'

It was impossible not to admire the fact that he said thank you and was so meticulous in his planning of how he gained exposure to all of his people. Contrast this with another CEO I worked with in the financial services industry. His business had offices in five countries. He was an infrequent visitor to each country and on the very odd occasion he dropped by he'd met the country manager in a hotel near the office.

'Why don't you go to your offices to meet them?' I asked, curious about this arms-length behaviour.

'I don't like the offices and I don't know any of the staff,' was the blunt response.

I could hardly believe what I was hearing.

'Let's start with your staff,' I said. 'Why don't you know any of them?'

'Because I don't go into their offices,' he shrugged, ignoring the obvious irony.

It was very evident this CEO was a numbers man. In his previous job as a finance director he had done an undeniably great job. When he was promoted to his current role, he had gone to an American business school on a leadership development programme. However, what this programme clearly hadn't taught him was how to engage with his people.

I suggested that the next time he went to the country offices he should allocate thirty minutes to a town hall activity with the staff. We would invite staff to submit questions to the CEO in advance of the meeting, which would enable him to identify the common themes and create answers that would satisfy the vast majority of the team. The CEO was initially a bit nervous, but we rehearsed thoroughly and I put him through his paces with some very challenging questioning.

The plan was to start small and build from there, so the first town hall activity was with a small team of about twenty-five people. The CEO did brilliantly. Thanks to the work that was done ahead of time he was very calm, concise and informative. He even did very well with the one or two questions that he was presented with out of the blue. The final town hall activity was with over one-hundred people.

The feedback from the teams he presented to was very good. For many, it was the first time they had seen the CEO and it was certainly the first time the majority of them had heard him speak. Everyone was unanimous that they would like more opportunity to undertake this type of activity in the future. The CEO agreed, which was a real result.

As a direct result of this experience, this CEO now plans 'people time' in his diary as a priority and divides his time fairly across all of the locations he is ultimately responsible for. His people see him more regularly and have the opportunity to listen to him in town hall forums. All of his direct reports know that he divides his time evenly and this makes a huge difference to them and their people. Meanwhile, the CEO himself, sees the value and benefit of allocating his time consistently across his teams.

I am surprised at how often I encounter leaders who spend very little time with their people. They attend monthly meetings with their direct reports but don't go much beyond that. Yet, it the value of getting out into the business and engaging with the team on a one-to-one basis has been proven again and again. There was even a television series called *Back to the Floor*, which tackled this beautifully. Chief executive officers from a range of industries went out to the front-line of their business to work alongside their staff. Regardless of the industry, all of the CEOs came back into head office with a list of really simple things that could be implemented immediately and cost effectively that would make a big impact on all of their people.

One episode I recall, in particular, involved Grant Whitaker, the Home Moving Director of removals firm Pickfords[2] who spent time on his removal lorries. Whitaker discovered that the people in the vans couldn't communicate with the team in the office who managed bookings. This oversight meant they frequently turned up for jobs that had been cancelled. The amount of time and money that was being lost was huge. A mobile phone in each van solved the problem. He also discovered that there weren't any first aid kits in the vans after he split his hand while carrying a piano. When he asked the supervisor to pass him the first aid kit, he was handed some gaffer tape and told to tape it up. That's what his frontline people had to do when they got hurt.

The Pickfords case illustrated very clearly that by spending time with people other than the 20 per cent

2. BBC *Back to the Floor, Series 2, 1998, Man on the Move.*

he would normally see, he was able to make cost savings and implement ideas that would enhance the morale of his front-line people.

The final scene in these programmes is always interesting. Without exception, the boss returns with an evangelical view on what needs to be done, which they deliver with a passion to a group of direct reports, who invariably don't seem to know what is really going on in their business and look a bit embarrassed. The episode then ends with a commitment from the boss that the senior team will spend more time on the front-line. Does it really happen I wonder? It certainly should.

Having seen so many leaders allocating their time so poorly, I have looked into the issue more thoroughly. I've asked a lot of leaders why they spend so little time with *all* of their people. There are lots of excuses, because excuses are what they are; for example, too much paperwork, a need to attend (often pointless) meetings and playing politics, amongst others. The reality is that getting around 80 per cent is often hard work because it means travelling, and it opens up the potential of being exposed to the complaining of those on the front line (regardless of the fact they may have legitimate concerns). I don't understand any of this.

When I was a young platoon commander serving with British soldiers, I thoroughly enjoyed chatting to the men over a cup of tea out in a cold and wet forest, or in a tropical jungle. That's when you get to know your people and they get to know you. I was aware of young officer colleagues who couldn't bond with their men and I found this very strange. One instance stood out in particular and that was a platoon commander colleague who spent his time with his direct reports but never with his men. Despite being their boss for six months, he didn't even know their names. His behaviour appalled me. Why would you want to lead people if you didn't want to spend time with them?

It is hardly surprising that when I took command of the platoon in question, their morale wasn't very good. The previous commander, who was young and inexperienced, had messed them around with a lot of unnecessary tasks. What was even more unforgivable was the fact that when the men were out on the streets confronting the terrorism that existed at that time, he had been back in the officers' mess, in a completely different barracks. While this section of eight men didn't need to be commanded by an officer all the time, an officer would have been needed to take command if something had kicked off and extra troops were deployed, This commander hadn't put himself in a position where he would be able to react quickly enough if something had happened.

I knew from my time in 2nd Gurkhas that if troops were exposed to risk, it was vital to be as ready as could be to provide support. From day one, when my troops were out on the ground, I was in the platoon office, dressed for ops with my rifle on my desk. My Landover was parked outside my office and my team were in the platoon-ready room with all their kit. I didn't do it just because I had to either. I enjoyed being on the streets with my soldiers. Indeed, I would often swop with a soldier and spend 12 hours acting as a driver for one of my direct reports. This gave me more opportunity to get to know the lads and see them in action.

I know that my commitment to spending time with the lads benefited me because I got to know them and they got to know me. It also showed there was no discriminating in the way the time was spent. I know that in this platoon on operations, my soldiers' perception was that I cared about them and took their safety seriously.

To lead people effectively you have to know them, their fears and concerns.

This is, in my opinion, pretty standard behaviour for a leader. Unfortunately, it isn't always replicated in corporate life.

To lead people effectively you have to know them, their fears and concerns. Creating the time to be able to do this isn't necessarily easy. Everyone is busy. However, there are enough examples of leaders allocating their time fairly to show it is possible. Spending more time with the team takes time and the determination to put other less important tasks to one side. It is always time well spent.

SUMMARY

1. Geography is no excuse not to engage with the whole team. Don't focus on the people closest to you physically and emotionally.
2. Don't ever ask anyone to do something you wouldn't be prepared to do yourself.
3. If you engage with the team it's surprising how much you'll discover about your firm.

PERSONAL DEVELOPMENT EXERCISES

EXERCISE ONE

People 80/20

Business benefit

You will spend your time equally with your people

Resources

Planning time

Format

Sit down with your diary or journal and add up the amount of time, in minutes that you have spent with each member of your team in the last four weeks.

»

Discount telephone calls and group events like team meetings. Create a table like the one shown here and complete it for your team.

Name	Time	%age
Total		

First , total the amount of minutes spent, then turn that amount of time into a percentage. This will tell you who've you spent your time with.

The second step is to rebalance who you spend your time with. This should be consistent unless you have a new member of the team who need s more of your time. If this is the case, subtract the time you are going to give them and divide the balance equally across the team.

After four weeks, complete the same task to see to what extent you have adhered to your plan.

PERSONAL DEVELOPMENT EXERCISES

EXERCISE TWO
People 80/20

Business benefit
You will use your time with your people more effectively

Resources
Planning time

Format
When you have started to spend equal amounts of time with your people, start to measure the types of activities you spend time on. As you know your business, you will know what activities people can spend time on and what activities people should be spending time on.

For your own benefit identify category A, B and C activities. Category A activities are those which make the biggest difference to the success of the business. Category B activities are still relevant but make a lesser contribution. Category C activities are activities that waste time for no gain.

Now measure the amount of time you spend with your people and measure where that time is spent. If the results require you to adjust not just the volume of time you spend with your people, but also how you spend your time, commit to spending equal amounts of time in Category A activities.

Then do it.

CHAPTER 14

AUTHORISE THE FRONT LINE

This year I've employed a young man to work on my marketing and Search Engine Optimisation (SEO) and I am already looking forward to the day he leaves. This is not because he is not doing a great job. No; far from it in fact. He is full of ideas, appears to have boundless energy and has already made a real difference. I would, however, be really disappointed if somewhere beneath this activity there was not an entrepreneurial desire, which is driving him forward to start up his own show in a few years time. That is the sort of person I like to work for me.

The problem with many bosses is they assume, or even insist upon, a 110 per cent dedication to their company, for life. There can be no deviation from that line and woe betide any poor wage slave who displays any ambition or free thinking.

This is just nuts. Imagine how effective your team

would be if they were all allowed to think, or behave, like entrepreneurs. Just think what could be achieved if you empowered your front-line to really stretch their minds and deliver their jobs in the best way they see fit.

Give them a license to operate and you'd be amazed at what can be achieved. I've worked with a number of companies on this basis and, to begin with, many of them have baulked at the idea. This was certainly the response of one sales director I worked with not long ago. He led a business that had 1000 sales people and 140 managers and invited me in to suggest what I would do to increase productivity.

'I'd authorise the managers,' was my immediate response.

Sensing he didn't immediately understand what I meant, I explained that I'd give the managers considerably more leeway. For example, I'd give them the opportunity to actually lead sales meetings with clients themselves. It is not common practice in many industries for those in position of authority to take time working in jobs 'below their pay grade,' but it is this lack of broad experience which stops the manager from leading from the front. Sure, they may have done these jobs years before on the way up the promotional ladder, but things change. Companies change too. If you don't get down to the ground floor now and again though, you'll never know that.

I know first hand that this can be hugely effective because I experienced it myself when I was a trainer and a locum manager. We were authorised to sell and the people we were leading knew that we were. This authorisation allowed us to lead by example and to really support the front line team.

Providing sales managers with the authorisation to sell was a new concept for the sales director, who was concerned about productivity and he was clearly not convinced. His immediate response when I made the suggestion was to shake his head and reply: 'Do you know how difficult that would be?'

I told him that he hadn't asked me to identify something that was not going to be difficult; he'd asked me what I would do to increase productivity. I could see this wasn't going to be enough though, so I explained more fully what I meant.

'Your management team is full of bluffers,' I began, quite bluntly. This was a good way to ensure his full attention. 'They don't spend any time out at client meetings and they don't spend any time coaching. They sit in their offices doing their best to avoid being exposed as people who can't do the job they are asking their people to do.

'For the first line of leaders, who have theoretically just left the sales role, it is very important they still get out there and sell. Too many of your managers only go out to client meetings with their people when they have to. In some cases that is just once a year, even though the manager is often only twenty or thirty miles away from their people. In the meantime, they manage their people by phone and have no idea what their people are doing at client meetings. They are not leading in any sense of the word.'

Although this appeared to convince the sales director, he was still worried about how this might actually work in practice, particularly since he had 140 people to manage. Now was the time I had to deliver the real kicker.

'I suspect that if you told them that you were going to authorise them, you'd probably lose about half of them overnight,' I told him. 'They would be so concerned about being exposed as incompetent that they would leave this part of the business and go back to the part of the business that they came from.'

If the sales director was nervous about the idea before I suggested it, he was now downright terrified of the prospect. However, before he could shoot the whole idea down in flames, I quickly explained why this was actually a *good* outcome. If he lost sixty or seventy managers who couldn't do the job properly, he could replace them with sixty or seventy managers who could. It is a brutal solution, but he could nearly guarantee productivity would rise after that.

In this case, to my disappointment, the director decided to ignore my advice. His view was they could muddle along the way they were because the business couldn't afford any disruption. He was clearly too focused on the short term to see any advantage in sorting out his first-line management team. From an outside perspective, this director was always doomed to failure. He was clearly not one to question anything, let alone everything and was in no way prepared to embrace the entrepreneurial spirit. He was too nervous of the here and now to think a way through a problem and come up with a creative solution, no matter how painful it may be in the short term. Plus, he was not prepared to utilise the resources around him, namely the handful of team members he did have who could do an incredible job if they were given half the chance.

Some leaders ...do everything they can to avoid any form of risk. This inhibits the entrepreneurial spirit of the people around them.

He left the business about six months after our conversation, switching out of sales at the same time and into a managing director's role. He brought me in to work with him on another project and, to his credit, the first thing he agreed to do was give his direct reports more responsibility and more authorisation to act independently. This was progress indeed. Looking back, perhaps it was just that the earlier step was too big for him to take and it took time to get used to the concept. It's a shame, but he got there in the end.

Some leaders never go out on a limb during their whole career, especially if they know they are going to be in a certain role for a fixed period of time. They do everything they can to avoid any form of risk. This inhibits the entrepreneurial spirit of the people around them who do have a flair and ambition to make a difference. Inevitably, this leads to the loss of those employees who do have the drive and determination that any business truly needs.

There is, however, a way to harness the entrepreneurial spirit without introducing high levels of risk. That way is the Goal Achievement Strategy (GAS). GAS is a simple approach, with the dual advantage that it enables a leader to both delegate tasks to their teams and harness their potential.

There are two components to GAS. These are:

1. **The goal or objective**. The goal must be communicated with absolute clarity, ensuring complete understanding by everyone involved. The leader must explain why the goal is so important and what achieving the goal will mean. This is summarised as 'what' and 'why'. What we're trying to achieve and why it is important.

To ensure that the 'what' is understood, it is perfectly reasonable to use brief back (see chapter six) to ensure your team have full understanding from the outset.

For example, when I was a relatively inexperienced trainer in a large company, I was tasked with creating a two-day programme that would be delivered to some of the most successful people we had in the business. My boss sat me down and explained what he wanted to achieve, which was to help our top performers become even more successful than they were. He defined success for me. Success was enabling our people to be more productive. This was also easily measureable as these people's business results could be tracked easily. The reason the business wanted to invest in these people was to ensure that they stayed up to date and also felt they were being invested in professionally.

2. **Defining the boundaries**. When the goal is understood and everyone is clear on the reason it is important, the second component of GAS is defining the boundaries within which the team must operate. The aim is to empower the team and allow them the latitude they need to harness their ideas without exposing the business to significant risk of loss, whether that's loss of profit or reputation.

Most people like to have some idea of the boundaries

they should be operating in. For example, when John F Kennedy said: 'we will send an American safely to the moon before the end of the decade,' the boundaries in this example were very obviously safely and time frame. The president made no mention of budget, for example, or indeed any other type of boundary. He made his priorities very clear and everyone had a distinct understanding of what needed to be done and how.

If time permits, there is great merit in providing any project team with an opportunity to establish the types of boundaries they would like the decision-makers to consider. There will be a number of factors that appear constantly across projects, like timeframe and budget, but even then it is worth emphasising the priorities; plus, if there are considerations that are project specific, they should be clearly identified and agreed from the outset. By setting out the objectives and boundaries beforehand, risk will be considerably reduced.

As I will show in more detail in chapter twenty, employing a stepped approach like this to the achievement of any goal is a practical way to overcome a challenge. This allows the leader to keep tabs on progress without inhibiting the entrepreneurial spirit.

Another useful tool for a leader who is keen to look at the possibilities of empowering his team, is the skill/will matrix. It is illustrated here in Figure 1.

All teams are made up of people who have varying levels of both aptitude and attitude. For example, there will be people who have a very inspiring *attitude,* but who don't yet have the required level of *aptitude* to make things happen. This lack of aptitude could be for a number of reasons. They might be new to the team, or they may have recently been asked to move into a newer, possibly more challenging, role. A person like this would occupy the top, left quadrant.

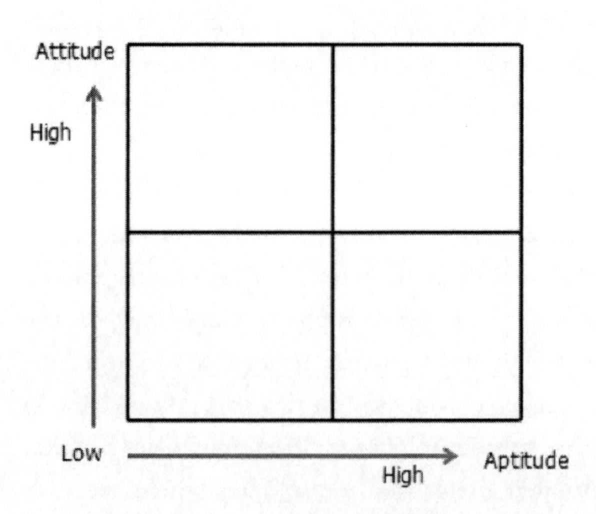

Figure 1. Where are your team

A person in the bottom, right quadrant is clearly very skilful, but for some reason their attitude is limiting them at this time. Again, there may be a number of reasons for this. It is possible that they might be bored, or dissatisfied, in their current role. There may be personal issues that are holding them back, or they may have decided to move on to a new employer and are marking time while they decide what to do. The bottom left square is generally occupied by someone who has just joined the team, or someone who is about to leave. Meanwhile, the top right square is the ideal outcome for all leaders because we should all aspire to help people grow high levels of aptitude and an inspiring attitude.

Any leader should take the time to work out which quadrant individual members of their team occupy. It is possible that a single person might occupy different quadrants at the same time, according to the varying components of their role. For example, they may be a high attitude/aptitude performer for 90 per cent of their time, while taking up a bottom left low attitude/aptitude place for a different part of the role. This might happen when, say, a highly capable and successful person is asked to speak in public. Although they'll be used to speaking on a topic they know a lot about, it doesn't guarantee they will enjoy the experience of speaking in front of a large audience, or that they will do it well. A leader has to be attuned to this type of challenge and be prepared to invest in the development of both attitude and aptitude of the people they want to move towards the top right quadrant.

Sometimes this will be relatively simple. Say, for example, there are concerns over some team members apparently languishing in the bottom right quadrant. In my direct experience, people in this quadrant are often those who have clocked up a long service and are simply feeling a little bored and uninspired. These people often want to be treated with respect (Who doesn't after all?) and may have been turned off by ineffective management. They may well benefit from being asked to work with newer members of the team. This has the dual benefit of allowing them to demonstrate their capabilities, while also bringing them back into the team quite quickly.

Another young graduate I worked with in our business was very definitely in the top left quadrant. He was very keen, but had no understanding of our sector. The most appropriate way to begin developing someone like this is to be direct, in other words, tell them what to do. This removes uncertainty and doubt, enabling the establishment of some basic understanding. In this instance, the direct approach is only the right tactic until a person is ready and able to take more responsibility. When this time arrives, continuing to be direct will frustrate them and may even lead to their leaving the business. It can be a bit of a balancing act for leadership, which is why it is worth doing this segmentation exercise on a regular basis. A leader should be very conscious of every individual's positions on this matrix. As the team members grow, the leadership style required will change.

One of the key questions raised in the context of authorising the front-line is how much control should be afforded to the team. People are all different, as we know, and some like more direction and control than others.

When I was a young second lieutenant with only eighteen months' experience, I was chosen to be the Reconnaissance Platoon Commander in 2nd Gurkhas. I was very proud to be appointed but also found leading that team was a great challenge. They were the best soldiers in the battalion and all very experienced in a variety of complex skills including demolitions, advanced first aid, satellite communication and long-range patrolling skills. I had none of these skills when I took command but that didn't really matter. My primary role was to lead the platoon, develop them as soldiers and leaders and plan and execute their deployment when we went on operations. I was capable of doing those aspects of the role; the specialist skills could be developed later.

I was sent to England to complete a three-week course to aid me in leading the platoon. The three instructors were world class and had undertaken dangerous reconnaissance tasks in conflict zones across the world. Reconnaissance patrols tend to operate in groups of four men. This group size enables a number of specialists to operate together and usually provides enough firepower if you bump into the enemy. The role is to gather information on enemy locations and often involves a lot of physical hardship and boredom as you observe an enemy's location for protracted periods of time.

As the platoon commander, I had eight, four-man, patrols under my command. All of these patrols were commanded by senior Gurkhas who often had eighteen years' experience. A lesson stressed repeatedly on the course was the need to develop each individual patrol member's ability to make sound tactical decisions. My instructors told me they had all experienced occasions when a patrol commander had been hurt or even killed. In these circumstances it was necessary for the team to act quickly and decisively, often without any input from a senior person who could have been fifty miles away.

When I got back to Hong Kong, my platoon was being prepared for a deployment onto the Hong Kong border. Illegal immigrants were trying to get into Hong Kong from China and the battalion was responsible for catching them at the border fence.

The border fence area was unusual. There were houses in the zone between China and Hong Kong and the people there did their best to get on with their lives, despite the fact that they were in the middle of no man's land. Some of them were known to be aiding and abetting illegal immigrants though. The police suspected about five people, in particular, and were able to tell us where these aiders and abettors (AAs) were based. My most senior Gurkha immediately suggested we deploy patrols led by our most experienced people to observe the AAs.

'They can undertake the initial reconnaissance, produce the observation plan, deliver the orders and lead the patrol on the ground,' he suggested.

To be fair, this was pretty standard procedure. I wanted to do things differently though. Remembering the lessons in England, my plan was to use less experienced soldiers to lead the patrols. The senior Gurkhas could be present but would act in a purely operational role, as opposed to a leadership one. This was clearly a new idea and, as I expected, it met with resistance.

The senior Gurkha was concerned about the achievement of the task and the reputation of the platoon. Being as it was an operational duty, meaning it wasn't a drill, he was worried the AAs would be armed and prepared to fight hard not to be caught. I shared these concerns, but I also felt we were being presented with a perfect opportunity to authorise some of our future leaders as patrol commanders. I really wanted to put into practice what I had learnt. I could see the quality that existed in our more junior soldiers who were both keen and capable. We just needed to give them the opportunity to lead.

I expected to receive quite a lot of resistance to this plan and I did. However, I wouldn't back down. I wanted to give all of my commanders an opportunity to command in the field and not just when we were practising on exercise. By allowing them to run an operational task, I hoped to show that I trusted them, which I did. After all, I could tell them I trusted them and then stay safe by allowing them to practise command, or I could put my money where my mouth was and really let them get on with it.

I held executive decision-making authority and could have imposed my idea on the team. That wasn't my style. I looked for a way to make it work for everyone.

One aspect of commanding a number of teams on the ground is that there has to be one person with a central view of everything going on to ensure that if something happens, additional teams can be deployed quickly and effectively. This role is usually the preserve of the platoon commander, that is, me, or the second in command. If I was really going to do this properly, I needed to pick a senior patrol commander and give him my role. By now this was starting to get a bit scary, but it seemed to make good sense.

I chose one man who was extremely capable, KP Pun, and he oversaw the initial planning by each of the patrols. One mantra in our platoon was that everyone was allowed to contribute to and challenge the plan, but the patrol commander had the final say. As I watched KP confidently challenge the rest of the platoon, while never once imposing his own ideas, I knew I had made the right decision. In fact, I knew then that he would one day become my second in command. In an instant I could see the leader he would become. He clearly got the idea I was trying to develop and embraced it fully. I'm sure I would have seen this over time if I hadn't done this exercise, but this gave me an almost instant indication of the strengths in both KP and the rest of the team. It also clearly demonstrated to the whole platoon that if something were to happen on operations, we had many other commanders who could step up and do the job effectively.

The upshot of the seven-day operation was that we apprehended five AAs who had been helping Chinese nationals enter Hong Kong illegally. As importantly for me though, a good number of my junior commanders received experience of commanding a patrol in an operational environment. The men on the ground had absolute control and really benefitted from the opportunity.

I often find it interesting when companies spend lots of money on hiring experienced and capable people, yet fail to take the very obvious step of looking within their ranks to see what skills their teams already have that are not being properly utilised. Worse still, having brought in these talented new recruits they frequently don't allow them the freedom to make the contribution they really could make.

Leadership is about backing your people and trusting their judgment without constantly looking over their shoulder. It isn't necessarily easy for a leader to do, but it is vital.

SUMMARY

1. Your team will be more effective if you empower individuals and promote an entrepreneurial way of thinking.
2. Any perceived risk can be mitigated by setting clear objectives and boundaries.
3. Allowing your team some leeway is an excellent way to identify future leadership potential.

PERSONAL DEVELOPMENT EXERCISES

EXERCISE ONE

Authorise your front line

Business benefit

You will further develop your team

Resources

Time at a team meeting/one to one

Format

Analyse the core components of your role with a view to identifying those you could develop within your people. An example of this would be leading part or all of a team meeting (although this would work equally well with other components and can easily be adapted).

Provide the team with a timetable of who will lead which meeting in the future and also provide clarity on:

- Meeting objectives: i.e. what must be achieved and why that is important
- Boundaries that need to be considered: time available, location etc.

Encourage innovation outside the boundaries.

Ask the team to come up with an initial version of their plan and to present this plan to you. Where possible, allow the plan to be implemented without too much change.

Implement.

PERSONAL DEVELOPMENT EXERCISES

EXERCISE TWO

Authorise your front line

Business benefit

You will further develop your team

Resources

Time a team meeting or one to one

Format

Ask the team to analyse your role as the team leader and feed their findings back to you in the form of a list of tasks. Next, ask them to identify a task that they think they are all capable of doing well. The task should be something that the team leader is required to do consistently and which you can pass to the members of the team for a week.

Provide the team with enough time to come up with an approach to achieving this task successfully and with no risk to the business.

Once the approach is agreed, oversee the implementation of the allotted task, measuring the benefit you as the team leader receive. Ensure that the team is fully aware of how you are benefitting as a direct result of their input.

At the conclusion of the project, each individual team member should be able to vocalise how they benefitted from the additional responsibility.

CHAPTER 15

BELIEF AND CONFIDENCE

There's a great expression that is used in both sport and in business to describe a period of sustained, high-quality performance. The person who is on this top form is said to be 'on a roll'. The implication is that once one has attained a degree of success for a period of time then the trend will continue unabated. As momentum builds, the success continues.

Being on a roll is great. Success breeds success and when everything seems this effortless, the results are usually great. It won't therefore require a huge leap of imagination to agree with me when I say that one of the key objectives of any leader should be to get his people on a roll.

Sounds great, yes? But how might that work in practice? Well, to begin with it is worth noting the main qualities that drive a team on a roll. Those qualities are a large amount of self-belief, which has the knock-on effect of provoking very high level of confidence.

Let's focus on belief first and look at how a leader can encourage this emotion among those around them. During my military career, I flew with a wide variety of helicopter pilots. It was one of these pilots who told me a story about the early stages of his training, which to me summed up just how easily you can encourage – or put off – those around you with just a few words.

The pilot described to me how the first time he went out with a qualified helicopter instructor (QHI), the QHI lifted the helicopter up off the ground into a hover. He then showed the trainee pilot what the three main controls were for, demonstrated them and gave the trainee pilot the opportunity to get the feel of them.

The power of our belief system is immense.

After a short run through, he turned to the trainee pilot and said: 'I would like you to take control of the rudder bars and when you are in control of that you can then take control of the collective and then you can take control of the cyclic.'

In essence, after just fifteen minutes of flying training, the QHI was telling the trainee pilot that that he was actually going to be flying a helicopter.

Outwardly, this plan didn't appear to get off to a

good start. When the trainee pilot took control the helicopter's nose started to veer a long way off from the point that the QHI had told him to focus on. Then, as he applied corrective measures, he found that while the nose was now pointing in the correct direction, he was hovering 50 feet above the ground instead of the 10-foot level he was supposed to be aiming for. Plus, he was starting to veer off towards the left, which needed additional corrective action.

In the trainee pilot's perception, the helicopter was going all over the place in an extremely uncontrolled way. Yet, when at last the QHI had retaken control of the helicopter and landed safely, he turned round to the trainee pilot, smiled and said: 'You're a natural.'

Now the trainee's story of the session would have used all sorts of words, other than 'natural'. But, because this positive review came from the QHI, how do you think the trainee pilot felt as he walked from the helicopter into the flight changing rooms? He felt fantastic, of course. After his first experience of having complete control of the helicopter he now saw his future with great optimism.

For the rest of the day as he went around the camp, sorting out equipment and becoming familiar with the layout of the flying school, there was one thought that kept reoccurring in his mind. That thought was: 'I'm a natural ...I'm a natural...I'm a natural...I'm a natural…I'm a natural.' As the trainee pilot went to bed, the last thing he would have thought before he went to sleep was, 'I'm a natural'.

We will never really know whether or not that trainee pilot was 'a natural,' but that isn't the point. All we need to know is that the QHI was a man with credibility. When he turned round and said to the trainee 'you're a natural,' he triggered a series of reoccurring thoughts in that trainee's head. He gave him the power of belief that saw him through the training and beyond.

The power of our belief system is immense. You have the ability to do something very similar to this with your own team. You can help them banish their limiting beliefs and make them a confident, effective unit. It really can be as simple as a few, well-timed words.

Obviously most of your senior team will be established in their jobs and will have gone well beyond the trainee stage, where the equivalent of a QHI can tell them they are a natural at what they do. However, this doesn't mean it isn't possible to transform ingrained bad habits by looking more closely at a team member's belief system. In other words, you can teach old dogs new tricks.

Let me give an example of how this might work in practice in a business setting. Not long ago I worked with a well-known FTSE 100 company. The contract involved analysis of their sales team, a two-day training programme and some infield coaching for a number of the sales people. I spent four days with one salesman called Mike and learned some interesting lessons to do with self-belief.

Mike was a very nice and genuine guy with a very good sense of humour who had been in his present sales role for about 11 months, having worked in a contact centre in an unrelated industry before that. His sales performance wasn't bad. He was hitting about 80 per cent of his target, which placed him about 550th out of one-thousand sales people. You could say he had made a good start to his new career.

Mike's job involved meeting clients, introduced to him by colleagues. While these colleagues had an existing relationship with the clients, Mike had usually never met them before. After observing him in action, I could see he was a very good communicator and adept at building relationships very quickly. He was also a very good listener and seemed to be genuinely interested in his clients. This was all boding well.

Mike's role meant that he had to present a recommendation to his clients, which he did very confidently. Indeed, as I observed a couple at one of the first meetings it became very clear that they believed Mike's recommendation was good and it looked as if they were ready to buy. Yet, when Mike finished making his recommendation, he simply stopped speaking. In one instant, he went from talking enthusiastically about what he thought they should do next, to saying nothing at all. A silence filled the very small meeting room.

After a short while, Mike asked the couple if they would like to think about his recommendation. They said, almost reluctantly, they thought they had better think about them and Mike said that he would call them in a week or so.

After the couple had left, Mike and I sat down to discuss the meeting that had just taken place. He asked me whether there was anything about his strategy he should change. I told him that while I admired his undoubted ability to build relationships as well as his strong listening skills, I was curious why he hadn't pushed to close the deal there and then.

'I think that couple really liked your recommendation and wanted to buy from you today,' I told him.

'I don't like to push people,' Mike responded.

This didn't surprise me. If anyone was going to do the right thing for his clients it was Mike. However, I tried to reassure him I'd be very surprised if there was anyone who thought he was pushy.

'I think you have to give your clients an opportunity to buy from you Mike,' I said frankly. 'I think by trying not to be pushy, you are discouraging them from buying something which is actually good for them.'

Mike was clearly surprised by this, but agreed to a strategy where he would ask his clients what they thought of a recommendation once he'd made it.

When the next client came in, Mike went through almost the same process as before, although this time it was specifically tailored for the new client. He duly made his recommendation, as he had before, and once again it all made very good sense, which was apparent to everyone. Then, Mike stopped talking and silence fell over the meeting room once more.

'Not again,' I thought.

Suddenly though, Mike looked over at the client and said: 'What do you think?'

'Sounds great,' the client said, virtually straight away.

'Shall I get the paperwork?' asked Mike.

'If that's what we need to complete the business then that sounds like a good idea,' said the client, without hesitation.

When the client had gone, I asked Mike for his views on the meeting. He believed it had gone well and the facts were borne out by the client signing then and there. I asked him what he had done differently and after weighing it up in his mind, Mike said he had asked the client what he thought of the recommendation.

'How was that?' I asked.

'It was easier than I thought,' admitted Mike.

Now I had evidence that Mike had some reticence

about posing what is known in sales as a 'closing question'. However, on the strength of his success, he agreed to continue with his new tactic. Whenever he got to a point where he thought that it was fair to ask his clients what they thought, he did so.

He used the question, 'shall I get the paperwork' as his way of testing a client's commitment to buy in an indirect way. As a style, it suited Mike. It produced remarkable results too. Clients liked his approach and responded positively. That small change in his approach, and the resulting leap in productivity, proved to Mike the worth of believing in himself and the value he was capable of giving to his clients. In a short space of time he became one of the top three performers in the firm and deservedly so. That is the power of self-belief. Mike is a salesman who is certainly still on a roll to this day.

In order to work out what you could do to give your team the power of self-belief, it may help to begin by understanding a little more about what lies behind beliefs.

Very often, beliefs are nothing more than very firmly held views. Indeed, there is occasionally never very much hard evidence to support the belief at all; yet, even then some people feel their beliefs so passionately they are prepared to die for them. One of the most famous historic examples of a firmly held, yet mistaken, belief is the once widely held conviction that the earth was flat. It was understandable why our ancestors might have thought that; after all, if the earth wasn't flat, why didn't the sea drain off the surface? Plato, the Greek philosopher, challenged that belief after concluding that the surface of the earth was actually curved. His rationale for revising this widely held opinion came from his observations of ships arriving at the port of Athens. He realised that the first thing he saw when a ship came into view was the tip of its mast. As the vessel got closer, the rest of it was gradually revealed until the whole ship was visible. Plato concluded if the surface of the earth was flat, you wouldn't just see the tip of the mast in the distance, you would see the whole ship. It would just be very small.

It is easy to follow Plato's logic today but, back then, people didn't yet get the idea of gravity. They couldn't fully engage with the idea because they didn't understand the alternative. When Plato's friends confronted him with 'evidence' such as water being poured onto a ball and cascading off, they could only see, and therefore believe, what was before their eyes.

Although we are now prepared to accept the Earth is round, thanks to widespread evidence, our core belief system has not developed much in the 2400 years, or so, since Plato was around. The bulk of our beliefs are part of our conditioning from parents, teachers, friends and experiences. Most were formed in our early years too because when we are young, we tend to believe what we are told, especially when that comes from a figure of authority. However, you don't just have to be young to develop a belief based on hearing something from an authority figure. Grown-ups are capable of this as well.

The risk with some of the beliefs we have is that they damage our confidence. If you believe that you will be unsuccessful, you will undoubtedly fail. If you believe that you've lost your edge that is how you will behave. Confidence and self-belief are very closely linked. I saw a prime example of this with several teams of highly qualified people, who were charged with pitching their company's business proposition at what are known as beauty parades. This particular company was involved in the investment management industry and each of their pitching teams was made up of three people, all from different parts of the business. Their task was to attend a potential client's office to show just why their company would make the perfect business partner. Success would mean a big deal, worth several millions pounds in revenue.

When I engaged with the people who had been pitching, it was clear their confidence was low. Each group had already delivered a series of pitches that year but, despite working for a market leading company, not one had won a single one.

In their favour, each group had asked for feedback on why they hadn't won, but collectively they were very sceptical about the answers they'd received. For example, they were repeatedly told their offering was too expensive, yet they thought that they were quite competitively priced. They became convinced that the actual truth was more likely to be there was something wrong with their products and services, but no one had the foresight to tell them.

This lack of success and the uncertainty around the real reasons why they were losing had a huge impact on morale. People who had previously had a strong track record of success lost their confidence. What was equally concerning was it was apparent their leaders didn't know what to do. In fact, the senior leaders in the business insisted this lack of success wasn't an issue at all. They told the pitching teams to continue as they were because it would come good in the end. Meanwhile, in such a high-value business, the pressure was mounting behind the scenes.

I was tasked with turning the situation around and my immediate solution was to work on building the confidence of all the pitching teams. With a pitch four weeks away, the pressure was on.

The pitch was scheduled on a Thursday, in London. I suggested that we devote the Monday and Tuesday of the week they were going to pitch in to training and preparation. The teams could then travel from their head office to the Capital on the Wednesday in readiness to pitch. Initially, there was some resistance to this plan because some people felt we were devoting too much time to it. I reminded them the business would be worth over a million pounds over five years if they were successful and they agreed that it was going to be time well spent.

We weren't able to change any of the pitching slides, because they were created and managed centrally. My challenge was therefore to use and hopefully inspire people who had previously been unsuccessful.

When the week of the pitch arrived, I spent two days working with three groups of three people. Each of the departments that made up one component of the pitching team was represented. We spent the first couple of hours ensuring that everyone was well briefed on the potential client and understood what each of their departments was responsible for.

I focused on creating an approach to the initial six minutes of the pitch that would create confidence in each team. We discussed the pros and cons of various types of introductions before settling on the one we thought worked best. We then rehearsed it thoroughly, including a session in front of a video camera. I gave feedback and made sure everyone stayed focused on the things they did well.

By now we had chosen three pitching teams, and they set about rehearsing all activities alongside the people they would pitch with. This familiarity soon started to create benefits. It became noticeable when they had to answer questions; they no longer shouted over each other. We instigated a system whereby one person was responsible for ensuring that the team understood the question before it was passed to the person who was best qualified to answer it. Simple ideas like this one allowed thinking time and ensured questions were answered confidently and concisely.

We devoted the second morning of preparation to rehearsing what each team would do if their proposed approach to managing the introduction was derailed for some reason. We did this through role play, where the team would be interrupted by one of the audience and would have to respond. This too was videoed and shown back to the teams. They made mistakes, but they learnt quickly from those mistakes. By lunchtime of day two, they were capable and confident in the face of any challenge we could throw at them

The final afternoon was spent rehearsing their responses to any questions they could expect to get. This was done with great focus and, again, there was an opportunity to practise in front of the camera. As we wound down, I was left with the strong impression these were all very capable people who had temporarily lost their confidence. My objective over the two days had been to build this confidence by showing them just how good they were and even though we'd not yet pitched, I already sensed a complete change in attitude. I was as eager as they were to see the outcome of their efforts. My job, though, was over and I had to wait to hear what happened.

A few days later, by complete coincidence, I met the general manager for the UK business, and the very first thing he said to me was, 'you might like to know but the team won on Thursday'. He'd only just heard because the business had taken forty-eight hours to confirm the decision.

I phoned the team leader, who was absolutely delighted. He told me the pitch had gone to plan, there had been no unexpected questions and that they felt confident coming out of the pitch. He was candid enough to admit this was a new feeling for a lot of them and they were even more relieved when they learned they'd won. The upturn in their fortunes didn't end there, either. Now well and truly on a roll, that team then won the next nine pitches in a row, accumulating a very high level of revenue for their business.

> One of a leader's primary objectives should be to build self-belief and confidence in their people.

What had changed? After all, the slides they used in their presentation were the same slides they had used when they lost pitches. Likewise, the messages in the presentation were the same as before. The key new element was the people delivering the message had changed. More specifically, the team's self-belief and confidence had been transformed. Thanks to the practice they had undertaken and the new mood among the team, they approached the pitch with confidence and self-assurance. They knew they could handle any curved ball that was thrown at them. Equally importantly, they had confidence in each other, because of the time spent in preparation with the other people in the pitching team.

One of a leader's primary objectives should be to build self-belief and confidence in their people. The two elements work hand in hand too. If you are able to help the individuals on your team to build self-belief, their confidence will grow and vice versa.

It will require an investment in time. In the examples quoted in this chapter, the approach to building confidence and self-belief, time was devoted to the intense practice of relevant skills and the application of team work. This approach is used extensively in the British Army. An army unit that isn't on operations is either recovering from an operational tour, or preparing for the next one. The army's role lends itself to being on operations for about one third of their time. This means that time can be devoted to building self-belief and confidence in both individuals and teams.

In an ideal world there would be adequate time

devoted to this practice in the commercial arena; however, I am realistic. Indeed, allocating any time at all to these types of activities isn't straightforward, where utilisation of people is often a key performance indicator. It's not likely to change any time soon, either. The time needed to really develop people in the corporate world will probably never be available, due to a perception of the costs involved.

This is where an effective leader's impact can have such enormous benefit. As we have seen here, a leader has the opportunity to develop their people's self-belief and confidence while the individuals are performing their primary roles. This requires skills like coaching and mentoring, which are addressed in other chapters, and a desire to enable others to grow. These are all core traits of an effective leader.

SUMMARY

1. A key objective of any leader is to help his team to be on a roll, success-wise. That requires self belief and confidence.
2. Helping individuals to be confident and believe in their abilities may only require a few well-timed words. Sometimes though, it will take an investment of time.
3. To understand why a team lacks self-belief or confidence, look at what lies behind these limiting emotions.

PERSONAL DEVELOPMENT EXERCISES

EXERCISE ONE

Build confidence and belief

Business benefit

Your team will know how to change limiting beliefs

Resources

Sixty minutes at a team meeting

Format

Put the team into groups of between two and four people. The number of groups will dictate the number of topics needed to enable the exercise to work effectively. Stress that for the first element of the exercise, each group is going to have to play devil's advocate. In other words, they are going to have to think with a glass half-empty perspective.

Give each group one topic from one or all of the following:

- the company (they work for)
- the competition
- the business environment
- their products/services.

Give each group five minutes to come up with between six and eight limiting beliefs that people might hold about the topic they've been given. They should write these down on a piece of paper, possibly a flipchart if you have one. Allow space

»

for them to write something else beside each of the limiting beliefs.

When all groups have their list, ask them for feedback. There is no need to debate the beliefs, they are after all firmly held views and the idea is that they were honest about them.

Once feedback has been taken from all groups, give them an opportunity to look at each of the limiting beliefs they have written down and beside it, write a more inspiring version. For example:

A limiting belief about the company might be:

'The company is very small'.

The inspiring version of that belief might be:

'Small is agile, small is good'.

The point of the exercise is to ensure people know that one person's limiting belief is another person's inspiring belief. They are, after all, only firmly held views.

It is worth noting that you are not asking people to believe any of this. It is simply a mechanism to show that for every limiting belief, there is a more inspiring version.

Once the team is happy with the process, you may like to encourage them to try it before each new project, so they list the limiting beliefs they might hold and then go through a process of identifying more inspiring versions. This activity will help people to start focusing on more inspiring beliefs from the outset. By starting with this focus, it is easier to retain it when the going get challenging, as it will.

PERSONAL DEVELOPMENT EXERCISES

EXERCISE TWO

Build belief and confidence

Business benefit
The team will develop their understanding of beliefs and the impact they can have

Resources
Time with your team

Format
Once the team has completed the first exercise, build on it with this exercise.

Ask the team to write down a personal goal. Let them know they won't be asked to disclose the goal. It should be something that matters to them that they haven't yet started. If anyone doesn't have specific ideas give them some examples:

- Raise money for charity.
- Lose a stone.
- Run a ten kilometre race.
- Learn a new skill.

When each individual has a goal in mind, ask them to write down five limiting beliefs that might be held about achieving the goal. Once completed, ask the team to write down the more inspiring version for each limiting belief. When each person has their inspiring beliefs, ask them to identify

»

one single step they could take to start to make progress towards the goal. For that one step, get them to write down three limiting beliefs about their ability to achieve that step. Finally, ask them to write down the inspiring versions of the three limiting beliefs.

Conclude the exercise by making the point that limiting beliefs can appear at every step of an activity, especially when you encounter challenges.

This exercise helps individuals to better understand limiting beliefs and consciously identify more inspiring versions until this becomes a habit. It can take time and practice, but if more inspiring versions aren't identified, the risk is that limiting beliefs will remain. Limiting beliefs will, of course, stop people from taking action.

CHAPTER 16

PAIN AND PLEASURE – THE DECISION MAKING PROCESS

We're all pretty familiar with the principle of short-term pleasure, which can bring long-term pain. That's why people smoke when the danger of cancer and other health problems are well known, or they steal from an employer, or are unfaithful to their spouse. At the back of their minds, they know they are not making the choice for the greater good in the long haul, but they base their actions on what feels good right now.

In good, wise, decision-making, it is often necessary to turn this principle on its head and suffer some short-term pain in order to secure some long-term pleasure. If you can look forward and embrace the importance of that long-term gain, it is possible to make the short-term pain bearable.

Decision-making is, of course, an intrinsic part of leadership. Clearly, you can't take decisions on the grounds that they will make you popular, but what is the right way to make the best choices? In this chapter, as we delve into the decision-making process, we will look at how to make sure you do the right thing, however painful in the short-term.

It may help to begin by getting down to the basics. Decisions generally fall into one of three categories:

1. simple and familiar
2. complex, but familiar
3. complex and unfamiliar.

Underpinning each of these categories is the likelihood that each decision may lead to short-, medium- or long-term pain, or possibly short-, medium- or long-term pleasure. Bearing this in mind, there are strategies for addressing each type of these categories.

SIMPLE AND FAMILIAR

Simple and familiar choices are exactly as they sound. These are issues and challenges that have been faced before and the leader knows exactly how to deal with them. The most effective strategy with these issues is to delegate the responsibility for addressing them to an inexperienced member of the team who will benefit from the opportunity.

A leader should bear in mind that while the issue

might seem simple and familiar to them, it may not necessarily be so for the person to whom the task is being delegated. Appropriate preparation/training and initial supervision and support might be required.

I encountered an example of a simple and familiar issue when I was a salesman. My boss had decided to run some seminars in the Wembley Conference Centre. He was the person best qualified to deliver these seminars, but he decided to give me a chance to participate. Even though this was a relatively straightforward challenge for him, it was daunting for me. My boss could see that I was capable of managing this effectively but made sure that I had the support to make it a success. While he didn't attend, he did allocate a senior colleague to participate in the seminar with me. This was a great opportunity for me and a good example of my boss using the opportunity of a simple and familiar challenge to add to the personal development of a member of his team.

COMPLEX BUT FAMILIAR

The familiarity aspect of this type of challenge is of big benefit. Though the issue itself is complex, it can be easily tackled by standard operating procedures, or defined business processes. If there is any hint that standard operating procedures (SOPs) won't address the issue, then the issue has been inappropriately diagnosed and should be placed into the final 'complex and unfamiliar' category.

I encountered a situation that fitted into this decision-making category in Angola. As the mining operations there gained momentum, there was a need to build and commission operating plants at various locations along the banks of the Cuango River. One such plant was sited beside a waterfall at a place called Tazua. It was imperative that the plant was commissioned with the most effective operating procedures in place from day one. The plant was a long way from Luzamba and I wanted leaders there who knew exactly what they should be doing and when. If we achieved this, it would mean that I wouldn't have to continue to return to Tazua, allowing me to focus on developing the other plants across the mining area.

The challenge was complex because there were many things we needed to get right the first time. I was in the fortunate position of having a high degree of familiarity with the potential pitfalls, because I had already been involved in resolving issues on plants that hadn't been commissioned effectively. However, while I knew the most appropriate SOPs, many of them were in my head. The first step in resolving the situation was to write them down in a logical and simple way because SOPs can be complex to people who are new to them. Having created the SOPs, my next challenge was to ensure that they were implemented effectively. We achieved this by extensive rehearsals of the processes and procedures, so the leaders in my team and the people in their teams knew exactly what to do. We also rehearsed likely scenarios that could go wrong, such as an industrial accident, so that the team were both confident and skilled.

When the plant was commissioned, I was there to play a hands-off, but supportive role to my leaders on the ground. They were confident in the execution of the SOPs.

COMPLEX AND UNFAMILIAR

No matter how experienced a leader is, there will always be issues and challenges that are very complex and which haven't been encountered before. Some businesses and teams allow themselves to be perplexed by these circumstances, while others rise to the occasion and see them as opportunities. Looking upon these tough calls in a positive way is clearly the better focus to have, particularly if you want to make your mark.

No matter how experienced a leader is, there will always be issues and challenges that are very complex and which haven't been encountered before.

In this case, the decision-making process will centre

on doing what is right for longer-term pleasure, while finding a way to manage any short-term pain into a tolerable position. The simplest and most efficient way to devise possible solutions for complex and unfamiliar decisions is to harness the skills of your team, because any leader who thinks they have all the answers is delusional.

I have seen numerous managers attempt to overcome complex and unfamiliar challenges by pushing through their own idea because they think this is the quickest, most efficient way to get a good result. Very occasionally this can work, but more often than not it doesn't. This isn't necessarily because the solution is flawed. It is often because the team who are required to implement it haven't fully bought into it. They feel as if the solution has been imposed upon them because they've played no part in the decision-making process.

A well-led team will tolerate significant short-term pain if they feel included and believe in the value of what they are doing. Of course, a leader must always be certain that the pain the team are being exposed to is justified by the goal, as well as the rewards that will come with achieving that goal, but if he is sure of this it will be a decision well-made.

We looked at how to create buy-in and engage the team in chapter four. This is especially pertinent in this type of tough decision-making, as you will see from this next story from the US Navy. It is a great example of complex and unfamiliar decision-making in action. It centres on a ship which at one time had the lowest score for employee engagement in the fleet.

A new captain was appointed, who was pleased to have inherited this unhappy ship. After all, its engagement scores could only really go in one direction. He set about finding what the problem with the crew could be. It quickly emerged that one of the key sources of their dissatisfaction was a new jacket they were required to wear. The crew complained it was uncomfortable and dangerous.

The captain tried one out by wearing it for a twenty-four-hour shift and couldn't help but agree that the jacket was indeed uncomfortable. He also established what the crew meant by dangerous, because if someone were unlucky enough to fall off the ship, the jacket had no integral flotation device. The jacket might possibly even hasten their journey to the bottom of the sea.

When the captain had established for himself that the crew had a case, he categorised the process of coming up with a solution as a complex and unfamiliar decision-making task. To begin tackling it, he told the crew that it was up to them to come up with an alternative, but that they had to do so for less than $130. Right then, the US Navy-issued jacket cost $155 per item. The captain knew that to make a case for something other than the issued version, he would have to prove its financial worth alongside any other positives. The crew quickly came up with a jacket that they all agreed was comfortable, safe and cost just $98 per item. Going a little beyond their brief, they also suggested the ship's name was placed on the back of the jacket.

The crew had provided the captain with a workable option, but the decision to accept this option was his and his alone. He considered the long-term gain was obvious. His crew would be comfortable, where they were currently uncomfortable, and would feel safer, where they currently felt vulnerable. In addition, the team morale would soar if he accepted their recommendation regarding the ship's name on the jacket. It was win–win, both directly for the crew and indirectly for the captain; a definite long-term gain. The short-term pain would be the challenge he would get from his superiors when they saw that he had decided to use a jacket that wasn't created by the US Navy.

After weighing it up, the captain decided that the case for adopting the jacket was too strong to be ignored. He told the crew to proceed with the development of enough jackets for each of the crew and to provide him with one too.

This decision had a considerable impact on crew morale. The jackets were adopted and were worn with pride. Where previously the crew had had to be told to keep their jackets in a serviceable condition, repairing rips and tears, now they did this voluntarily.

The next time the captain was faced with a complex but unfamiliar challenge, he adopted the same strategy; he gave the challenge to the crew, but always with strict parameters. On every occasion the crew came up with a workable solution that always exceeded his, by now, high expectations. He adopted all of their ideas, some occasionally with a degree of adjustment, and morale soared.

In the first evaluation of the crew's engagement since the captain had taken over, the results were totally different from a year before. The ship now had one of the most engaged crew's in the US Navy. Not only were their engagement scores high, but their performance in exercises and operational activities had also improved out of line with any reasonable expectation.

There is one final element to this story, which is worth noting here. Some time after the jackets were introduced, the captain was challenged by his boss, who told him the men must take off their non-regulation jackets and replace them with the officially approved version. When the captain refused to obey this order, he was threatened with court martial.

His reply to his boss?

'If you're going to court martial me for implementing an idea that has saved the US Navy nearly $60 per item and which has made a direct contribution to some of the highest engagement scores in the US Navy, go ahead.'

It was a brave move. The captain himself took the short-term pain for long-term gain. He took the pain as opposed to his team taking the pain.

Although executive decision-making authority always rests with the leader (the buck after all, stops at the top), outlining the scope of the issue and any parameters within which the team must operate when tackling complex and unfamiliar decisions, is the inspired choice. Try it yourself and once you've got the team on board, ask them to evaluate the short-term pain alongside the longer term pleasure in their options.

In the commercial world, I have seen weak leaders introduce consensus when it wasn't necessary or appropriate.

Of course, one of the key aspects of decision-making is that we don't always get weeks or days to weigh them up, even if they are complex and unfamiliar. Sometimes, decisions need to be made under stressful situations. Despite this, the same rules should always apply.

Let me give you another example from my time in Angola. When the mine was attacked in October 1992, we were not in a position to defend it and were forced to withdraw into the bush, about three quarters of a mile from the mine. Once everyone was accounted for,

I had a decision to make. Because the attack had come in unexpectedly, we didn't have the clothing, footwear or equipment to attempt to escape to either Zambia or Zaire. This could have been an option, albeit a risky one, if we'd had the right kit, but we didn't. As the leader of these people, my only purpose then was ensuring their and my survival. Whatever this took, I was going to have to do it and fast. The only real option I had was to walk back into the villa of Luzamba and attempt to speak to the rebel commander in a bid to persuade him to treat my men fairly.

Was I scared returning to camp and speaking to the commander? Of course I was, but a quick appraisal of my options told me that this was the one that was likely to get the best long-term outcome. If I had sat in the bush and not made a decision, my credibility as a leader would have been lost forever. I could have sought consensus from the team, but there was no benefit in doing that in these circumstances. In this situation, I actually needed to remove the idea of consensus and take away the prospect that I was going to ask for input. There was no point; I knew what the best option was. I needed to get on and take action.

In the commercial world, I have seen weak leaders introduce consensus when it wasn't necessary or appropriate. The reason they did this? They wanted to give themselves an opportunity to avoid having to make a tough call. Making tough calls is part of leadership, though. Too often, leadership teams debate key issues in their businesses and, as they start to identify the possible solutions, you can actually see them analysing the possible results and the implications, for them as individuals, of making what is seen as a bad call. We all know that you need hindsight to establish with certainty whether the correct decision has been made. As we know hindsight is a wonderful thing or, as a friend of mine in Dublin said, 'hindsight is the foresight of a gobshite,' and I agree.

There are, of course, two steps to any decision-making process. The first step is to make the decision based on the different options outlined above and the second is to communicate that decision and make sure it happens the way you'd like it to. Whether he knew it or not, the captain from the example earlier employed what some people know as the eastern front decision-making process, particularly when it came to communicating the alternatives.

For those unfamiliar with the eastern-front process, let me recap. In the Second World War, the Eastern Front developed a reputation for being an extremely unpleasant place to be. For a start it was incredibly cold. Minus 50 degrees wasn't uncommon and German soldiers weren't equipped for that type of temperature. Life was very hard and then there were the Russians, who were hell-bent on revenge and being driven mercilessly by their own leadership.

The Western Front was still a battlefield, but while the chances of dying were still fairly high they weren't quite as awful as the Eastern Front. The weather was a bit better and the British and Americans were perceived to be better people to fight against than the Russians.

In the art of decision-making where all your courses of action come with a price, as opposed to a prize, the eastern front strategy works as follows: You begin by describing the set of circumstances that are the least appealing; in other words, the eastern front. It is made very clear this is an option, but the strategy is designed to play on everyone's dislike for it and to encourage them to think about any alternatives that you might have for them. If the eastern front version is delivered with sufficient clarity, the western front explanation will seem like a far better bet than if you just led with the western front option in the first instance.

The US Navy captain who had to communicate to his boss his refusal to give a direct order to ditch the non-regulation jacket chose this tack. The eastern front choice was inviting the senior man to put him into a very public court martial for letting his team create a jacket that was more comfortable and safe, not to mention cheaper than the regulation one. The western front choice was to embrace everything they had achieved.

A good example of well-communicated decision-making concerned a regional manager in a retail bank. He took over a part of the business that had forty-six branches and about six hundred people, spread over a sizeable geographical area. The business hadn't been doing well, sales were poor and staff engagement was awful. On the plus side though, the new regional manager had been an area manager before undertaking a planning role in head office. He knew the nuts and bolts of the business very well.

As soon as he was in the role, the new manager's first step was to give all of his people absolute clarity on when and how he would come and talk to them. His staff knew immediately that they would see and hear him face to face. With forty-six teams it was going to take some time, but he created a plan so that everyone knew exactly when he was going to be in their branch.

Having set the expectation, the next step was to decide what he was going to say. His approach was to focus on building the engagement of his teams. He spent time with his branch managers to help him define the strategy for engaging their people. He refined their ideas into three components of a plan focused on an iterative approach to developing their team, their customers and their results.

Before he engaged with his people face to face, he reconvened the leadership team and shared his vision.

When he visited their branches for quarterly meetings he asked each manager to tell him what progress they were making to develop every member of their team, how this was benefitting their customers and what impact this was having on their results. He made it very clear he expected to be able to track their progress. Once the managers understood his approach, he engaged face to face with his people for no more than ten minutes. Rosters were agreed to enable him to have time with every member of his team.

His message was simple. He valued all of them and wanted to invest in their professional and personal development. He wanted them to learn new skills, to contribute their ideas and to be able to fulfil many functions in the business. He reminded them this would make them very employable if they wanted to change their roles and would protect them against uncertainty in the banking sector.

Everyone understood the strategy; if they contributed to growing their knowledge, skills and confidence, everyone would benefit. When this regional manager met his branch managers, he was able to track progress and this was the starting point for all their meetings. He kept an eye on their business results, of course, but his main focus was on how business lines were doing. If a business line wasn't doing well, he expected his managers and their teams to have a recovery plan.

In the three years that he led the region, he stuck to

the same focus. Engagement scores were the best out of the eleven regions in the business and his team were in the top two for all business lines during his tenure. Inevitably, before long, someone wondered if he would be able to deliver the same performance with a bigger team. At the time of writing, he now has a team of 1250 people and his strategy hasn't changed.

He summarised it to me this way: 'My objective was to minimise the short-term pain for long-term pleasure that most change programmes require. I needed my managers to engage with their people so that the teams would see short-term pain for long-term pleasure. My managers were amazed at how readily everyone committed to a tailored and stepped development plan. The mood in the place shifted almost immediately and we've never looked back'.

SUMMARY

1. Decision-making usually breaks down into one of three categories: simple and familiar; complex and familiar; and complex and unfamiliar.
2. Frequently, there is a need to suffer short-term pain for long-term gain. You must be prepared for that.
3. It is a mistake to seek consensus as a delaying tactic to avoid making tough calls.
4. Pay attention to how you communicate your decision; it can be just as important as the decision itself.

PERSONAL DEVELOPMENT EXERCISES

EXERCISE ONE

Understand the decision-making process

Business benefit

The team will understand the decision-making process

Resources

Format

Begin by asking the team to identify one aspect of their life that they would like to develop but haven't done anything about, e.g. fitness, weight loss, increasing energy. Assure them that they won't have to make the topic known to you or anyone else.

Ask them to identify and write down at least five things that are good about their current state of affairs. Next, can they list ways the current situation might develop over the next five years? Then ask them to write down what the impact will be in ten years' time if they have done absolutely nothing about the matter they have identified. Finally, get them to write down one small thing they could change immediately that would make a contribution to achieving their goal.

Emphasise that they should focus on one thing that is easy to do but does make a difference.

Before the session concludes, ask the team

»

to identify, for themselves, the reason why they might be prepared to make the one small change and why it matters to them. The aim is to help them to understand how they have arrived at their decision.

PERSONAL DEVELOPMENT EXERCISES

EXERCISE TWO

Understand the decision-making process

Business benefit

The team will develop additional skills

Resources

Time at a team meeting/one to one

Format

In a team meeting, or one to one, explain you are going to take them through an exercise that will help them make a decision about the development of one capability that will make a big difference to their professional performance.

Help them discuss and choose a capability, which will be one that they know will add value, but under normal circumstances, they would have done nothing about.

Once they have agreed a topic, ask them to consider and then write down what impact doing nothing about the development of this capability

»

will have for them: first in five years' time; then ten years' time; and finally fifteen years' time. Allow them a couple of minutes to complete each timeframe.

When the team have completed the three stages, ask them to put a deadline on taking the first step and tell you what they have decided. Make a note of the timescale and tell the team you will follow up at the appropriate time.

Before the session concludes, ask the team to identify the reason why they are prepared to make the one small change and why it matters to them.

CHAPTER 17

FEAR MEANS GO – DON'T HESITATE

Fear is a feeling that can inhibit action and cause paralysis. It comes in many forms too. In the corporate world there is the ever-present fear of failing, together with the fear of embarrassment and even fear of rejection. Within those natural human emotions, there are many other sub-categories of fear that can creep up on us and stop us in our tracks– if we let them.

Right now we need to tackle the thorny issue of what to do when a course of action terrifies you. Even though you know something needs to be done and it is for the good of the company, it just makes you feel weak-kneed at the thought. For some people it may be tackling a sensitive subject with a valued client, for others it might be reducing headcount. Or, there could be a thousand other different reasons. We are talking about an action that ties you up in knots and stops you short. Or, even if you are able to tackle whatever it is that scares you, your deep-set feelings may even impair performance.

If you don't face-up to this potentially damaging emotion, your day-to-day fears will blight what might otherwise be a very exciting and fruitful period of leadership.

To begin with, it may help to explore a little more about fear. After all, there is little point in saying that whatever it is that worries you probably won't turn out to be that bad in the end. Deep down, you probably already know that.

It is very common to mix-up, or confuse, other emotions with fear. If you don't know what you are dealing with, it is very difficult to, well, deal with it. For example, many people tie themselves in knots far in advance of something they fear. This expectation is not fear in itself. It is anxiety; this is an expectation that something is going to be unpleasant. Fear is the reality of actually confronting something that is unpleasant. The two emotions need to be tackled in different ways.

Think about it the context of someone who is about to deliver a speech to a large group of their peers in two weeks' time. The chances are he may feel uneasy about the task ahead. That is anxiety. He will be in anticipation mode and, for some reason, is making the assumption that his speech is not going to go well. Conversely, if in two weeks' time, this same character is standing at the podium and about to speak, he is now on the cusp of the experience so that now qualifies as fear.

I've made this point with a number of corporate clients over the years, in particular in the run up to a big presentation, or new business pitch, and have had interesting results. Any major presentation or new business event can be stressful because the party involved will either win or lose. If they win there is usually some sort of financial incentive or bonus, while if they lose they will inevitably be exposed to scrutiny. It doesn't matter if the parties doing the pitching are experienced teams; this still doesn't guarantee they are anxiety free in the days leading up to the pitch.

Experience has shown that, for some reason, most people find acknowledging they are anxious less threatening than acknowledging that they are scared. There seems to be an almost universal reluctance to accept fear. While most people reluctantly admit to experiencing anxiety, they do feel reassured when they are told that the discomfort they are experiencing in the lead up to a big event is just anxiety. This is a very important first step. It proves that if you can break-down the emotion and recognise it for what it is, it is easier to embrace and deal with it. Once you tackle the anxiety, it is much easier to tackle the fear.

My approach with teams I work with is to first help

them understand the difference between fear and anxiety. This realisation is followed by intense preparation. For the next stage of my plan, I ask the team to pitch without any form of interference. Then, once the team has achieved a good standard of performance, I make life more difficult for them with constant disruptions. They never know how they are going to be disrupted, but just know the disruption will come. I use video cameras to record their responses to my interruptions and then show them the videos. The exercise shows there is often a huge disconnect between a presenter's perception of how they've managed disruption and the reality. People automatically assume they haven't done as well as they wanted. The video camera demonstrates that even though they felt uncomfortable and believed that they didn't perform to their best abilities, they still managed to get a good outcome.

Most people find acknowledging they are anxious less threatening than acknowledging they are scared.

This strategy is hugely effective in showing presenters that while it is possible to feel anxious and, indeed, they probably will feel this way, they need not worry about being perceived as an accomplished presenter. Anxiety can be easily managed.

But, what if it is not anxiety at all? What if it is an all-consuming, mind-numbing, fear? It does happen and

I have personally come across many examples of people being literally paralysed by anxiety or fear. The most extreme manifestation of this I have witnessed is during firewalking exercises.

I am accredited firewalking instructor, authorised by the Fire Institute to run firewalking seminars. I first became interested in this discipline after a seminar in London in 2008. One aspect of the seminar was an opportunity to complete a firewalk. We were put through six hours of extensive preparation before being taken outside to a fire-lane. We were encouraged not to look down at the fire-lane as we walked across barefoot and to think of walking on cool moss as we did so. I was torn between doing what I had been told to do and trying to feel if my feet were experiencing any heat. It took me five steps to walk the length of the fire-lane and when I got to the other side and my feet were hosed down I wasn't sure whether I had walked on a real fire or not.

Despite that uncertainty, it was a good experience and like other experiences I have had in my life in the army and Angola, the anticipation was worse than the actual event. I was curious about firewalking. My curiousity took me to Sweden in the summer of 2008 to attend the accreditation course. At this point, I had no intention of using firewalking at any of my events.

Part of the accreditation was a challenge to walk

across a ten foot fire-lane 108 times in succession. The instructors assured us it was possible. I've always liked challenges, but I do remember watching the fire burning and thinking that it looked longer than ten feet and incredibly hot. We were told we would cross the fire about thirty times before we had to stop and rake in new, hot, embers to ensure that it stayed hot.

The five students there on the course all managed thirty crossings before the new, red-hot embers were raked in. Once this was done satisfactorily, one other student and I both started walking across the rejuvenated lane again. What surprised me was that the other three students didn't move. For some reason, they couldn't bring themselves to resume the firewalk again, despite the fact that we had only stopped for about three minutes. My colleague and I did what we could to get them to make just one more crossing on the basis that if they did one more, they'd do lots more. However, they wouldn't change their minds. Only two of us completed the 108 crossings.

When I spoke to one of the guys afterwards, he told me he just couldn't re-engage. He was, in his own words, paralysed with fear and couldn't explain it. Even though he could see the pair of us crossing repeatedly, it seemed so dangerous he just couldn't do it.

Following my accreditation, I now run my own firewalking events. Unlike a lot of other companies in this field, I encourage attendees to walk across the fire up to three times. I work hard to produce a fire that is hot but not so hot that people will be badly burnt. I use a thermometer to measure the heat and show the temperature to the firewalkers. I don't want to hide anything from them.

The first time is always the worst. I don't shout at people when they are about to firewalk. On the contrary, I am very calm. I tell them that they are capable of it and that they just need to take one step. I move their focus from walking across the fire to just taking one step. This seems to work.

People are usually in a state of high anxiety before they complete their first firewalk and literally grow in confidence when they complete one for the second and third time. For me, this is a great example of people stretching their comfort zones. The first firewalk is a step outside the comfort zone. By the time they have completed three crossings of the firelane, this activity has become part of their comfort zone. Some people are almost blasé on the third crossing, while very few are blasé on the first crossing. Each person who completes the firewalk has confronted a fear and overcome that fear.

If your role requires you to act, or to lead, by example, then being paralysed by fear or anxiety is something you must work to overcome. If you feel fear, yet stretch yourself, you'll inevitably discover new limits. If you find these new limits, you will grow as a person and this can be a very enlightening experience.

My biggest taste of this was during my four and a half month tour of the Falklands in 1986. One of my unit's principle tasks on West Falkland was guarding two radar sites, one at Byron Heights and the other at Mount Alice. We used to spend a week on the radar sites rotating camp duties, settlement patrolling and training.

Three months into our tour, our commanding officer decided that it would be a good idea to move our Company from Fox Bay to Port Stanley. The night before we left we celebrated our prospective move to the relatively 'developed' town of Port Stanley with a somewhat liquid leaving party. I remember leaving the sergeants' mess at one o'clock in the morning very much the worse for wear.

It felt like I had only had my head down for three or four minutes before I was shaken awake by my colleague, who was telling me that we had been 'stood to', which means that we'd moved to a war footing; this is, of course, very serious. The Commander of British Forces Falkland Islands had put the whole of the Island security force onto red alert.

Over the course of an eventful morning, it emerged that a Chinook had crashed, at least one person had been killed and many injured. I immediately grabbed my kit and ran to the waiting Sea King helicopter. As we flew towards the crash site, I started to think about what we might find when we got there. I assumed the worst. I had never seen the results of a helicopter crash, but I had to prepare myself that I would be confronted by dead and badly mutilated people. This unsettled me and I started to feel physically sick. I wasn't sure how I would react to what I would see on the crash site. These people weren't strangers after all; they were friends and colleagues.

I made a decision to stop speculating about what I was going to see and instead think about how I would deploy the men when we landed. I focused on my first aid training and how we had to make sure the men were safe from any additional hazards such as fire, or an exploding airframe, before we started to attend to their injuries.

My second in command was sitting beside me and I shouted over the noise of the helicopter to explain what I thought we were going to have to do. This planning and shouted conversation was the distraction I needed at that time. My focus had switched from worrying to problem-solving.

We were all straining to see our first glimpse of the crash site. When we did eventually see it, about three or four hundred feet below, the enormity of the situation sank in. The large twin rotor Chinook was lying on its side and both sets of rotors had completely disappeared. The snow and ice around the crash site were stained the most vivid colour of red. My worst anxieties were being confirmed.

There had been four RAF members of the crew and twelve Gurkhas in the troop-carrying compartment. It's likely that the helicopter had hit the mountain and bounced forward at speeds in excess of one hundred knots. We had had no information regarding casualties, but I now expected them to be very heavy. As I looked out at the scene I had to ask myself how I was going to cope with this.

Once we landed I was told that one of the RAF loadmasters was dead and the other one was badly injured. The pilot had been thrown out through the front of the helicopter and was still fastened to his seat. The co-pilot was stuck in the wreckage of the cockpit. The twelve Gurkhas in the back of the aircraft were still alive but were very badly injured.

We picked the three most seriously injured casualties, which included the platoon sergeant, and loaded them onto the Sea King. Sergeant Toya Bahadur was doing his best to refuse all of our efforts to get him into the Sea King. He was very seriously injured but adamant that he would not be separated from his soldiers. Tragically, he later died of his injuries and I was truly gutted.

We endured between six and seven hours of almost

complete chaos at the crash site as we loaded all of the remaining casualties into the second Chinook helicopter. All of the men were in a very bad way. It didn't help that their advancing states of hypothermia meant it was virtually impossible to establish intravenous drips because we couldn't find veins in their arms.

Left behind, my men and I worked to help the injured onto another Chinook, but soon discovered the helicopter had damaged rotors, so we had to work fast to transfer them to another one, while keeping its rotors turning to ensure the same thing didn't happen again. This was a hell of a job and made all the more difficult because the rotors on the damaged Chinook were flapping in the high winds. If a stretcher party had been hit by rotor, more people would have been killed.

The eleven men we managed to bring in that day were all badly hurt, but they survived. The sad conclusion to this whole episode was that as well as Toya Bahadur, two other members of the Royal Air Force lost their lives as a direct result of the crash. Everybody else survived and was able to return to normal active service.

My experiences in those twenty-four hours taught me many things about fear and anxiety. If you begin with the attitude that things might change, then you'll be prepared to react when you need to. That way, when it does go wrong, it won't be a big shock.

The most effective way I had to manage my own

fear was to get as fully involved in what was going on as possible. Taking action to rescue and save my injured colleagues was all I could do. This helped me overcome my fear when it could easily have paralysed me into inaction. When you are immersed in trying to make the best out of something, your entire focus shifts from the problem through to building the best solution imaginable. This shift ensures that you then focus on the positives and not the negatives.

I undoubtedly suffered some form of traumatic disorder in the weeks that followed the crash. However, the most important thing was that, when the chips were down, I was able to function and indeed take control of the rescue effort. If I am totally honest, I was initially absolutely terrified.

While there is no comparison between attending a helicopter crash and establishing your own business, when I did set up the business in October 2001, three or four days after the premature birth of my first son, I know that I experienced a lot of fear and self-doubt. My strategy for coping with both the fear and the doubt was to keep myself distracted. I made sure that I got up early, had an extensive list of things to do, which was easy, and worked relentlessly on the activities that would help us to be successful. I also made sure to keep a list of all of the things I had achieved on a daily basis. This meant that at the end of the day I was able to reassure myself that we were making progress.

Full immersion in a process is one of the most effective ways to combat fear. Shying away from what needs to be done, or avoiding it altogether, only amplifies the initial feeling. It also opens the way for a whole load of new fears.

In my corporate work, I am constantly amazed when people are not prepared to step up because they don't feel up to the job, or believe there is a possibility they may damage their credibility in front of their people. Very often, these same business leaders and managers are very demanding of their own people, fully expecting them to take risks themselves. Indeed, they can often be impatient with those lower down the ranks who don't step forward themselves. They may even use fear as a control mechanism, or to 'motivate' their people. While most people need a kick up the backside from time to time, consciously creating fear to try and get them to do what is needed is a very misguided strategy.

> All bullies ever really achieve, in addition to making everyone around them unhappy, is to inhibit some potentially good work.

When I was on secondment to a British unit back in my army days, one boss used this approach with the men. This boss seemed to have a massive 'chip on his shoulder' for some reason and, as a result, treated our soldiers in a very disrespectful way. He constantly picked them up on the minutest detail, predominantly on stuff that really didn't matter at all.

Hardly surprisingly, my men feared him. The implication of this behaviour was that they avoided him at all times and when they did meet him, they told him what they thought he wanted to hear. This wasn't how I ran my platoon. If something was wrong, I wanted to know. If an issue was going to be left to fester, I wanted to sort it out.

One day, my Sergeant told me that one of our men, a private soldier, was having a problem at home. His wife was experiencing post-natal depression. In the Gurkhas, a compassionate case like this always gets priority and rightly so. I was taught that it is better to have the wool pulled over your eyes ninety-nine times than get one of these cases wrong. I obviously knew the soldier and wanted to get him back home in record time. I spoke to my boss and told him that we could cover a quick run home for the private.

'He's useless,' said my boss. 'Tell him to piss off.'

I shared this with my sergeant. He told me that there was a car that went back into our barracks every day, we could get the lad into this car and he could have an hour or so with his wife. It was my call; I was his direct boss. I didn't hesitate for a moment and took the decision to send this lad back. I was taking the law into my own hands and was happy to do so.

Why was I prepared to do this? I was, after all, going against my boss's wishes. I didn't use fear to make my men do what I wanted them to do. On the contrary, I treated my men with respect and, while I was demanding of them, their welfare was a very high priority. 'Look after your men and they will look after you' is a fair mantra.

As luck would have it, the car that was carrying this private broke down and the boss found out about the deception. I won't describe what he said to me. He shouted and swore and swore a bit more, all in full earshot of the men. He never once asked me why I had done it, or how the soldier's wife was.

What would I do if I was faced with the same issue again, knowing that it might go against me? I'd do exactly the same thing. In my view, I did the right thing.

People who act in the way this boss did in the workplace are bullies and all bullies ever really achieve, in addition to making everyone around them unhappy, is to inhibit some potentially good work. I'd like to think that my soldiers respected me before that event. I didn't make the decision to curry favour though. I made it because it was the right thing to do, for that one lad and for the rest of my people. If your team believes you will look out for them, rather than trying to force them into submission, they will look out for you.

It is the job of a good leader to build confidence among those around them and part of that means removing fear. That needs to start close to home.

SUMMARY

1. Learn to differentiate between fear and other emotions such as anxiety. Then deal with each one appropriately.
2. When you do experience full, paralysing fear, stretch yourself by throwing yourself into what scares you and getting as fully involved as possible.
3. Don't ever be tempted to use fear as a tool to motivate, or subdue your team. It will always backfire.

PERSONAL DEVELOPMENT EXERCISES

EXERCISE ONE

Fear means go

Business benefit
The team will remove the concept of fear of failure

Resources
Time at a team meeting

Format/Context
Talk to the team about the concept of fear. Tell them the only way to overcome a fear is to confront it. This is easy to say, but most people then reply by asking:

'What if I fail?'

»

Explain you believe in win/learn/change as a strategy for overcoming fear, specifically the fear of failure. Win/learn/change simply means that when you undertake any form of challenge, you must initially take time to understand your goal and, most importantly, you must know why it is important to you. When you know this you can identify a series of small steps to start to make progress towards your goal. In considering your first step, you must specify what achieving that goal will be like; if you don't, you won't know whether you've achieved it or not. Then take action. Go and do it and measure the results that have been achieved.

The aim is to get the outcome that the individual wants, which we call 'a win'. If, however, 100 per cent of the outcome is not achieved, they should note what has gone well, because that is still a win. If there is something that hasn't gone quite so well, that is what we call 'a learn'. It means an individual has just had a very valuable lesson. They should identify why it was a learn, then modify or change their approach and take action again.

This process of win/learn/change will enable people to eradicate the concept of failing completely, ensuring that they can undertake any activity safe in the knowledge that the worst thing that can happen is that they will learn.

Ask the team to think of examples where they have taken action towards a particular goal but not achieved what they set out to achieve. Ask them to think about the lessons they learnt from

»

this experience and, where possible, ask them to explain how they have used that learning in other aspects of life.

Take feedback.

PERSONAL DEVELOPMENT EXERCISES

EXERCISE TWO
Fear means go

Business benefit

The team will remove their fear of failure

Resources

Time at a team meeting/one to one

Format

Ask the team to think of one fear they hold in open forum and note the fears on a flipchart (unless people would rather not share the fear). Encourage them to identify how they would feel if they were able to overcome this fear.

Now ask the team to identify five steps they could take to confront that fear. Encourage them to make the first step simple and easy to achieve, while still relevant. When the team have their five steps, ask for feedback on the first step only.

When you have insight into the various first steps that the team have identified, ask them when they might undertake that step. Without forcing

»

anyone to take an action that they really don't want to take, ask the team to engage with you to go forward and confront that fear.

The goal is for the team to come up with a plan. While they might still feel challenged by their fear, the only way to confront it is to do precisely that, confront it.

CHAPTER 18

NO PLAN SURVIVES FIRST CONTACT

The battle for Goose Green during the Falklands War in 1982 was planned with seven stages. These stages, as in any combat situation, indicate the commander's view on how the battle will unfold. They are usually interdependent, meaning stage two can't occur until stage one has been completed successfully, and so on.

As it turned out, the whole plan for the attack on Goose Green changed during the implementation of stage one. Despite a huge amount of contingency planning and numerous hours being spent on trying to second guess what could go wrong, something that no one could have predicted did happen. As the Paras launched the first phase of what was supposed to be a seven-stage assault, they encountered higher numbers of enemy than they were expecting, lost a number of senior leaders and had very little cover to use to support their advance. These three challenges meant that the commanders on the ground had to revise the plan, on the hoof, while in the middle of a battle.

This story is just one of many in military history that proves the view firmly held by anyone in this sphere that no matter how good the plan, as soon as anyone starts to implement it, the plan will become ineffective to some extent. The scenario is not unique to the armed forces, though. It occurs in nearly every walk of life too and no less so in business. It is how you react to those unexpected changes which threaten to seriously disrupt the achievement of your goals that separates those who will be successful and those who just manage to survive.

Well-run businesses spend a lot of time planning, just the same as any well-run military unit. The planning process involves identifying goals, communicating these goals, often to a lot of people and engaging people to the creation of the plan.

The objective of planning is to create a strategy that, in the ideal world, will be implemented to the letter. Everyone wants a good plan to succeed as expected. However, if you go one step further and accept this hardly ever happens and are fully prepared for that and can deal with it, you should still get a good outcome. Accepting that when the plan is then implemented it will almost certainly need some adjustment is not a limiting belief, far from it

This was certainly something that came to mind

when I first went to Angola in late 1991. The moment I arrived in the mining town of Cafunfu, on the Cuango River, I was more than a little taken aback with what I saw. The airfield terminal that greeted me and my team of Gurkhas was an old container, the type you see on a forty-foot lorry. As we got off our small plane, we were met by a member of the local mining police, complete with an AK47 assault rifle slung casually over his shoulder. Seeing AK47s everywhere would become the norm quite quickly but, at this stage, it was new and a little unsettling.

The person who was supposed to be meeting us was unable to do so. He had been called away to deal with an incident at the mine we were about to go to. It turned out that the chief of the mining police had just been shot dead by one of his staff. Apparently, there was a disagreement about which members of staff were allowed on a truck that was being used to ferry people from Luzamba to Cafunfu. The chief of the mining police had climbed up onto the truck and started trying to get people off by slapping them with his hand and then hitting them with his baton. At some stage, one of the people on the truck got the chief's pistol out of its holster and shot him. He died about ten minutes later.

Wow.

By now I was starting to wonder about the fifteen men I had with me. While we had a job to do, my major concern was making sure that nothing happened to any of them. My view about my ability to achieve this objective was starting to be challenged, as were my perceptions of a place that I didn't yet know. This made me uneasy.

My men would be providing industrial security to the diamonds during the extractive mining process. We had recruited mature men who'd be good at being vigilant for long periods of time. While these men were still Gurkhas, with all the strengths that go with their heritage and training, a lot of them were in their late forties and early fifties. Were they too old for the environment into which they were going to be pitched?

> In most plans there are interdependencies, just as there are in military strategies with their various stages. For B to happen, then A must happen the way we expect it to.

As I was thinking about this, one of the senior Gurkhas came out and stood beside me on the veranda. His name was Prem and he'd served in a rifle regiment for over thirty years. Prem was closer to sixty than fifty and I was already starting to worry about his ability to withstand this place.

'Well Paddy, things appear to be a little different to the original brief,' he said in a completely unflustered way. 'This place reminds me of Malaya, except there's more rubbish.'

In the nicest possible way, Prem was reminding me

that he, and the other men in the team, had been to places like this before. I was the new boy. I was grateful for this.

'I think we're going to have to revise the plan Prem,' I said.

'Sure, wasn't that always going to be the case,' he said, with a twinkle in his eye.

It was at this moment I really understood for the first time that I was leading a small team that would have to work unsupported by any other units, or people, in a very hostile environment. This was new to me. I had always led within a very well-defined framework. There had always been plenty of other officers to give me guidance. My ability to adapt to an ever-changing environment could mean the difference between life and death, for all of us. We were going to have to revise our plan in the knowledge that as soon we started to implement our new plan, it would not survive contact.

As I thought about this, I realised that the only thing that was really new was the lack of support. As a young officer I had been trained and practiced in the ability to both react and respond to external influences. Angola would be no different, but the stakes were higher.

If we got into bother, which seemed highly likely, we would have to get ourselves out of it. I knew I had to impress this on the team. They couldn't afford to think there would be back-up. When we conducted our planning we had to be certain that we had enough people on the ground to make us a formidable team. The moment I accepted I had to react to the changes in our circumstances as they happened, my task became instantly more manageable.

Of course, the obvious retort to the no plan survives first contact scenario is: If no plan really does survive contact, what is the point of planning in the first place? The answer lies in the level of detail that you seek to create within the initial plan. In the chapter that follows I will go into more detail on creating a plan, but let's for now look at the issue in a broader sense.

In most plans there are interdependencies, just as there are in military strategies with their various stages. For B to happen, then A must happen the way we expect it to. If A doesn't happen the way we expect it to, then B will be different and so will C, D and E, for example. However, what you need to bear in mind at all times is, although the plan might change, the direction in which you are seeking to take the team or business may not.

In chapter six the concept of strategic intent was introduced. In the example of the care home business, a team of people from the business were given the goal of achieving full occupancy in the homes. The goal came from the senior leadership team and was defined as the strategic intent for the business. Full occupancy would lead to greater profit which would allow the business to grow by taking over other homes, creating opportunities for promotion for people already in the business. The team from the business played a central role in identifying the four core elements they thought would generate full occupancy, as well as the teams of people from within the business who could deliver the strategy.

The benefits of planning at this stage were many:

- There could only be joined-up action with a plan. There were five separate homes. If the team were to grow occupancy, there had to be a consistent approach. How the business went about developing full occupancy would have a huge bearing on the quality of life of the residents. The residents' quality of life was their priority and also their brand. This was too important for unstructured, unplanned and ill-considered changes.
- Planning allowed other members of the team to make a contribution with their ideas. Many good ideas came from people who weren't in the leadership team.
- People who were involved in the planning inevitably talked about it when they were back in the homes they worked in. This created an interest from others, as they made their own contributions and a positive focus for everyone. All people in the team were now thinking of ways in which they could make a direct contribution with a great deal of clarity; this, in turn,

led to higher levels of engagement from the staff.

- Adopting ideas into the plan demonstrated to the people in the business that they were being listened to and that their ideas mattered.

The plan provided a reference point from which the business was able to track progress and monitor successes and lessons learnt. It did change as they encountered and overcame unforeseen challenges. However, their strategic intent didn't change. The direction they were taking didn't change, even though the route itself might have changed.

So, if you accept the need to plan and that a plan might change and indeed probably will, how do you react when things are obviously not going the way you expected?

When you encounter disruption to any plan, the first step is to accept that it has happened and remove, as quickly as possible, any form of emotional reaction. It is not unusual for plans to unravel as a direct result of actions that other people have or haven't done. If you feel let down, it is perfectly reasonable to experience some form of disappointment, but a good leader must strive to be even in their emotional response to things that don't go well. It is fine to be quietly disappointed, but there is nothing to gain and plenty to lose by giving way to unrestrained emotional outbursts in front of the team.

If you have taken action in pursuit of a specific goal and you haven't achieved your goal, don't blame other people. Too many organisations operate a blame culture. Indeed, in one company I worked with they said 'we don't have a blame culture, until something goes wrong'. In a blame culture, people spend huge amounts of time making sure that the implications of a bad decision cannot be traced back to them. This dilutes the focus on achieving the goal, leading to poor results. Forget appropriating blame.

Leaders have to encourage their people to take action with confidence. The reality of any action delivering exactly the result that you are looking for is extremely remote. This shouldn't stop people from aiming for perfection, but you can't beat people up when you get a less-than-perfect result.

The first step in dealing with plans that have not worked-out is to understand what has gone wrong. Usually, plans go wrong for one or more of the following reasons:

- The information that was used to formulate the plan was either incomplete, or wrong. A lesson my father taught me was to report facts, not opinions, and if I didn't know the answer to something to say so. When I was a reconnaissance platoon commander I impressed this upon my men. We knew what we were looking for when we recce'd an enemy position, but we had to be sure to only report on what we'd seen.
- The plan isn't communicated effectively. Here, a

senior leadership team may know what they want, but there is either ambiguity, or a lack of clarity, in what they are trying to achieve. For example, I once worked with a company in the Middle East and was told the strategic intent was 'productivity'. When I asked each of the five directors what they meant by productivity, they all said something different. If the five directors didn't know what they meant, what hope was there for their twenty-eight direct reports? If you don't understand the strategic intent, how can you plan? If you can't plan how can you engage your people?

- Ego. Ego is often an issue in the commercial world. People are less inclined to get behind someone else's plan than their counterparts in the armed services. Soldiers might grumble about a plan, but when push comes to shove they'll get behind it. Some managers I've worked with have even blatantly lied about what they are doing (or indeed not doing). They assume they know better, even though that is not always the case.
- Murphy's law – or, what can go wrong will go wrong. My own, personal, most ridiculous example of this rule occurred on an ops posting. Two of my men's radio antennae got entangled while we were in the back of a covert vehicle on the border in Northern Ireland. When we all tried to get out quickly and

quietly these two were literally joined at the shoulder. In the ensuing minutes there was a lot of messing around, which could have compromised our entire operation. They were eventually separated when one of my Corporals kicked one of them in the arse as hard as he could. You can't plan for that type of occurrence.

If appropriate corrective action is to be taken, you must know your starting point. Don't tie yourself in knots by making excuses for why things haven't gone to plan, or attempting to remove any possibility of blame. What you should be doing is accepting what has happened and getting on with finding a new way towards the original goal.

Even if you've had a bloody nose, you must still act with determination and commitment as you refine your plan. It is the ability to take the punches and come back fighting that separates great teams from average teams. As the leader, your ability to enable this to happen is a key leadership trait and skill.

Returning to my arrival in Angola, let me share with you how I changed my plan to accommodate the situation. Remember, my men and me were still reeling from the somewhat unsettling news of the death of the chief of the mining police. We also subsequently learned that the mob had turned on our new boss.

Myself and my senior Gurkhas had to reformulate

our plan, specifically how we would make an initial impression with the workforce. If we were too heavy handed, it would look as though we had been brought in as a direct result of the murder of the chief of the mining police. If we didn't make an impression, we would be on the back foot.

We agreed that seeking counsel from Rob, the man on the ground, would be the best course of action. He also told us that curiously, the murder of the chief of the mining police had calmed things down. A bigger issue would have existed if he hadn't been killed.

'If you are perceived to have done something wrong, the local people will do everything they can to get their revenge,' he told me. 'There is still a threat which we have to manage; you'll be a part of that.'

We agreed that the unpredictability of the situation was the key consideration. We couldn't make a concrete plan because we didn't know what was going to happen. There were sixteen of us destined to work closely with the diamonds, although production hadn't started and wouldn't start in earnest for another three weeks.

It was decided my team would have a presence on the ground, supported by Angolan security guards. My men would always operate in pairs and there would be two pairs in both of the key locations of the mine. That meant that eight men would be on the ground at any time. There would be a back-up group of men at all times in the operations room, and they could be deployed at any time if an issue was escalating. The men on the ground would not be armed and would exert a firm but friendly approach. The senior Gurkhas and I would do our time amongst them, as well as manning the operations room and visiting the two key locations on a consistent basis.

This plan was put into effect immediately. I am sure that having even sixteen Gurkhas on one site made everyone feel more secure. We built a good relationship with the Angolans quite quickly. This enabled us to change the plan again. We were able to reduce the number of people on the ground and place more people into reserve. This made life a little less onerous.

The success of the initial engagement in Luzamba demonstrates that when plans need to change it is not always negative. In the planning phase, people can only estimate how the plan might unfold. It is also possible that certain aspects of the plan will be achieved more easily than people might have imagined. While this is good thing, it still means the plan needs to be changed.

When I think about the leaders and the businesses that I work with, one trait that sets them apart is their ability to respond when things don't go the way they expected. Great leaders are like test pilots who take new or prototype aircraft up into the sky for the first flight. While the people on the ground will have done all they can to make the plane as safe as possible, there will always be unforeseen issues. When a test pilot is confronted by an issue they automatically go into issue resolution mode.

Of course, some of the most intrepid, brave and courageous test pilots were the men who first flew in space. A member of my family met Jim Lovell, the commander of the ill-fated Apollo 13, which was destined for a lunar landing; but the crew of Apollo 13 had to abort when an oxygen tank exploded, crippling the space craft. The three men inside were adrift in space with limited power, loss of cabin heat, shortage of water and few options. It was Jim Lovell who uttered the now famous line: 'Houston, we have a problem.'

When Jim Lovell was asked later on how the crew felt when they found out there was an issue, his response was: 'We had all been test pilots; we've been fixing things for years. We just started fixing this.'

Plans should have contingency built in but, most importantly, it is how people respond when the plan doesn't survive that will make the difference between success and failure.

I have consulted on a number of projects that have included the design and delivery of IT, specifically bespoke software solutions. In my experience there are consistent themes and challenges across all IT projects and they almost always relate to the disparity between the original view of the size of the challenge when the project was being scoped and the reality that's encountered as the plan unfolds. Very often, the petty politics that surround this mismatch will blight a project completely.

My first experience of this was at a marketing organisation, where one division was building new software from scratch. I was brought on board with no less than twelve senior consultants to ensure the new system landed perfectly. The moment we were brought in, the senior man who had recruited us visibly relaxed. It was clear to me his motivation for employing us was to have someone to blame if it didn't go to plan. The consultants were his buffer zone.

> The adage 'under promise and over deliver' is acknowledged to make a lot of sense. Why is it that people who know that all plans will require flexibility can't seem to apply it?

It didn't take long to discover that the software would be delayed, which isn't unusual in these projects. We duly reported back and were amazed at the ensuing debate which went on for days. The senior staff wanted to tell the team there was only a minor delay of a few weeks, or so. To me this was completely missing the point. While the management focus was entirely on whether or not we should delay, what they should have been concentrating on was the delivery of the software to a team who were not particularly technically savvy. In my view, the project success criteria were that the new IT platform would a) be readily taken up and b) there would be very few calls to the help desk. These were both measureable and seemed to be sensible goals to us.

It was soon clear that people in head office were prepared to compromise the success of the project to ensure an on-time delivery. I knew the target audience. The team was managing without the system at that time and could continue to do so for another six months, which was what we were going to need to deliver the project.

Finally, after much debate, we managed to convince the boss to change the plan so that we could deliver the best possible solution, even though this was going to mean a delay. In the meantime, three senior consultants, of whom I was one, spoke directly to the teams who were ultimately going to benefit from the platform. This plan was adopted, the delay did last six months and the delivery was seamless. Our two key success criteria were met and the business results improved immediately.

When I look back on the amount of time that was taken while people debated what should be done, I am still amazed. The adage 'under promise and over deliver' is acknowledged to make a lot of sense. Why is it that people who know that all plans will require flexibility can't seem to apply it?

SUMMARY

1. Everyone wants a good plan to succeed as expected, but it hardly ever does. If you prepare for that eventuality though, the outcome will still be good.
2. The fact that no plan survives first contact does not reduce the need for careful planning.
3. Don't waste time on the blame game when things don't go to plan. Get on with finding a viable solution.

PERSONAL DEVELOPMENT EXERCISES

EXERCISE ONE

No plan survives contact

Business benefit

You will further develop your team's ability to create new plans

Resources

Time at a team meeting/one to one

Format

Brainstorming exercise: Explain to the team that they have twenty-four hours to travel from their home location to a city at least five hundred miles away. The team should not travel by air to reach

»

the other location, but the budget is unlimited.

Ask them to agree how they plan to make the journey and allow five minutes for discussion in an open forum.

When the team have presented their idea to you, inform them that they now have a budget of just £25 per person. Tell the team that they have ten minutes to come up with an alternative plan for achieving the goal.

Take feedback.

PERSONAL DEVELOPMENT EXERCISES

EXERCISE TWO

No plan survives contact

Business benefit

You will further develop your team's ability to respond

Resources

Time a team meeting or one to one

Format

Divide your team into smaller teams and nominate a leader for each team. Give each team a simple challenge to complete such as creating the tallest tower possible, using eight pieces of flip chart

»

paper and some sticky tape. Allow twenty-five minutes to plan and complete the activity.

Ten minutes after the teams have started assembling their creations, tell them that they have only five minutes left to complete the exercise. Observe how the teams manage the reduction in time.

When the exercise has finished, take feedback on what they think they did well and what they would do differently if they faced the same challenge again.

CHAPTER 19

CREATING A PLAN THAT WORKS

One Sunday evening in Hong Kong, I was with six of my fellow young officers at a weekend retreat called Gurkha Haven. It was an old fisherman's house that had been made available to us so that we could escape for a couple of days from life in barracks, or in the field. We'd spent the day waterskiing, sailing and snorkelling before settling down for a beer and some freshly cooked food from the barbecue.

One of the officers there was called Peter. He was a good friend of mine. We'd been in the battalion together for over five years. Peter led the Mortar Platoon, which was a very important role. He had over seventy men in his platoon and their role was to provide fire support to the whole battalion.

Out of the blue, Peter said: 'I want to become a doctor.'

No one seemed particularly interested, so he pressed his point.

'I've been thinking about it for a while. I want to leave the army and become a doctor,' he stated, with real conviction.

This was the first I'd heard about this and I was probably his closest friend. I asked him what qualifications he had and it turned out his 'A' levels were in the classics.

'So you'd have to do more 'A' levels before you could even start your degree?' I said.

He said: 'I think I could get away with just doing biology and chemistry. It can be done in a year, if I work full time at it.'

Not only had he thought about it, he'd done some research.

'See how you feel in the morning,' said one of the other young officers, dismissively.

I knew Peter. I knew he'd feel the same way in the morning. The next morning we packed up and made our way to Gallipoli Lines, our barracks. Peter hadn't said anything to anyone that morning and when we got back, we all went our separate ways.

About three o'clock the following morning I was woken by Peter.

'I've just been on the telephone to an education authority in Oxfordshire,' he said. 'They will give me a grant of £600 per month. If I sell my motorbike and use public transport I should have just enough money to last me for a year.

'If I study full time, I should be able to get my two 'A' levels completed in one year. With this level of grant, I could be starting my medical degree in about fourteen months.'

But there was more. He'd already spoken to the senior officer in the battalion who had said he could be on his way back to the UK in three weeks if the Colonel accepted his resignation, which was quite probable. That is exactly what happened too. Within three weeks, all of the officers from our battalion were down at Kai Tak airport in Hong Kong for the traditional send-off for one of our friends. Peter shook hands with everyone and headed for the door. He didn't look back once.

Many months later, I visited Peter in Oxford. When we had been in Hong Kong discussing Peter's plans, the amount of time it was going to take him to qualify was a point of debate. Here we were, almost at the end of his A-level year, after which he would start his medical degree. The time had flown and even more so because he was immersed in a subject he loved.

We had different objectives and so were going in different directions. Peter was training to be a doctor. I wanted operational service with a highly trained unit within the British Army. When you analysed the principles of our plans, they were exactly the same.

If a leader is going to inspire people to undertake challenges that the person thinks is impossible, being able to share the component parts of a plan that will enable them to achieve their goal can provide the confidence needed to get started.

> 98 per cent of the people don't have goals and if they do, they haven't been created in sufficient detail, neither have they been written down.

There will always be challenges that need to be overcome by you and the people in your team. Challenges are often not as insurmountable as they seem, once you've started. The key to success is good planning. Defining a goal and believing that achieving it is possible are the starting point.

There are seven components to any plan:

1. Have a goal and take time to visualise it everyday: journey.
2. Take action: model excellence.
3. Bite-sized chunks: identify what you need to learn.
4. Evaluate your results: be prepared to change/win/ learn.
5. Be prepared to take a step back.
6. Invest in yourself.
7. Enjoy the journey.

HAVE A GOAL AND TAKE TIME TO VISUALISE IT EVERYDAY

This sounds so simple, yet 98 per cent of the people don't have goals and if they do they haven't been created in sufficient detail, neither have they been written down.

Everyone I've met has things that they want to achieve and things that they want to avoid. We've seen this in the chapter on the decision-making process. I had direct experience of this when making the decision to go back to Angola. My strongest motivator was the desire to avoid being considered a coward. I wasn't interested in being described as brave, but I was very concerned about my bravery being questioned.

In this example, making the choice that would help me achieve my goal was straightforward. I only had two real courses of action available to me. I could leave Africa and not go back to Angola, or I could take the risk and go back. My goal was clear and the choices were clear. Even if I had wanted to prevaricate, which for some people is an option, circumstances dictated that I had to react almost instantly. Prevaricating wasn't an option.

For most people, there is usually no pressure on them to create goals. Added to this is a perception that goals are only applicable in their professional lives. There can be an element of 'What's the point?' It is a real shame. Why do they have this attitude?

I liken some people's take on life to their being on

a raft on a relatively fast-flowing river. Most are pretty comfortable on a journey over which they think they have at least some control. They may, for example, experience white water occasionally, which would be both scary and/or exhilarating, depending on their response. It is difficult to steer a raft in white water, but if everyone pulls together, it is possible to make minimal changes to the raft's direction. White water is often endured, not enjoyed, so people live in the hope that the rapids will soon peter out and they will once more drift into a calm stretch of predictability. Others don't like calm water, finding it boring. They may even choose to deliberately steer into a tributary that looks a bit more exciting.

Having a plan can help people overcome the concerns about choosing the best course for them. It also means they can confront the unknown if they wish. It is impossible to do this unless you know exactly where you are going and that you really want to go there.

I have always had goals. I am a bit of a restless spirit and have never been satisfied with the status quo. These goals don't just encourage me to take action. They also give me absolute clarity on what I am trying to achieve before I start to act.

In the corporate world, there is frequently confusion between goals and targets. Even more unsettling is the fact that some businesses don't release the targets to their people until the accounting year is over a third complete.

I like targets because they give clarity on results, but leaders must be very good at helping their people to articulate their goals before targets can then be applied

When you have goals, you should take a moment to remind yourself why you have the goal and why you want to achieve it. This will help with keeping you focused and motivated.

TAKE ACTION

This point may sound incredibly obvious, but I raise it because of the number of people I meet in large companies who actually do have professional goals, but who are apparently unwilling to take action. The prime reason for it is usually fear of failing and/or being embarrassed if they aren't as successful as they would like to be.

I know this feeling. When I was working for a big company in 1999, I wanted to become self-employed. I had aspirations for a certain lifestyle and income and thought that the only real way I would be able to achieve that would be to set up my own business. In 1999, my wife and I both had really good jobs, earned very good incomes and lived in a really nice house in a beautiful part of England. Life was really comfortable on many levels and in some people's eyes we were successful. I toyed with the idea of taking the first step towards self-employment and went to speak to a training company in London. They offered me a job as a training consultant. This was to be my first step towards running my own business. I declined. It sounds appalling to say this, but it all looked a bit too much like hard work! I was working hard, no doubt about that, but I would have had to commute to south London from Buckinghamshire, I'd have been away from home a lot and wasn't going to be paid well until I started drumming up business for them. It was too easy to stay in my old role and so that's exactly what I did.

Within twelve months our professional lives changed in an instant, as so often happens. Our employer was taken over and I was given some cash while still keeping my original job. I was determined to use this spur to enable me to follow my goal and now I was prepared to act. With hindsight, I may have needed a boost like this to take the action I knew I needed to take.

When I speak to others about helping their people to change direction, the assumption that is often made is that the change has to be instant and drastic. It doesn't. Anyone who is about to make the change must be assured that most actions can be taken without unmanageable risk. Alternatively, if the risk is deemed to be too great, people will at best prevaricate and at worst do nothing.

BREAK THINGS DOWN INTO STEPS.

While the aim may be overnight success, it is worth recognising that any goal is best achieved by breaking it down into bite-sized chunks, or a series of steps. This simple technique can make an ambitious goal seem very achievable. The steps themselves may still be substantial, but having a route planner can be a great source of encouragement.

Let's take the example of Peter, whose story opened the chapter. He was twenty-eight-years old and had spent seven years being trained to be an army officer. Training to become a doctor was a substantial change in direction. The most important part of the change programme was his desire to achieve his goal. With the desire fuelling his change, Peter knew that he had to:

1. Leave the army.
2. Pass biology and chemistry 'A' levels.
3. Complete a medical degree.
4. Progress from House Officer to Consultant.

Time needed – probably about fourteen years.

Each of these steps had a number of component parts, some of which are substantial in their own right. Gaining a medical degree is no mean achievement on its own. I kept in touch with Peter as this journey progressed. I can honestly say that he loved every minute of it. His goal made all the effort very worthwhile.

NOTICE THE RESULTS

When you start to act, you get results. If you want to be sure that your actions are making a contribution to the achievement of your goal, you must be able to evaluate the quality of what you do with objectivity. If there is no objective measurement, you can't be sure that you're making progress.

People who achieve great things are rigorous in their evaluation of the results that they get. They look for evidence that they are doing things right (and wrong) and do not delude themselves if they are making mistakes. The aim is not to be too hard on yourself, but you must be very clear about your success criteria and be sure that you either get what you want, or that you learn from the experience.

Most great success stories involve people taking action, noticing their results, learning and then taking action again. This simple formula is at the heart of success and a leader's role is often to encourage those around them to ensure that they continue to take action.

People are often conditioned to focus on the things that go wrong. I've seen that when my sons come home from school with the results of a spelling test. They'll have got fourteen out of fifteen right, but if we're not careful we can fall into the trap of focusing on the one they got wrong. When I look back on all of the tests I've done, I'd very happily settle for fourteen out of fifteen as an average. I've chatted to people who think that it isn't necessary to give praise for the fourteen correct answers, because it is so obvious that they've done well. I've never seen a child or indeed an adult react negatively to sincere praise and thanks for a job well done.

As an aside, I've seen lots of insincere praise delivered, usually just before the criticism starts and it's very obvious that it is insincere. I've had it done to me and I don't like it. As the old saying goes, 'if you've got nothing good to say then don't say anything at all'.

I've seen lots of insincere praise delivered, usually just before the criticism starts and it's very obvious that it is insincere.

Good leaders make sure that their people do focus on all of the good things that they've done. This can require effort, because people can be naturally drawn to what has gone wrong. This is not to say you should ignore anything that has gone wrong. You should. However, always do so with the objective of understanding why it has gone wrong and what you can learn.

Analysing what has gone wrong in order to learn is something I refer to as win/learn. This means that when anyone takes action and notices their results, they either get the result they want, which is a win, or they learn.

This is the principle that removes failure. Of course,

the aim is always to get the outcome that is wanted and needed, but we must also accept that this will not happen all of the time and we will 'fail' or learn spectacularly on some occasions.

BE PREPARED TO TAKE A STEP BACK TO GO FORWARD

I am a fan of perseverance and dogged determination, but you must be going in the right direction. If you find that you aren't going in the right direction, you have to change. If this involves taking a step back then that is what you have to do. For me, too many people view a change in direction as failure. I don't agree with this at all. The world we live in is changing so dramatically that we have to be prepared to change and ready to take a step back to be able to go forward.

I worked with one senior leader on seven major change projects. He's an ambitious person, which means that he changes roles every couple of years. He called to tell me that he'd changed roles and that he envisaged our working together in the very near future. When I asked him what he thought we were going to do, he told me that the business he had joined had already made one attempt to re-structure and it hadn't worked. He had been in the new role for long enough to have gathered the evidence that he needed to make a business case for taking 350 people back to square one.

'It's easy for me,' he said, 'I wasn't part of the planning

team who got it so badly wrong when they started a year ago but some of my senior managers were and they are going to be part of the team when we re-launch'.

'What are they going to say?'

'That we got it wrong and we're going to start all over again; what else can they say?' was his response.

I admire honesty in senior leaders. It was clear that this was what had happened and taking the step back was actually a lot easier to communicate than any spin on what had been a bit of a disaster.

As I write, the change programme is in full swing. I played a small part in the launch of the new business and they are making great progress. This senior leader's people admired the way he stood up, and told them that 'we, the senior team' had got it wrong and that 'we' are now going to get it right.

ENJOY THE JOURNEY

There are some people who believe that if they can just get to their desired outcome or goal that everything will be all right once they reach it. They focus so intently on the goal and work so hard at achieving it that they forget to enjoy the journey. When they have finally achieved their goal, they find another one and start working doggedly towards the achievement of the new one.

Impatience can help people achieve goals, but a leader must ensure those around them are given the opportunity to enjoy the journey. Highly task-driven leaders can attract other highly task-driven followers. This usually results in a highly task-focused team, which is fine as long as the dynamic doesn't change. In my experience, teams that are solely focused on task run the risk of burning out and often don't devote enough time to staying up to date with changes in their sector or industry.

I've seen this in occur frequently in IT project management. Really good people are driven at a relentless pace for too long. Task-focused leaders don't allow people to enjoy the journey, preferring to drive out results. When I've analysed why some leaders adopt this approach, it is often because they don't know what else to do and, in some cases, can't be bothered to learn or adapt their style.

We know that success is a journey not a destination, so work at creating the situation whereby your people can enjoy each day, safe in the knowledge that what they do on a daily basis will make a direct contribution to the results ultimately achieved.

CELEBRATE AND SAY THANK YOU

The pace of life is hectic and demands on people are great. Good leaders will have teams of people who work damn hard on their behalf. They will work very willingly because they are committed to the team goal, their own goals and to the other people in their teams.

All being well, results will inevitably follow.

It's important to take time to say thank you and to celebrate success, but it doesn't happen often enough and regrettably budgets for this type of thing are getting tighter. Yet, the actual cost of doing something for a team often isn't that much in comparison with the goodwill it can generate. Conversely, not spending a relatively small amount of money can generate a lot of ill-will.

When I was working in Angola, it became clear my unit was going to be there for the festival of Dashain, which is a Hindu festival that we had celebrated in the army. Two of the senior Gurkhas, who were there with me, agreed that it would make a big difference if we were able to celebrate Dashain properly. I recalled that in Hong Kong I had been present when goats were sacrificed as part of the festival. This wasn't an absolutely necessary part of the celebration, but it would be a bonus if I were able to make this happen.

In the weeks leading up to Dashain, I spent my free time with an Angolan member of the Human Resources team who spoke the local dialect. My aim was to locate and purchase three black goats that could be sacrificed and made into curry. I had a number of adventures in the pursuit of this ambition and finally acquired three goats that were deemed suitable.

We were able to celebrate the festival in a way that was very close to the format that would have been followed in

Nepal. All of the team were involved and we enjoyed an evening of eating, drinking and dancing, Nepalese style. It was a real highlight of our time in Angola. My objective in investing my time in some dangerous parts of the local bush, seeking out goats, was to tell the Gurkhas in my team that I recognised the importance of their festival and to thank them for the efforts they had made on our behalf. The festival and the evening's celebration were talked about for a very long time afterwards.

It's important to take time to say thank you and to celebrate success.

A well-timed and sincere thank you takes very little effort but makes a huge difference. It is poor leadership to subscribe to the idea that 'it's their job, that's what they're paid to do'. Treat people the way you would like to be treated and that means saying 'thank you' and setting time aside so people can celebrate their achievements.

If leaders are to enable their teams to achieve demanding business goals, both the leader and the team are going to have to have a workable plan that inspires confidence. In chapter eighteen we addressed the fact that no plan survives contact. The principles that underpin effective planning acknowledge this and allow a high level of adaptability. Occasionally, business goals will change and leaders will have to refocus their people on the new goal. Helping the team to devise the new plan will encourage the engagement that leaders need if goals are to be achieved. The important part of this is to understand the need to plan in the first place.

The well known adage 'fail to plan, plan to fail' is known by most business people. The quality of both goal-setting and planning varies greatly among teams. However, when a workable plan is devised and implemented, there is always a very noticeable increase in results. It's that important.

SUMMARY

1. Have a goal that inspires you – the journey may well be very tough but if you know that you're going towards where you want to go, that will help
2. Take time to look forward to achieving the goal and the rewards that this achievement will bring
3. Enjoy the journey.

PERSONAL DEVELOPMENT EXERCISES

EXERCISE ONE
Creating the plan

Business benefit
You will have clarity on your goals

Resources
Your own time

»

Format
Think about your goals. Write down exactly what you want and by when and, most importantly, why your goals really matter to you. Then note what achieving your goal(s) will mean to the people around you.

Keep this document with you at all times, and take a minute or two to think about it everyday.

Identify the first step that you need to take to start your progress towards your goal. When you have taken this first step, email me at bryan@bryandunlop.com adding 'First step done' in the title bar of the email. We'll send you a download from our series on 'Creating Success' as a gift and to say well done.

PERSONAL DEVELOPMENT EXERCISES

EXERCISE TWO
Creating the plan

Business benefit
Your team will have the plan template

Resources
Time with the team

Format
The next time you need to create a plan for the

»

achievement of a team goal, give this responsibility to your team.

You should ensure that the team know the objective and why it is important. You should also agree the boundaries within which they must operate. Give the team the time they need to create their plan, which will then be presented to you by the team.

Unless you have real concerns about the plan, allow the team to implement their plan. Let the team know under what circumstances they should engage with you.

Each member of the team should keep a log of what they do, what goes well and what they learn in the process.

When the task has been completed the team should create and deliver a presentation on:

Their original plan

Which elements of the plan were implemented successfully

The changes they had to make

The lessons they have learnt as a direct result.

CHAPTER 20

RESPOND DON'T REACT

It's easy to be a great leader when everything is going well. What happens though, when things don't go to plan? The recent global economic crisis gave any observer of leadership behaviour a perfect opportunity to gauge what can happen when an average, or even weak, leader is thrown into unknown territory.

In the economic boom that preceded the bust, most, if not all, leaders found it very easy to deliver excellent results. Staff entertainment budgets were unlimited, conferences were lavish and bonuses were being shared across the entire business. Not surprisingly, everyone was happy, profits were great and these leaders were proclaimed as the ones driving extraordinary levels of success. Meanwhile, as the poor leaders were savouring the moment and believing their own hype, the truly great leaders were taking the time to understand that the situation was unreal and were attempting to establish when everything would return to normal.

When the wheels came off, the ineffective leaders struggled, immediately. Results dropped off a cliff, morale dived and the leaders didn't know what to do. Perhaps unsurprisingly, many didn't stay the course. Yet, the effective leaders dug in and reacted because they were fully prepared. They put their energies into keeping their people focused on the goals that mattered and re-emphasised why they mattered. After all, when the team is focused on the goal, it is far easier to harness their ideas and skills and make the goal a reality.

I've always been fascinated by how people react when times are tough. Average or poor leaders always struggle when suddenly everyone is under pressure and results aren't as easy to deliver. As results spiral down, they often don't know how to deal with the fall out, let alone regain their former position and generally react negatively. One of the worst manifestations of this sort of negative reaction can often be described as 'going off on one'. You know the sort of thing; it is when someone engages without much thought after they see or hear something they don't like. This is an emotional reaction, which may involve anger or aggression, or other equally unhelpful feelings. In other words, they explode and start ranting and raving.

This knee-jerk reaction usually exacerbates a usually

poor situation, particularly if a team is used to dealing with a relaxed and happy boss. Now, as well as knowing they have to tackle the issue that caused the explosion, they will also be faced by a leader whose reaction to any issue or challenge is to lash out at those around them.

This is clearly a poor approach for any leader to take. If a team knows the boss is quite likely to overreact when confronted with news that they don't like, they will either learn to avoid saying anything at all, or at the very least avoid telling the boss themselves. Whatever way you look at it, these are poor outcomes. At a time when a leader needs to know exactly what is going on, their behaviour is encouraging people to conceal information.

I worked with one leader in large telecoms business. I liked him and enjoyed his company. Yet, when as part of a consultancy project I organised a 360° feedback survey from his people, I was amazed to see how concerned they were about his lack of consistency. This clearly needed to be followed up. The general view was that the team didn't know which version of their boss was going to show up. It wasn't even as simple as which version of him was going to show up *each* day. He had an ability to change completely between nine o'clock in the morning and five o'clock in the afternoon. It had got to the stage where the beginning of each meeting was devoted to trying to establish which version of their leader was present that day.

This encouraged a timid and careful approach among the team, until they were sure they knew how to manage him. This also meant that everyone would decide on the hoof whether or not they should tell him the latest news. There were good days to reveal bad news and bad days to reveal bad news. Everyone was acutely aware that if they got it wrong, he'd react in a very aggressive and intimidating way.

This leader's default setting was to react.

A reactive leader can have a really negative impact on a business. In this case, for example, it put numerous projects in jeopardy. Project managers knew what they were trying to achieve, but also knew they wouldn't get to their goal without some mistakes being made along the way. Yet, they were also aware, anything less than instant perfection was a disaster. It put them in an untenable position. They couldn't afford to take any risks.

Although they bravely pressed on, they often had to consult their boss for authority to make the changes to the plan. The leader insisted that when results were presented, they focused on four things:

1. What they had done that had gone well
2. What they had done, in good faith, that hadn't gone well
3. What they had learnt in the process
4. What they now planned to do as a result of what they had learnt.

To make matters even more difficult, the boss always

focused on what they had learnt, except he called it 'what had gone wrong'. Then, because his focus was on what had gone wrong, he easily glossed over what had gone well and what the team had learnt in a positive sense, even though these were two vitally important aspects of the implementation. The team was increasingly frustrated that each time they presented their ideas for the next stage of implementation, the boss was perpetually distracted by what had gone wrong. He even fixated on what had gone wrong far back in the mists of time. Projects were doomed to fail from the beginning.

Aside from his fixation on 'what had gone wrong,' this leader also suffered from acute inconsistency. He would react differently to different stimulus on any given day.

Compare this leadership style to one where the leader never reacts in an uncontrolled way, or an inconsistent manner. If a good leader is presented with the four elements above, which analysed the success or otherwise of a specific project, they would ensure they allocated focus and time across all four components. In particular, they would direct their attention to what had gone well, what had been learnt and how the learning would shape future action. By taking this approach, the team will automatically engage with total honesty. It will be far easier to get a successful outcome, while also maintaining a team who feel valued and confident.

Any leader who feels they may be guilty of habitually reacting must train themselves to respond rather than react. This was certainly what I had to do with the boss of the telecoms business I described above. My role then was to stop this executive from reacting in an aggressive way and enable him to develop the ability to respond.

A good starting point is to begin by thinking that you should treat people the way you would like to be treated by them. When someone in a position of leadership thinks about what they are going to ask people to do and how they are going to tell them, this is a good mental test to pass a proposed plan through.

Any leader who feels they may be guilty of habitually reacting must train themselves to respond rather than react.

Next, it is time to break a habit. Some people think they are conditioned to react explosively and that is all they will ever be able to do. This isn't the case. As our behaviour is learnt from babyhood onwards, it must be possible to learn new ways. After all, while we may be creatures of habit, as Aristotle said, 'excellence is a habit'.

Most people associate habits with behaviour, which they are. A lot of people overlook the fact that we also have habitual patterns of thought. Reacting is a habit of thought and, like many thoughts that reoccur consistently, can become beliefs. People who react by getting aggressive must believe that what they are doing is right or, at best, not wrong. If they didn't hold this belief, they wouldn't behave this way.

With this in mind, my challenge was to help the telecoms boss to change his habit. For clarity, let's define a habit as 'an acquired pattern of behaviour regularly followed until it has become almost involuntary'. This definition is very relevant and has two very important parts: an 'acquired' pattern of behaviour and the 'almost involuntary' part. If something is acquired that indicates other habits can be acquired and the 'almost involuntary' bit that tells us that it is not completely involuntary. If you follow this thought pattern through to its logical conclusion, it shows that when something is not involuntary, it can be changed, if necessary.

Habits drive everything that we do. They are parked in the subconscious part of our mind and can encompass simple activities like waking-up at a certain time, through to much more complex ones such as driving a car, riding a bike, or using technical equipment and how we behave when we are given news we may not like. Some habits are learned consciously, like driving. We go through a very specific series of steps that enables us to develop a competency that we can then repeat. We repeat them so often that it becomes something that we can do without thinking about it. Some people refer to this competence that we can do unconsciously as our second nature.

Changing a habit is actually quite straightforward. The starting point is engagement from the person who needs to change their habit and an understanding why changing will be of value to them. I have found that when people have a 'why' for doing something, the 'how?' is relatively straightforward.

This guy understood he needed to respond with a more measured approach, rather than falling back on intuitive, knee-jerk reactions. If his reactions were going to be replaced with a response, the starting point had to be self-awareness. As you will see in the personal development exercises, the first step in this endeavour is to consciously ascertain the negative triggers that will provoke a reaction. It is usual that people react to the same thing, or the same influences, on a consistent basis. Once you are aware of the triggers that are likely to get you angry, you can then employ a different strategy or approach.

This executive and I carefully considered what triggered an aggressive reaction from him. It boiled down to him being very impatient. When he got angry, he wasn't actually annoyed with his people, he was annoyed that the projects appeared to be being delayed. When he had been a project manager, he would have done whatever necessary to get things back on target, regardless of the cost to the other people in the project team. He couldn't understand why others were so laid back about projects that he thought were business critical. His view was that he could sharpen people up by being aggressive and, if he kept people on their toes, they would be more committed to staying on track.

Clearly, this approach was having the opposite effect. People were distracted by it and they couldn't concentrate fully. It was difficult for me to measure the exact impact, but I did know that people went out of their way to avoid him, even during lunch in the company dining room, because they knew that he would ask about their projects. What sort of leader encourages their people to avoid them?

I had no choice. I had to tell him exactly what his behaviour was doing to his people. There wasn't much point in telling him that he was hurting their feelings, because he didn't really care about that. I knew that he did care about the efficiency of his projects so that was the angle to take. I suggested that his approach was making a contribution to projects getting behind. By constantly following up with his team, he was distracting them. While he might have thought he was encouraging them to greater efforts, he wasn't. He was losing impact, because he did it too often.

He agreed that we had to do something, the question was what? I had a suggestion based on the old idea of simply counting to ten when confronted with a negative trigger. This is as sound a strategy as it ever was and works very effectively when confronted with a negative trigger without any warning. The reason for counting to ten is to avoid any type of immediate reaction.

There will be occasions when the best strategy is not just to count to ten, but to actually buy yourself even more time to manage your reaction. This isn't as easy as it sounds, because the modern business world often requires leaders to make instant judgement calls that can have far reaching consequences if they go wrong. Some leaders believe that they have to react very quickly to grab or maintain competitive advantage. This is a high-risk strategy. As we've seen in the chapter on the decision-making process, even battlefield commanders are trained in the art of making a considered choice, even when bullets are flying. Knee-jerk reactions when emotions are running high do not constitute effective leadership. If your people are trying to put you under pressure to make ill-considered decisions, this needs to be addressed as there are often ulterior motives at play.

However, if the trigger is likely to take you well beyond ten and you can't withdraw to consider the issue more fully, it is worth remembering the formula:

E + R = O

In the formula,

E is the event, or trigger.

O is the outcome you want to get out of the event.

R is the response that you will need to adopt in order to get the outcome you want.

Here's an example.

If you've ever flown, you'll be aware that flights get cancelled. For frequent flyers, in particular, this can be a very negative trigger and it is easy to understand why. Regular exposure to these issues doesn't necessarily make them any easier to deal with. On one occasion, I was sitting in a plane that was due for take-off when we were told that the plane wasn't safe to fly and the flight was cancelled. I was as annoyed as everyone else, but there were one or two people who were clearly more upset than me. We were told that we had to go to the ticket desk to rebook on the next available flight. I was lucky to be at the front of the group as we walked towards the ticket desk. As I queued I thought through my E + R = O.

My E was the cancellation of the flight. My O was a seat on the next available flight and ideally a place in the business lounge where I could work, even though I didn't hold a premium ticket. To get my outcome, I decided that my R, or responses, was going to have to be pleasant, understanding and polite. After all, it can't be a lot of fun for the airline staff who have to deal with people who have had their flights cancelled. I am sure they were watching our approach with heavy hearts.

My response worked very well. Having told the member of ground staff that I understood that these things happen, it was out of their hands and that the next flight would be fine, I asked in a very polite way:

'Do you think I could go into the business lounge from now until the next flight departs please? I have a lot to do and need power for my laptop, which isn't available in the terminal.'

The ground staff assured me that that would be fine. As I took my ticket and turned to walk away, I could hear the next man begin to 'go off on one'.

'Third bloody time this week…' he fumed.

Needless to say, I didn't see him in the business lounge and not on the next flight, as I recall.

Three weeks later, I was on the same flight. Approaching the gate, I searched my usual suit jacket pocket for my passport and discovered it wasn't there. As luck would have it, the person checking the boarding cards was the person I had spoken to when the flight had been cancelled.

E – no passport

O – get on the flight and be able to get back

R – polite

Happily the lady remembered me.

'Have you got two other forms of identity? Credit cards or debit cards?'

I had two.

'Shouldn't really be doing this but...'

I got on the flight and I got back that evening.

It is not always straightforward and some times will be harder than others. There was another occasion I vividly remember when I was a young officer, working with the United Nations in Korea. I was asked to send two Gurkha pipers to Japan, where the then British Prime Minister Mrs Thatcher was visiting a cemetery. The two men in question didn't speak great English and I was a little concerned as I watched them disappear into the US military transport system. After twenty-four hours I received a call from the Defence Attaché in Tokyo, who announced there was no sign of my men with just twenty-four hours until the Prime Minister arrived.

I spent fourteen hours trying to locate the two men. I even elevated my rank to Colonel from Lieutenant to give me more impact on the phone. This was risky but the alternatives weren't that great. Every time I phoned the Defence Attaché in Tokyo, I was prepared. I spent ten minutes drafting the key facts that I needed to impart and I made sure that when we spoke on the phone, I came across as calm but determined. My preparation meant I could pre-empt most of his questions so I was unlikely to be put on the back foot, which might have made me begin blabbering in an unstructured way.

The soldiers did turn up on time and were a great

success. The Prime Minister's office wrote to my boss saying how great they were. A copy of this found its way to me and I passed it on to the two men. Nine months later I went to see my Colonel to get my annual confidential report. The Defence Attaché in Tokyo had written to my boss to say: 'Dunlop is to be commended for keeping his head when all about him appeared to be a total disaster.' It was unexpected, but a nice complement to get, even though I wasn't as relaxed as he thought. Success in changing your response is a lot to do with training.

With the telecoms executive I was coaching, we agreed that he would identify the precise triggers that were likely to make him angry, he would then identify the ideal outcome and he'd then work back to defining his response.

My final tip to him was to remove the frustration and introduce fascination. If the team said that they had implemented something, his objective was to be fascinated. This would enable him to establish what had gone well and what had gone wrong, ideally in that order. If he got this right it would be a big change from the early days, where he couldn't help but focus on what had gone wrong before focusing on what had gone well. It had to be a stepped approach.

We made progress and he became a more consistent responder, although it did take time. Changing from a reactive nature to a responsive one does take thought and time. The change process can go on for a long time because some habits are so ingrained.

Reacting is a natural way to behave, we have a fight or flight instinct and certain triggers encourage those reactions. The key is to know the triggers and respond in a measured way when the triggers occur.

Counting to ten is the simplest strategy and failing that, the E + R = O is a method that is well worth practising and perfecting. Being fascinated, or in other words asking questions and not making assumptions, will make a massive difference as well.

Counting to ten is the simplest strategy.

Is developing the ability to stay calm really that big a deal for a leader?

Absolutely. Even people who don't know very much about understanding the impact of body language will seek to interpret your response to bad news or some form of provocation. We know that a little knowledge is a dangerous thing, so the slightest non-verbal reaction will often be misinterpreted. A huge part of body language is facial expressions. The ability to retain a neutral expression in the face of extreme anxiety or provocation is vital. The alternative, some form of over emotional reaction is a no-no for a leader. It's OK to acknowledge something isn't right, but this has to be done with a calmness that you may not actually be experiencing from the inside out.

I've watched leaders in extreme circumstances, when the bullets were flying. All were calmness personified. I've adopted that approach when the bullets were being aimed at me. I was inwardly scared but outwardly calm. A colleague who heard me speaking on the walkie-talkie when bandits were shooting directly at me was initially unaware that I was on the receiving end. It wasn't easy, but it was important and the consequences had an impact on the confidence of my team.

It was a habit I had learnt.

SUMMARY

1. Any one can lead, but it is only when the going get tough that a true leader will prove their worth.
2. A reactive leader, who flies off the handle at the slightest provocation, can have a highly negative impact on a business.
3. If counting to ten doesn't work, try E + R = O.

PERSONAL DEVELOPMENT EXERCISES

EXERCISE ONE

Respond don't react

Business benefit

You will respond not react

Resources

Time

Format

Use the box below or recreate the E + R = O table in a Word document. Think about the events or triggers that inspire the worst reactions from you and write those triggers in the event column. For each trigger, consciously identify the best outcome you could have from that event. Also consider the outcomes you don't want. Finally, think about which responses you need to employ to help get the outcome you want.

To make this work for you, the next time you see or hear a negative trigger, consciously count to ten while thinking about the outcome you want. Then employ the responses you need to help you get it.

Now practise.

Event (Triggers)	Outcome	Responses

PERSONAL DEVELOPMENT EXERCISES

EXERCISE TWO

Respond don't react

Business benefit

You will enhance your leadership impact

Resources

Time

Format

One trait of leadership that people admire is the leader's ability to be consistent in their dealings with their people. As we've seen, a leader who is inconsistent makes life difficult for their people. People aren't sure how they ought to behave and waste a lot of time trying to ascertain which version of their leader has appeared that day.

Take time to identify what type of behaviour you think is aligned to being a consistent leader. What is it that leaders who behave consistently actually do?

Your next step is to ascertain how consistently you apply this type of behaviour. If you think there is an opportunity to adapt a behaviour, or adopt a new behaviour, establish what that behaviour is.

The aim is to become a more consistent leader.

Create a plan for implementing this change now.

Act.

AFTERWORD

Recording these twenty habits in this book, together with my own life experiences, has given me the opportunity to really think about the things that great leaders do, the type of people they are, how they work with their people and their teams and how they lead when they are faced with great challenges. Why is it that some are great and some aren't? Why do some leaders inspire their people, yet many don't?

When I led a team in Angola, I had thirty men spread over a huge geographical area in a very hostile country. When the mine was attacked and we were taken captive, my role was to behave like a leader, no matter how threatened or scared I was. I certainly had to behave like one when I negotiated with the UNITA commander on the day of the attack. Later, when I was presented with the decision over whether to return with my men to civil-war-torn Angola, I was presented with another crucial leadership moment.

Although we were facing exceptional circumstances, which changed by the minute, each of my decisions had to be made with great care throughout this period. This care wasn't just important for my own personal well-being, much less so self-aggrandisement, but for the safety and well-being of my team.

When I made my decisions, I drew on my military training, my experience in the field, the habits I have acquired and probably just a little touch of sheer bloody mindedness, because I wouldn't allow myself or my team to be brought down by the circumstance. I was also utterly focused and determined to achieve a good outcome. I certainly wasn't stymied by rules or any pre-ordained approach to my situation. How could I? My situation was unique, just as every challenging leadership scenario will be.

Since turning to leadership training, I've met lots of really great people in big companies, all of whom face a wide range of challenges. I am constantly amazed at how much they are required to do, yet they are invariably prepared to meet their challenges with focus, determination and good humour. It is inspiring.

I really believe in the commercial value of effective and innovative leadership. I have seen businesses transformed by the arrival of just one person. Crucially though, this success is not just down to that individual. In a transformation like this, what I am really seeing is that the people already within that business were always able and ready to perform; it's just that they were never given the chance. The new person unlocked that potential and that is the essence of leadership.

Leadership is a profession. It is a full-time job and at times it can be a very testing one. My hope is this book will prove to be a useful tool when tackling the day-to-day challenges and the odd times when something really extreme comes along and threatens to throw you off track completely. Although we all have different styles and ways of approaching challenges, the habits outlined here should enhance any leader's impact.

Acquiring a habit takes time and focus, which is why I would recommend starting with just one or two of those outlined here to begin with. Identify one habit that relates to you as a leader and how you lead your team, or perhaps one that relates to a particular challenge you may be facing right now. After going through the relevant chapter, devise a plan of how you might implement the habit. The exercises that complement each chapter are designed to enable you to put the habit into practice. They've been used with real people and real teams and proven to be effective. I'd encourage you to read around the topic as well. If you would like ideas on further reading please email me at bryan@bryandunlop.com

While the leadership habits in this book are straightforward, it doesn't mean to say that applying them consistently is easy. It isn't. If it was, everyone would be doing it and they aren't. Acquiring new habits requires practice and application.

Being a leader requires the highest standards of thought and deed on a daily basis and that means walking the walk, as well as talking the talk. Too many managers expect their people to do what they say, while adopting a different form of behaviour for themselves. This isn't leading. This is taking advantage of the title or position. As I have emphasised again and again in this book, leading by example is an absolute necessity. There can be no compromise. You can't choose the days when you are going to be a leader.

The hard work and effort will be worth it. Working with people and leading a great team is one of the most fulfilling things a person can do. Confronting seemingly impossible challenges together, delivering amazing results and enjoying the rewards of this success combine to make being a part of a team very rewarding. Watching people grow both professionally and personally is a real privilege. I have seen the quality of people's lives being changed forever by the impact of great leadership. I have benefitted from the impact of great leadership myself and, as a direct result, so has my family. This has impacted where we live, where our sons go to school and how we can afford to spend very high-value quality time together. This is the impact that leadership can have. Quite simply, you can change people's lives for ever.

Don't be shy about sharing your achievements. If,

as a result of reading this book, you change a habit and make some real progress, I'd love to hear about it. You can email me direct at bryan@bryandunlop.com. I write an ezine on a weekly basis, where I cover various leadership topics with advice and tips on specific elements of leadership. If you would like to receive the ezine, please visit the website at www.bryandunlop.com and sign up. When you do so, we will send an ebook entitled 'Motivated people – better business results' as a gift.

As leaders, we all need to keep moving and learning all the time. We need to develop new effective skills every day. Adopting just one of the habits outlined in this book will help you become a better leader. Perfect all twenty and who knows what you will be able to achieve?

Great leaders won't always have all the answers, but at the critical moment when things get difficult they will instinctively know the best way forward thanks to the deeply ingrained habits honed through hard work and application. Their approach may not be text-book, but it gets the job done. What could be better than that?